THE ROMAN COOKERY BOOK

a critical translation of

THE ART OF COOKING

by APICIUS

for use in the study and the kitchen

by

BARBARA FLOWER

and

ELISABETH ROSENBAUM

With drawings by
KATERINA WILCZYNSKI

Martino Publishing
Mansfield Centre, CT
2012

Martino Publishing
P.O. Box 373,
Mansfield Centre, CT 06250 USA

www.martinopublishing.com

ISBN   978-1-61427-239-7

Cover design by T. Matarazzo

Printed in the United States of America On 100% Acid-Free Paper

THE ROMAN COOKERY BOOK

a critical translation of

THE ART OF COOKING

by APICIUS

for use in the study and the kitchen

by

BARBARA FLOWER

and

ELISABETH ROSENBAUM

With drawings by
KATERINA WILCZYNSKI

BRITISH BOOK CENTRE
New York

First published in Great Britain 1958
by GEORGE G. HARRAP & Co. LTD
182 High Holborn, London, W.C.1
© *Introduction, translation, and notes, E. Rosenbaum* *1958*

Composed in Imprint type and printed by
William Clowes and Sons, Limited, London and Beccles
Made in Great Britain

PREFACE

The idea of this new translation of Apicius was conceived by Barbara Flower at one of her supper parties in the winter of 1952. For both of us it was to be a kind of recreation from our daily work. We began by cooking some of the dishes at random, in order to get the right touch for Roman cooking. When we felt we had acquired a certain skill we became more systematic and more ambitious, and regularly arranged Roman dinner parties to which we invited friends who could judge our interpretations of the recipes. We then proceeded to discuss the recipes one by one, and only after we had gone through the entire book in this manner did we start to write down our translation.

When Barbara Flower died in July 1955 we had worked through the whole book together, and the translation of most of Book I, the whole of Book II, and most of Book III had been written. In the following winter I resumed work alone. Had she lived to see the final result it would certainly contain fewer faults.

The book is meant to be used as a cookery-book rather than read as a curiosity of literature. The introduction is arranged for the convenience of those who are equally at home (as good scholars are apt to be) in the study and the kitchen; those more interested in the practical cookery side might start reading it at page 18.

I wish to thank all those who gave their criticism and advice: Professor P. Maas, who kindly gave me his advice on technical problems in the edition of the Latin text; D. M. Davin, E. Frankfort, and D. P. Walker, who helped to correct the English; J. Liversidge and V. Scholderer, who contributed chapters to the introduction; H. Buchthal and A. M. Meyer, who read part of the proofs; M. Webster and A. Williamson, who typed the manuscript; J. Chadwick, C. Mitchell, and

J. Reynolds, who helped in various ways ; and all the friends who bravely came to our dinner parties.

I hope our new Apicius will serve the purpose we and he intended. May it give those who use it as much delight as it gave us while we worked on it together.

June 1957   ELISABETH ROSENBAUM

NOTE

Thanks are due to the Teubner Verlag, of Leipzig, who have given permission for the use here of the Latin text of Apicius, published by them, and edited by C. Giarratano and F. Vollmer.

CONTENTS

INTRODUCTION

I. THE TEXT AND ITS AUTHOR

Cookery-books seem to have been numerous in antiquity, but only one has come down to us, and that is in Latin. It bears the name of Apicius. It is preserved in two ninth-century manuscripts. One of them was written in Tours during one of the most important periods in the history of the Tours scriptorium, under Abbot Vivian (844–851); the other was probably written in Fulda. The Tours Manuscript, now in the Vatican Library (Urb. lat. 1146), was not made for everyday use; it is distinguished by a decoration which could hardly have withstood the atmosphere of the kitchen: the tables of contents of the first book are framed by arches in a way usually reserved for the Canon Tables of Gospel books.[1] The other manuscript was brought from Fulda to Italy in 1455, came into the Phillips Collection in Cheltenham in the early nineteenth century, and is now in the Library of the Academy of Medicine in New York.[2] Both manuscripts derive from a common archetype which we know to have been in Fulda, and from which Poggio had excerpts made in the early fifteenth century.[3]

Apart from these manuscripts, some excerpts—made by a certain Vinidarius, an Ostrogoth living in North Italy in the fifth or sixth century—have survived in an eighth-century manuscript.

The cookery-book aroused the interest of the Renaissance humanists, and especially that of the physicians among them, who were attracted by its importance for diet. A number of fifteenth-century manuscripts, probably all depending on the Vatican codex, exist in various libraries of Europe, and we can gather from the early printed editions that the educated society of Northern Italy appreciated a text which afforded an insight into the daily life of the Romans.[4]

9

The earliest date connected with the printing of Apicius'
text is recorded in Panzer's *Annales* (Vol. II, p. 64, No.* 350),
where he quotes from an earlier source the note of an edition
signed by Guillermus Le Signerre of Milan "Anno domini.
MCCCCLXXXX. die. viii. mensis Ianuarii," but only to
stigmatize it as "editio spuria," adding "cf. edit. ann. 1498."
Panzer is unquestionably right in his condemnation, the
supposed edition of 1490 being a 'ghost' raised by some mis-
reading of the colophon of the true edition printed "Mediolani
per magistrum Guilermum Signerre Rothomagensem Anno
dñi. Mcccclxxxxviii. die. xx. mensis Ianuarii." The erasure,
deliberate or otherwise, of the two x's after 'die' in a copy of
this would be enough to account for the error. Two issues of
the 1498 edition are known, one in which the title reads
APICIUS DE RE QUOQUINARIA with Le Signerre's device
below and the three following pages devoted to a dedicatory
letter from Antonius Motta to Ioannes Mollus, secretary to the
Duke of Milan, and some verses by Motta and Bernardinus
Mollus, while in the other issue the title reads "Appicius
Culinarius" with the device of the publisher Ioannes de
Legnano, and is followed by a letter of Blasius Lanciloti to
Bartholomæus Merula and a "carmen subitarium" of Ludo-
vicus Vopiscus addressed to Ioannes Antonius Riscius. The
rest of the book is the same in both issues. (For a full descrip-
tion see the *Gesamtkatalog der Wiegendrucke*, No. 2267.)

On November 9, 1497, the Duke of Milan granted a privilege
of copyright for five years to one Ioannes Passiranus de Asula
in respect of six classical texts, one of which was "Apicius de
cibariis." This obviously refers to the present edition, which
was shared between the printer and Legnano, as the title-pages
of the two issues show. Legnano's copies seem to have been
destined for the Venetian market, where customers were likely
to be attracted by the dedication to Bartholomæus Merula,
"preceptor of the children of the magnific Georgius Cornelius"
—*i.e.*, the Venetian patrician Giorgio Cornaro, brother of the
Queen of Cyprus. This issue was reprinted about the turn

of the century at Venice, anonymously and without date (no doubt with a view to avoiding any difficulties which the Milanese privilege might raise), but with the types of Bernardinus (de Vitalibus) Venetus, and having two tracts of Suetonius incongruously subjoined (*Gesamtkatalog*, No. 2268). This edition in turn served as a model for that of Ioannes Tacuinus (Venice, 1503), from which, however, Suetonius is again omitted.

The anonymous Venetian edition has been accepted as the *editio princeps* by the editors of the Teubner Apicius and others, but all the circumstances go to show that this honour belongs to Le Signerre's work of 1498. His issue of it is the only homogeneous printing of the three in question, inasmuch as both the dedication at the beginning and the verses at the end are Milanese, and if the Venetian edition were earlier it would be hard to understand why the preliminaries should point to Venice and yet the addenda to Milan.

The first critical edition of the text by Albanus Torinus was published in Basle in 1541. It gives a kind of translation into humanist Latin, and has many arbitrary conjectures and additions. The next edition, by the physician Gabriel Humelberg (Zürich, 1542), is a masterpiece of classical philology of the time. Humelberg based his text on good manuscripts, among which he names an "antiquum manuscriptum exemplar" now lost. The next editor was the personal physician of Queen Anne of England, Martin Lister. His edition, following Humelberg fairly closely, was published in 1705 in London and in 1709 in Amsterdam. Of the other editions, that of Theophilus Schuch (Heidelberg, 1866 and 1874) deserves mentioning because of its badness. He abolished the division by chapters and paragraphs extant in the manuscripts and numbered the recipes right through. Moreover, he incorporated the excerpts of Vinidarius, inserting them in places where in his opinion they fitted best. Above all, he disfigured the text by numerous baseless conjectures.

The latest and, by our standards, the only reliable edition is that by C. Giarratano and F. Vollmer (Leipzig, Teubner, 1922).

The style of the cookery-book and the name of its author present a number of problems. The admirable study by E. Brandt, the last scholar to investigate these problems, has solved them at least in broad outline, and in such satisfactory manner that we may in general consider his results as facts.[5]

The humanists give the name of the author as Apitius Caelius. Vollmer has shown[6] that the name Caelius is their invention. It seems to originate from a misunderstanding of the corrupt form in which the title of the book is given in the Vatican Manuscript: on the first folio we find API CAE. Vollmer read this Api⟨cii artis magiri- or opsartyti⟩cae ⟨libri X⟩. This leaves us only with the name of Apicius to get on with. Of the various people known by this name, only one is reported to have written books on cooking. This is M. Gavius Apicius, who lived at the time of Tiberius. He is mentioned by several authors. A number of anecdotes are told about him, and his name is linked with several culinary inventions. Seneca is the first to give an account of his death: when, on counting his fortune, he found one day that, after having spent a hundred millions of sesterces mainly on food, he had only ten million sesterces left, and the prospect of starvation before him, he poisoned himself. He wrote, apparently, two cookery-books, one a general recipe book, the other a special book on sauces. His fame hardly diminished with the passage of time; he is mentioned by various Christian authors—for instance, St Jerome; Odo of Cluny speaks of him also. His books must have attained equal fame: Isidorus even states that he was the first to write a cookery-book.

Since Apicius lived in the first century, one would expect his style to be at least as classical as Columella's. The language in our cookery-book, however, is far from classical, or even silver, Latin. It is therefore obvious that what we have before us cannot be Apicius' original book. Brandt has shown that as it has come down to us the cookery-book is the work of an

editor who lived in the late fourth or the early fifth century.
This person—whose name we do not know, as he published his
book under the name of Apicius—made a compilation from
various sources. He wanted to combine in one book recipes
for the average middle- and lower-class household in town and
country with recipes for the more luxurious table. The
cookery-book of Apicius offered him only recipes of the latter
kind. So he supplemented it from a book on agriculture and
domestic science by Apuleius, a book of which fragments have
survived in the *Geoponica* and which is probably also reflected
in Palladius' book on agriculture; from a Greek book on agriculture; from a dietetic cookery-book, probably also Greek;
and from various other sources, chiefly medical writings part
of which ultimately go back to Marcellus, a physician who
lived under Nero. The popular Latin which permeates the
entire book is chiefly due to this editor, although the editions of
Apicius and Apuleius which he used may already have contained some popular elements. About three-fifths of the
recipes of our book come from Apicius' work. The edition
used by our compiler was certainly a fairly late one which
already combined Apicius' two books, the general one and the
book on sauces—our Books IX and X are almost exclusively
recipes for sauces—and which contained also some additions
made after Apicius' lifetime. There are, for example, a number
of recipes named after emperors or gourmets of repute which
had probably slipped into the various Apicius editions made
before our compiler set to work. That such different editions
of Apicius' book existed is also proved by the excerpts of
Vinidarius. He must have used one that contained, apart from
Apicius' original recipes, a Greek cookery-book of the Imperial
period or at least extracts from such a work.

The arrangement of our book is entirely the work of the
fourth- or fifth-century compiler. He seems to have had the
titles of the various books before him, although they hardly
come from Apicius' original work, and he arranged his material
according to these titles. This led him occasionally into

difficulties.   He took, for instance, recipes out of the context in which he found them because he thought they belonged to some particular book, and then forgot to delete them in their original place, so that several recipes occur twice.   The compiler is also responsible for the tables of contents at the beginning of each book.   He took as his guide the titles of the recipes.   The chapter headings were then inserted into the text from the tables of contents, either by himself or—more likely—by a yet later editor of his compilation.   Here too things have occasionally gone wrong.   Some headings in the tables of contents are not found in the text, and vice versa.

Comparatively little can be deduced from the compilation about Apicius' original book.   It must have contained recipes for a great variety of dishes, and if in our compilation there is only a small number of sweets, this is probably the fault of the compiler.   It made use of a great wealth of spices.   But the recipes rarely include any indication of quantities, and the ingredients are often simply enumerated without any direction on how they should be used.   This means that only experienced cooks could have used Apicius' book.   The style is simple and to the point, frequently colloquial, and in general very much like the style of cookery-books down the ages.   At one place there is a reference to the illustration of a pan (IV, ii, 14), and we may therefore assume that the book was originally illustrated.

The bulk of our Book I, and most of the short recipes of Book III and the following books, come from the work of Apuleius.   Some of these recipes are clearly addressed to the farmer—for example, those which tell how to make bad honey good enough for sale (I, xi, 2), or how to make red wine white (I, v).   All the recipes for preserving fruit, meat, and so on, and those on what to do with food in danger of going bad (e.g., I, vi), also come from this source.   They often add remarks referring to the result of whatever action is recommended.   About half of these recipes have parallels in Palladius and in the *Geoponica*.

The Greek agricultural book is the source for the recipes for spiced wine (I, i, 1–2), Roman vermouth (I, ii), *amulatum* (II, ii, 8), and *apothermum* (II, ii, 10). These recipes are markedly different in style from the rest. Some expressions make sense only in a Greek book: for example, the title "absinthium Romanum" or—in II, ii, 8—"quod Romani colorem vocant." Some of these recipes are different from the majority also in giving precise quantities.

The Greek dietetic cookery-book is represented by such recipes as IV, ii, 4, 5, 8, 9, 29, 31, 36. All these give precise indications of the quantities required. Some of them direct the dishes to be cooked "in thermospodio,"—*i.e.*, hot ashes— and the Latin translation of "thermospodia," "cinis calidus," occurs as well, in one case side by side with the Greek word.

The remaining recipes, taken from various medical writings, are also clearly recognizable. Some have "ad ventrem" in their titles (III, ii, 2–3, 5), others have remarks stating the effect of the dish on the digestive system, and usually they give precise quantities (*e.g.*, I, viii, xviii, xx, 1–2; III, xviii, 2–3).

To judge by the style, our compiler probably translated the Greek recipes himself.

II. Translations ; Some General Remarks on Roman Cooking

Apart from the editions mentioned and discussed above, there are a few modern translations: two Italian ones, by G. Baseggio (Venice, 1852), and by P. Buzzi (*Romanorum Scriptorum Corpus Italicum, curante Hectore Romagnoli*, Villasanta, Milan, 1930; re-edited under the title Apicio, *La cucina di Roma*, Veronelli, Milan, 1957); two German translations—R. Gollmer (Breslau–Leipzig, 1909, 2nd ed. Rostock, 1928), and E. Danneil (Leipzig, 1911); a French one, B. Guégan (Paris, 1933); and an English or, rather, American one by J. D. Vehling, *Apicius: Cooking and Dining in Imperial Rome* (Chicago, 1936). We have been unable to see copies of Baseggio's Italian translation or Danneil's German one. Gollmer's, obviously based on Schuch's edition of the text, is arbitrary to the point of becoming a mere paraphrase. Guégan's translation into French has considerable merits. It is made by an expert on gastronomy who is at the same time an historian and well versed in classical literature. Guégan's detailed introduction (with a list of manuscripts and printed editions) and his excellent commentary are so exhaustive that we felt in the present edition we could dispense with a great deal of annotation relating to the species of animals, fish, birds, and vegetables. Wherever we considered it necessary to add notes we are greatly indebted to Guégan's commentary. Any reader who wishes to know more about the nature of the ingredients in our recipes will be well advised to consult this book. Guégan's translation is marred by only one thing: it is based on imperfect editions of the Latin text. Guégan was well aware of the uselessness of Schuch's text, and claims to have based his translation on Humelberg, keeping Schuch's arrangement of the recipes and some of his so-called emendations. But it looks as if he had used rather more of Schuch's edition than the mere arrangement. In any case, it is difficult to understand why he did not use the Teubner edition, which had appeared more than ten years before the publication of his book. In consequence, though he attempts to adhere faithfully to the original, his translation is frequently wrong, in some places so much so that one hardly recognizes the recipe.

Vehling's translation is the only translation into English known to us—it claims to be the first. Vehling was (or is?) a professional cook, and therefore approaches his subject from the practical side. According to the foreword (written by a friend), he acquired his knowledge of Latin at school—which he attended, however, only up to the age of fourteen. It is therefore understandable that his text is so full of mistakes that it becomes almost useless as a translation. But he rightly states in his introduction that the crux of the Apicius question lies in the fact that the scholars who dealt with it before him knew nothing about cooking. Being himself a renowned practitioner of the culinary art, he felt justified in treating his

PLATE 1

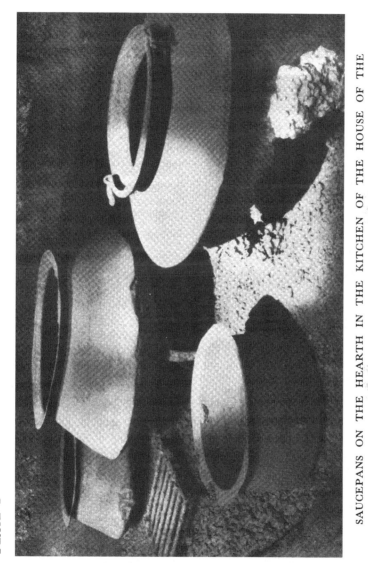

SAUCEPANS ON THE HEARTH IN THE KITCHEN OF THE HOUSE OF THE
VETTII, POMPEII

By courtesy of Istituto Geografico De Agostini-Novara

PLATE II

BRONZE VESSELS IN THE TOWNELEY COLLECTION

(1) (?)*Patella*. (2) Bowl of type probably used for *bain-marie* cooking.
(3) (?)*Patina*. (4) *Caccabus* or small *ahenum*. (5) Strainer.
(6) Frying-pan.

By courtesy of the British Museum

17

text without too many philological scruples. Unfortunately, he tried his hand at philology as well—he even gives a stemma of all the Apicius editions, manuscripts and printed books alike, including his own translation—and proudly announces that he made use of both the Teubner and the humanist editions— evidently believing these to be independent sources. The result is very curious, and, had he given the Latin, it would look even more grotesque. Whole sentences inserted by the sixteenth-century editor Torinus out of his own imagination appear, along with insertions by other people. Terms which Vehling did not understand are—without much regard to rules of textual criticism—replaced by others which looked more likely to him. This method was bound to lead him astray even on culinary matters. To give an example: disregarding all the literary evidence, he boldly claims that *garum* is a fish sauce of which little is known, whereas *liquamen*[7] simply denotes any kind of liquid, and may therefore be translated as the occasion requires by 'broth' or 'stock' or 'court-bouillon.' His method of translation can be tested by his rendering of recipe V, viii, 2 (B and C), which reads as follows: "*et elixati, sumpto.* Boiled sumptuously. And cook the beans, in a rich manner, remove the seeds and serve (as a salad) with hard eggs, green fennel, pepper, broth, a little reduced wine and a little salt, or serve them in simpler ways, as you may see fit."

The most useful part of Vehling's book is his appendix "Apiciana," which gives a full list with description of all the relevant manuscripts, printed editions, and translations.

Paolo Buzzi's translation, which appears to have escaped the notice of both Guégan and Vehling, became known to us only while the present edition was already in the press so that we could not make full use of it. Qua translation it is probably the best of the existing ones. It prints the Latin text opposite the Italian version; there are a few notes, concerning mainly names of plants and fishes, but there is no commentary. The Latin text is obviously a reprint of the Teubner text (without the apparatus criticus), although this is nowhere stated. In
2—R.C.B.

some cases the translation seems to be based on a text different from that printed in the edition.

Every translation is by its nature partly interpretation. The translation of a cookery-book—and one as concise in places as this—must be interpretation to an even greater extent than other translations. Although we have some experience in cooking, we cannot claim to be professional cooks, and there are some recipes which we understood as little as our predecessors did. We have therefore decided to print the Latin text opposite the English, so that the reader can form his own judgment. We have in general reprinted the text of the Teubner edition, without its apparatus criticus, and we have also omitted the excerpts of Vinidarius printed as an appendix to that edition. We have made a few alterations to the Teubner text; these are partly emendations or restorations of the text of the manuscripts made by Brandt in the book cited on p. 12 or in the footnotes and appendix of the Teubner edition itself; partly they are emendations made by ourselves. Only where our text differs from that of the Teubner edition do we give an apparatus. We have not indicated every instance where we have changed the punctuation of the Teubner edition. We have kept the normalized spelling of the Teubner edition even in cases where our text accepts the corrections of Brandt, who adopted the spelling of the manuscripts. His method is certainly the correct one in a case like Apicius', but as we did not aim at a new text edition we considered the normalized spelling to be more convenient for the reader. In order to enable the reader to compare Guégan's translation, Schuch's recipe numbers are added in italics at the end of each recipe.

Our aim in making this translation was mainly practical. We have tried out many of the recipes, and we found that many could become welcome additions to our menus. In addition, Apicius gives a number of useful hints which could be adopted to vary modern recipes.

The Roman cookery-book was not meant for beginners. The lack of indication of quantities in most recipes makes a basic knowledge of cookery necessary. But we found that with common sense and a little imagination one cannot go wrong on the quantities. We have nevertheless in some cases added the quantities we think correct in a footnote.

Most of the herbs are obtainable in London, at least dried. A number can be obtained from herb-nurseries (seeds or plants). We also found that one may safely omit one or another of the herbs without essentially altering the taste. Recipes for several of the basic ingredients (not given in our book) and some notes on a few of the most important condiments are given in Part III of our introduction, and some explanations and hints will be found with individual recipes and in the Index.

In general we found ourselves in disagreement with the criticism of Roman cooking expressed by a cook on the cook-market in Plautus' *Pseudolus* (1, 810 ff.)[8]:

I don't season a dinner the way other cooks do, who serve you up whole pickled meadows in their *patinae*—men who make cows their messmates, who thrust herbs at you, then proceed to season these herbs with other herbs. They put in coriander, fennel, garlic, and horse-parsley, they serve up sorrel, cabbage, beet, and spinach, pouring into this a pound of asafœtida, and pounding up wicked mustard, which makes the pounders' eyes water before they've finished. When they season their dinners they don't use condiments for seasoning, but screech-owls, which eat out the intestines of the guests alive. That is why life is so short for men in this world, since they stuff their bellies with suchlike herbs, fearful to speak of, not just to eat. Men will eat herbs which the cows leave alone.

Nevertheless, the cookery-book shows very clearly that the Romans abhorred the taste of any meat, fish, or vegetable in its pure form. There is hardly a single recipe which does not add a sauce to the main ingredient, a sauce which changes the original taste radically. Some of the more complicated recipes contain so many different things that no single one can be tasted. And at least one of the recipes for a substitute belongs already to the original book of Apicius (IV, ii, 12). With a certain pride, Apicius says at the end of this recipe: no one at table will know what he is eating. Petronius' feast of Trimalchio offers grotesque examples of the Roman passion for the disguise of food, both in appearance and in taste. There is, for instance, the hare done up as Pegasus, which is paralleled in our book in a more humble form in the recipe for 'salt fish without salt fish' (IX, xiii, 1), where a kind of liver paté is shaped into fish. But, then, Mediterranean cooking of to-day shows the very same tendencies. When eating pizza, or bouillabaisse, or Spanish rice, or Spanish omelette, or paella, and a hundred other delicious Southern dishes we may—after having become acquainted with Apicius—feel an additional pleasure to that of the palate—namely, that of gaining practical experience of the survival of antiquity.

A Roman dinner of the more elaborate kind consisted of three main parts: the hors d'œuvre or entrée, called *gustum, gustatio,* or *promulsis*; the main course, *mensae primae*; and the dessert course, *mensae secundae*. The *gustatio* was accompanied by *mulsum.*[9] It could consist of eggs prepared in various ways; vegetables raw and cooked, including asparagus, cucumbers, and pumpkins; herbs; lettuce; mushrooms; salt fish; oysters; mussels; snails; also the famous dormice—all these prepared in a variety of ways, so that most of the contents of our Books II–V, VII, and IX–X could be used for the *gustatio*. The *primae mensae* were devoted to roast and boiled meat, poultry, some meat delicacies (which could, however, also be included in the *gustatio*). The recipes in Books VI and VIII, and some in Book VII, would chiefly refer to this course. During this course wine was drunk, usually mixed with water, and in fairly moderate quantities. The *secundae mensae* consisted of fruit or various kinds of sweets. Originally savoury dishes were also served with the third course, and in Trimalchio's feast mussels and snails are included in the *secundae mensae*. But fruit and sweets were the more normal practice in later times. In our cookery-book very little is to be found that could be used for the sweet course—only in Books IV and VII do we find a few recipes suitable for a *secundae mensae*. Sometimes the serious drinking began with the third course, but it usually began after the meal. Apart from the very elaborate feast of Trimalchio, a few simpler Roman menus are recorded. We find, for instance, in Martial's epigrams a few that contain an invitation to a meal. In one he promises his guest a variety of raw herbs, lettuce, eggs, fish, and sow's udder for the *gustatio*, kid, chicken, ham, and sausages for the *primae mensae*, and fruit as dessert. In another it is herbs, lettuce, eggs, cheese, and olives for the *gustatio*, and fish, mussels, sow's udder, and poultry for the *primae mensae*. In Juvenal we find a menu consisting of asparagus and eggs for the *gustatio*, kid and chicken for the *primae mensae*, and fruit for the *secundae mensae*.

III. Fish Sauces ; Wine Preparations ; Cheese ; Starch ; Silphium

In our version we left some of the terms untranslated, as no proper English equivalents exist. These are above all the various basic sauces used for seasoning and the preparations of wine and must used for sweetening and colouring. The first place in importance is taken by the *garum*—or *liquamen*, as it is called in almost all our recipes. This sauce was made in factories, and its use may be compared with that of sauces like Worcester sauce, except for the fact that it was apparently used in lieu of salt. Readers who do not wish to go to the trouble of making their own *liquamen* could therefore use salt instead. One must, however, be aware that without *liquamen* the authentic flavour cannot quite be attained.

Several towns were famous for their *liquamen*—for instance, Pompeii and Lepcis Magna. From Pompeii we know an inscription on a small jar saying: "Best strained liquamen. From the factory of Umbricus Agathopus."[10]

The *Geoponica* give a number of recipes for making *garum*. Chapter 46 of Book XX is entirely devoted to it:

(1–4) The so-called *liquamen* is made as follows: the entrails of fish are thrown into a vessel and salted. Take small fish, either *atherinae*, or small red mullet, or sprats, or anchovy, or any other small fish, and salt all this together and leave to dry in the sun, shaking it frequently. When it has become dry from the heat extract the *garum* from it as follows: take a long fine-meshed basket and place it in the middle of the vessel with the above-mentioned fish, and in this way the so-called *liquamen*, put through the basket, can be taken up. The residue is *allec*.[11]

The Bithynians make it in the following manner: It is best to take large or small sprats, or, failing them, take anchovies, or horse-mackerel, or mackerel, make a mixture of all and put this into a baking-trough. Take two pints of salt to the peck of fish and mix well to have the fish impregnated with the salt. Leave it for one night, then put it in an earthenware vessel which you place open in the sun for 2–3 months, stirring with a stick at intervals, then take it, cover it with a lid and store it away. Some people add old wine, two pints to the pint of fish.

(6) The best *garum*, called *haimation*, is made as follows: take the entrails of tunny fish and its gills, juice, and blood, and add sufficient salt. And leave it in a vessel for two months at the most. Then pierce the vessel and the *garum* called *haimation* will flow out.

These recipes certainly refer to the factory-made *garum*, though a country household, too, could provide the facilities necessary for these lengthy processes. Fortunately, the same chapter of the *Geoponica* contains also a recipe for a quick process:

(5) If you wish to use the *garum* at once—*i.e.*, not expose it to the sun, but boil it—make it in the following manner: Take brine and test its strength by throwing an egg into it to try if it floats; if it sinks the brine does not contain enough salt. Put the fish into the brine in a new earthenware pot, add origan, put it on a good fire until it boils—*i.e.*, until it begins to reduce. Some people also add *defrutum*. Let it cool and strain it two and three times, until it is clear. Seal and store away.

This is the kind of *liquamen* we made and used (we did add the *defrutum*), and the *liquamen* prepared in this way was so good that even considerable quantities could be used without leaving an unpleasant taste.

Liquamen was mixed with water, wine, vinegar, and so on, and was then called *hydrogarum, oenogarum, oxygarum*, etc. Sometimes other spices were added to the mixture.

A by-product of the *liquamen* manufacture is the so-called *allec*, or *hallec*. It is mentioned in the first *liquamen* recipe as the residue that remains when the *garum* is extracted. Pliny tells us (*Nat. Hist.* XXXI, 8, 44 (95)) that it was also made separately from very small fish that were otherwise useless. It then began to rise from a waste product to a luxury article. Countless varieties were made, and it was used in various ways. It was, for instance, like *garum*, mixed with old *mulsum* until it became sweet enough to be drunk. And it was served with oysters, sea-urchins, and innumerable other delicacies. Pliny mentions also its therapeutic qualities.

Apart from plain wine (*merum* or *vinum*), several wine preparations were used for cooking. It is generally known that cooking-wine has to be reduced in order to impart its full flavour to the dish. Nowadays we do this usually as part of the preparation of the dish in question. If, for instance, we make a sauce or gravy with wine we add the wine and let it boil fiercely until it is sufficiently reduced. The Roman cooks had this done beforehand, and used wine or must reduced to various degrees ready made. According to the degree of reduction, it was called *caroenum, defrutum* (or *defritum*), or *sapa*. The definitions given by various classical authors do not all agree with each other. According to Varro and Columella, *defrutum* is must reduced by boiling to one-third of its volume; according to Pliny, it should be reduced to half of its volume. Palladius gives the following definitions (XI, xviii):

Now about the preparation of *defrutum, caroenum*, and *sapa*. Although all three are made from the same substance, namely from must, the method of their preparation modifies both their names and their properties. For *defrutum* has its name from "boiling down," and it is ready when it is reduced to a thick consistency. *Caroenum* is ready when it has lost one-third of its volume with two-thirds remaining, *sapa*, when it has been reduced to one-third. The latter is improved when quinces are cooked with it and fig wood is added to the fire.

We usually made *defrutum* from tinned grape-juice—fresh must being unobtainable—which we reduced to one-third of its volume. It gives an excellent flavour to all kinds of sauces, and adds a very pleasant slight sweetness to the dish. We made our *caroenum* of white or red wine according to the dish it was used for, reducing the wine to two-thirds of its volume.

Another specially prepared cooking-wine is the *passum*. Like *defrutum*, it was used to sweeten sauces. It is not only sweeter than *defrutum*, but has a different flavour. Palladius (XI, xix) even says that one can use it like honey. Columella gives two elaborate recipes for the preparation of *passum* (XII, 39):

> Mago gives the following directions how to make the best *passum*, and I have made it myself like this. Gather early grapes when they are fully ripe, removing mouldy or damaged berries. Fix in the ground forks or stakes 4 feet apart to support reeds and join them together with poles. Then place the reeds on top and spread your grapes in the sun, covering them at night so that they do not get wet from the dew. Then, when they have dried, pick the berries off the stalks and put them in a cask or wine-jar and pour the best possible must over them so that the berries are completely covered. When saturated put them on the sixth day in a wicker basket and press them in the wine press and extract the *passum*. Next tread the grape-skins, having added freshest must which you have made from other grapes that were left to dry in the sun for three days. Mix together and put the whole mash through the wine-press, and this *passum* of the second pressing put immediately in vessels which you seal so that it does not become too rough. Then, after 20 or 30 days, when it has ceased fermenting, strain it into other vessels, seal their lids with gypsum immediately, and cover with skins.
>
> If you wish to make *passum* from the "bee" grapes gather the

whole grapes, clear away damaged berries, and throw them out. Then hang them up on poles. See to it that the poles are always in the sun. As soon as the berries are sufficiently shrivelled pick them off and put them without the stalks in a vessel and tread them well with your feet. When you have made one layer of them sprinkle old wine on and tread another layer of grapes over it and sprinkle this also with wine. Do the same with a third layer and, after having added wine, leave for five days. Then tread with your feet and press the grapes in a wicker basket. Some people prepare old rain-water for this, boiling it down to a third of its volume, and then, when they have made raisins in the manner described above, they take the boiled-down rain-water instead of wine, doing everything else in a manner similar to that described above. This process is very cheap where there is plenty of wood, and in use it is even sweeter than the *passum* described above.

Instead of *passum* we have used very sweet Spanish wine, being aware, of course, that this wine provides only the sweetness required, but not the original flavour.

Mulsum, wine mixed with honey, occurs in our recipes only on a few occasions. But as it is the drink that accompanied the first course of a Roman dinner it is of equal importance with the other wine preparations. Columella gives a recipe for its preparation (XII, 41):

> Best *mulsum*. Make in the following way: take right from the vat must called *lixivum*, which is that which has come out from the grapes before they have been too much trodden, but make it with grapes from vines that grow winding around trees and that have been gathered on a dry day. Take 10 lb. of best honey to three gallons of must, mix thoroughly, and put it in a wine-jar which you seal with gypsum. Have it placed in a store-room. If you wish to make more add honey in the proportion indicated above. After 31 days the jar should be opened, and the must has to be strained into another vessel, which again is to be sealed and then placed in the smoke.

Pliny has other ideas about *mulsum*. He says (*Nat. Hist.* XXII, 24, 53 (113–114)) that it is always better to make *mulsum* from dry wine, since it mixes better with the honey, a complete mixture being impossible with sweet wine. The *mulsum* made from dry wine has other virtues besides—for instance, it does not cause flatulence. It whets the appetite for food. When drunk cold it relieves stomach-ache. It also makes you stout. Pliny proceeds to tell an anecdote about Pollio Romilius, who, asked by Augustus how he had managed to become a centenarian, answered, "By using *mulsum* for the inside and oil for the outside."

For our *mulsum* we used dry white wine. We did, however, not let the mixture stand for a month, but used it fresh. The proportion given by Columella works out at roughly 6 oz. of honey to a pint of wine, but we took about two tablespoonfuls to the ordinary bottle of wine. It is a very refreshing drink, an agreeable apéritif, and one can use very cheap wine, which in its pure form would hardly be drinkable.

In some of our recipes cheese is mentioned among the ingredients. There was a great variety of Roman cheeses. Apart from Vestine cheese, in the immediate neighbourhood of Rome—which occurs in our cookery-book—Pliny mentions (*Nat. Hist.* XI, 42, 97 (240–242)) cheeses from the region of Nîmes; from the Alps; from the Apennines; Sarsina cheese from Umbria; Luni cheese from the border district between Etruria and Liguria. This latter could weigh up to 1000 lb. Columella's cheese-making recipes give us an idea what Roman cheese must have been like (VII, viii). He mentions thin cheese that is to be sold as quickly as possible, as it does not keep. Hard cheese that keeps longer is made from fresh milk not mixed with water. It is curdled with rennet from lamb or kid, or with the flower of wild thistle (or artichoke), or seeds of saffron, or with the sap of fig-trees. But the best cheeses contain only very little of any of these things. The proportion of rennet to milk must be at least the weight of one silver denarius to the pail. The milk is to be kept at a certain temperature, but not put on the fire. As soon as it has thickened it is transferred into wicker baskets or moulds so that the whey can percolate.   One may either let it drain away slowly or promote the draining by pressure.   The cheese is then taken out of the baskets or moulds and put in a cool place on clean boards sprinkled with pounded salt.   After hardening it is pressed again to make it quite compact.   It is once more treated with salt and compressed with weights.   Then it is set in rows on wicker-work trays to drain thoroughly.   This cheese is suitable for export overseas.

Cheese to be eaten fresh is taken out of the baskets and dipped into salt and brine and then dried a little in the sun.   Hand-pressed cheese is made by breaking up the slightly curdled milk, then pouring hot water over it and making the shapes by hand or in box-wood moulds.   Columella also mentions smoked cheese, which is first hardened in brine and then coloured in the smoke of apple-tree wood.

Most of the sauces in our book are thickened with *amulum*. We have translated this word for the sake of convenience as 'cornflour,' for this is the starch most frequently used for this purpose to-day.   The *amulum* was, however, wheat-starch. Pliny relates how it is manufactured (*Nat. Hist.* XVIII, 7, 17 (76)):

> Starch is made from every kind of wheat and fine wheat, but the best comes from three-month wheat.   For its invention we are indebted to the island of Chios.   And from there comes the variety most highly praised to-day.   It takes its name from the fact that it is made without a mill.   Next to that made of the three-month wheat comes that made of the lightest wheat.   It is soaked in fresh water in wooden tubs so that the grain is covered, and the water changed five times a day.   It is better if this is done also during the night, so that it gets mixed evenly.   Before the softened grain goes sour it is strained through linen or through wicker baskets and poured on a tiled floor spread with leaven, and left so as to thicken in the sun.   Next to starch from Chios that from Crete is most highly praised, then that from Egypt—it is tested by its smoothness, its light weight, and its freshness—and it has also been mentioned by Cato among ourselves.

Finally, at least a word must be said about the famous *sil-phium*, also called *laserpitium* and *laser*. Pliny has devoted a long chapter to this herb (XIX, 3, 15 ff. (38 ff.)). From him and Theophrastus (*Hist. plant.* VI, 3) we gain a great deal of information about it. The silphium grew in abundance in Cyrenaica, and was one of the chief exports of that province. It had become a kind of symbol of Cyrenaica, so that it appears on the coins of Cyrene, and even on reliefs. But in spite of all this no one has been able to identify the plant. In fact, it was already extinct in Cyrenaica in Pliny's time. He says that only a small quantity could be discovered under Nero, and this was sent to him. Otherwise it was only from Persia, Armenia, and Media that silphium was still imported, but this was of far inferior quality to that of Cyrenaica. The silphium from Cyrenaica was apparently expensive even when it was still grown in great quantities. Pliny mentions that under the consulate of C. Valerius and M. Herennius (93 B.C.) thirty pounds of silphium were sent to Rome and given to the State.

Although the identity of the Cyrenaican silphium cannot be established, that of the Persian variety is fairly certain: it was most probably the asafœtida, also called Devil's dung. This plant has retained its importance in the Middle East to this day, and it is used for pharmaceutical purposes also in the north.[12]

We know from Pliny that the juice of both the stem and the root was used. Its costliness is well illustrated by our recipe I, x: how to make an ounce of silphium last. The Cyrenaican variety is mentioned expressly only twice in our book; usually it simply prescribes 'laser.' Apicius himself may still have known and used the Cyrenaican silphium, but our late fourth- or early fifth-century compiler could only have known the Persian or Armenian varieties.

In recipes where *laser* is prescribed we have used asafœtida extract obtainable at chemists. It is very strong, and must be used with the utmost caution. The tiniest drop gives just enough flavour. If more than a minute quantity is taken the entire dish may be spoiled. But, used with care, it gives a delicious flavour, especially in combination with fish.

IV. Roman Kitchens and Cooking Utensils

by Joan Liversidge

The type of Roman kitchen about which we know most is well illustrated by the discoveries made during the excavations of Pompeii, where several of them which had obviously been in use at the time of the eruption of Vesuvius in A.D. 79 were found. Their most recognizable feature is the hearth, which consists of a raised platform of masonry faced on top with tiles, sometimes edged with a curb, and with a coating of *opus signinum* along the front. Arched openings in the front of the platform nearer the floor-level lead to fuel bins that are roughly constructed of rubble and tile.[13] Arrangements for providing water for cooking and washing-up are also sometimes found, as are the supports for the stone or wooden tables used for the preparation of food.[14]

Much of the cooking was done on small iron tripods and gridirons over burning charcoal. Pl. I shows in greater detail the hearth in the kitchen of the House of the Vettii at Pompeii, with cooking-vessels still standing on three-legged tripods, and a tripod and a gridiron found on Scottish sites appear on Pl. IIIa. Both of these can be paralleled from occupation sites in many parts of the Roman world, although the arrangement of the gridiron bars and cross-bars varies a little; and there does not seem to be much room for doubt that when Apicius refers to a *craticula* he means a grid-iron of this type.

Other fuel beside charcoal, however, must have been used, as Apicius refers to certain dishes being smoked. Possibly wood was also burnt on the raised hearth, the smoke escaping through a vent in the kitchen wall, while the sausages or the sucking-pig were hung on a well-placed hook over the fire. It is interesting to remember that the kitchens in the House of the Dioscuri may have been unroofed, apart from a canvas awning which could be spread out in bad weather, and so a larger wood fire lit on a brazier or some form of portable hearth would be a possibility. One of the discoveries made at Pompeii was a cooking-stove consisting of a low iron frame with a cement hearth which could presumably have served for either wood or charcoal. Four movable cross-bars are placed across the frame at one end, and there are two rounded supports for pans.[15] Some of the very ornamental water-heaters that were found at Pompeii may have been used for reheating or keeping dishes warm, or for cooking by the *bain-marie* process. One very elaborate bronze heater is in the shape of a square battlemented fortress with a tower at each corner covered by a hinged lid. Water could be poured in through the top of the towers to stand inside the hollow frame which formed the castle walls. It could also be drawn off by a faucet in the centre of one side, and was heated by a fire which was placed in an iron pan in the centre.[16] Other heaters were cylinder-shaped, with the fire at the bottom and a water container on top, usually covered by a lid.[17] Large bronze bowls with flat rims have sometimes been discovered in the rich Belgian barrow burials, usually accompanied by smaller, shallower dishes which just fitted on the top of the deep bowls. Their use is uncertain, but as they show no signs of ever having been placed on a fire it has been suggested that the large bowl was filled with hot water, and food was placed in the shallower bowls to cook or be kept hot. This would be an even closer approximation to the *bain-marie* process than the big heaters (Pl. II, No. 2).[18]

For such dishes as the sucking-pig suspended in a basket in a cauldron of boiling water (VIII, vii, 4) these hearths and braziers seem a little cramped, and perhaps in country kitchens at least the older method of slinging the cauldron over a large wood fire still prevailed, the smoke escaping through an aperture in the roof. A clear picture of this appears on the side of a Roman altar found at Bonn.[19]   It shows the iron chain hanging from a stout ring apparently fixed into the ceiling or a crossbeam, with a hook on the end with the cauldron handle looped over it. On the other side of the altar a servant is seen approaching carrying a pig on his back.   Numerous cauldron chains of this type have been found in Roman and pre-Roman contexts in Britain and elsewhere.[20]   Boars and other larger animals were also roasted on spits[21] over a wood fire, and Apicius himself refers to the smoke of the burning laurel and cypress branches when he is advising the careful housekeeper how to purify stale *liquamen* (I, vi).   He also says, when cooking pork in recipe VII, x, "brown its fat on a glowing hot brazier," and here one can imagine the cook's assistant plying the bellows at a charcoal fire; but for *conditum paradoxum*, described in I, i, 1, as heated in a brass vessel over a fire of dry sticks, wood must have been employed, and from the quantities the brass vessel must have been a large one, which would hardly fit over the small tripods and gridirons.

The ovens used for baking and roasting were constructed of rubble and tiles, shaped like a low beehive, and provided with some kind of flue in front to provide a draught.[22]   Wood or charcoal fires were lit inside them, the ashes were raked out as soon as the required temperature was reached, and the food was put in, the mouth of the oven being covered over to retain the heat.   Small rectangular ovens working on the same principle were actually discovered standing on the hearth in the kitchens in the House of the Dioscuri at Pompeii.   They may have been used for baking pastry, as a pastry mould was found near by. Some recipes, such as III, x, 2, for leeks cooked rolled in cabbage-leaves, or IV, ii, 4 or 33, for *patinae*, direct that the leeks or the pans containing the *patinae* are to be placed "among the coals" or "placed in the ashes" (*thermospodium*); such directions may refer to one of these ovens before all the ashes were removed, or they might mean among the ashes of a portable hearth.   Then there was the *clibanus*, a small portable oven of earthenware, iron, bronze, or occasionally of more precious metals.[23]   This was also chiefly used to bake bread or cakes and keep dishes hot, as it could be placed on a table in the dining-room.   Apicius directs that the *clibanus* was to be used for roasting mutton in a frying-pan (VII, v, 5); while the stuffed dormice mentioned in VIII, ix, are either to be placed on a tile and cooked in the oven (*furnus*), or else put in the *clibanus*.   From literary sources we know that this form of small oven had a rounded vault wider at the base than at the top and double walls.   A charcoal fire must have been made under the inner floor, the heat percolated between the walls, and the fumes escaped through small holes in the outer covering.

In some of his recipes Apicius refers to the various kinds of cooking vessels to be used for various dishes.   With the possible exception of the frying-pan (*fretale* or *sartago*) none of them can be identified with absolute certainty, but the collections of kitchen equipment sometimes recovered from military sites and the various discoveries made at Pompeii enable us to suggest some strong probabilities.   One such hoard has been preserved from the Roman legionary fortress at Newstead, Scotland, and it can now be seen in the National Museum of Scottish Antiquities in Edinburgh.   It includes a gridiron and seven cooking-vessels of various shapes and sizes, all showing traces of burning and hard usage; several of them have been repaired with bronze patches soldered into place (Pl. III*a*). At Pompeii a further selection of cooking-vessels was found *in situ* on the hearth in the kitchen of the House of the Vettii (Pl. I).   Possibly the Latin word *caccabus* (which is the word most frequently used by Apicius, and which must include pans of several different sizes and shapes) applies to cooking-vessels of these types.   They are widespread, and similar examples have been found at Gneisenau, Germany,[24] and in Pannonia.[25] Some of the Pompeian examples have lids attached to the handles by small chains to help pull them off when hot and to prevent them getting lost.

PLATE III

(a) BRONZE VESSELS AND IRON GRIDIRON FROM
NEWSTEAD; IRON TRIPOD FROM CARLINGSWARK
LOCH HOARD

By courtesy of the National Museum of Antiquities. Scotland

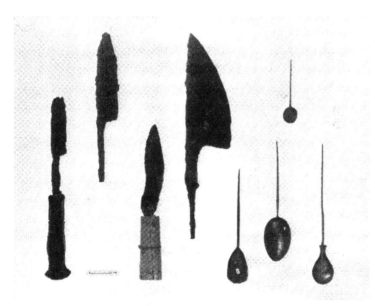

(b) BRONZE SPOONS AND IRON KNIVES, TWO WITH
ORIGINAL BONE HANDLES. BRAYBROOKE COLLECTION

By courtesy of Cambridge University Museum of Archæology and Ethnology
Photo L. P. Morley

PLATE IV

(*a*) TYPICAL ROMANO-BRITISH COOKING POTS

(*b*) (1) MORTARIUM. (2) BOWL PROBABLY USED
FOR COOKING

By courtesy of Cambridge University Museum of Archæology and Ethnology
Photos L. P. Morley

When Apicius tells the cook (*e.g.*, III, ii, 5; IV, ii, 22; VI,
i, 3; or VI, ix, 13) to take a clean pan or a new pan he presumably means an earthenware cooking-pot, even when he still
uses the word *patella*. Bronze pans would be too expensive to
replace frequently, and they could also be got surprisingly clean
with sea or desert sand. But sand is not such an efficient
cleaning material for earthenware, and, with no soap available,
these vessels, which were often made of very coarse pottery,
must soon have become foul and unfit for service. They were
also cheap to buy. Their shape and fabric varies at different
places, as they were often made locally. Pl. IV*a* illustrates a
few British examples.[26] In some cases Apicius is more explicit,
and in VII, iv, 4, the Latin actually reads *patellam fictilem*,
as opposed to *patellam aeneam* in IV, ii, 15. Elsewhere he
uses the word for a pottery vessel, *cumana*, and this occurs in
IV, ii, 11, as the casserole in which a *patina* of anchovies is
cooked, or in VII, xiii, a recipe for an egg and milk sweet, to
give only two examples. The *pultarius* used for cooking
sauces or sea urchins may have been a small pottery or metal
vessel.

For large joints, or for the soldiers' porridge, cauldrons of
the type shown on the Bonn altar must have been needed. In
VII, vii, 1, and VIII, vii, 11, the word *olla* is used for the vessel
full of water in which the cook boils the sucking-pig or pig's
stomach. In excavation reports *olla* is the term often used for
the ordinary small cooking-pots. Here it must indicate something very much larger, more in the nature of a cauldron or a
big camp kettle of the type sometimes found on military sites.
One found at York bears a series of inscriptions telling us that
first the century of Attilius Severus had it, and then it was
passed on to the century of Aprilis—an interesting testimonial
to the fact that these bronze vessels would be expected to remain
in use for some time.[27] Other cauldrons have turned up on
sites in Pannonia[28]; and, like the cauldron chains, several
examples of Roman and pre-Roman cauldrons have been found
in Britain.[29] The word *zema* which is used by Apicius in

3—R.C.B.

VIII, i, 10, and VIII, vi, 6, must also mean some kind of cauldron.

The Roman frying-pan (*fretale* or *sartago*), of round or oval shape, and with a lip for pouring, is quite well known. Several bronze[30] examples have been found in Pompeii, and Pl. II, No. 5, illustrates a frying-pan now in the British Museum. Iron frying-pans were also used, and fragments of one discovered in London show that it had a movable handle which folded up when not in use.[31] Similar pans of a more oblong shape, and with folding handles with incised decoration and holes for suspension when not in use, are among a collection of Coptic cooking equipment found in Egypt, and now in the Royal Ontario Museum.[32] From the same collections come rectangular iron trays with handles, and also a lip at each corner, designed for roasting or frying.[33] Possibly the *angularis* mentioned by Apicius in VII, iv, 1, was a vessel of this type, but it must have been deeper to allow for the layers of meat and oil-cake.

In Book IV Apicius refers frequently to pans he calls *patellae* and *patinae*, and here our evidence becomes very inconclusive. The *patella* is usually identified as a round, shallow pan with a handle, little deeper than a frying-pan[34]; it could appear at table as well as in the kitchen, and may have been the secular form of the *patera* used for religious purposes. A possible example of it is illustrated by Pl. II, No. 1. From the recipes, with their description of dishes built up with layers of oil cake, the *patina* must have been a deeper vessel. One authority describes it as a large, open pan of oblong form, and we wonder if certain oval or round bronze vessels usually lifted by a handle on each side or else provided with a long handle thicker than that of a frying-pan were not also *patinae*. One two-handled example was found at Pompeii,[35] another vessel which originally probably had a long handle has been noted from Carnuntum,[36] and the example illustrated (Pl. II, No. 3) comes from the Towneley Collection in the British Museum. The flat pottery bowls often found on Roman sites may also have been used for this purpose; they are rather like a round pie-dish, and the traces of soot occasionally found beneath their rims prove that they were used for cooking (Pl. IV, No. 2). Reference has already been made above to an earthenware *patella*, presumably a shallower bowl of this type.

Equipment for preparing and dishing up food resembles the implements in use for similar purposes to-day. Knives of all sizes are frequently found, usually made of iron, with bronze, wood, or bone handles (Pl. III*b*). Many examples of spoons are also known, made of bone, bronze, or silver, with round or oval bowls. The *cocleare* was a small spoon supposed to be used for eating eggs, and with a pointed handle convenient for picking snails or shellfish out of their shells. Larger spoons of bronze or iron, ladles and dippers (*trullae* and *simpula*), and meat-hooks were other items used in kitchen or dining-room. The strainers (*colae*) which are often mentioned in the recipes are a greater problem, as the long-handled bronze strainers with holes arranged in ornamental patterns are usually associated with the more decorative bronze vessels used for serving wine. Excavations have produced pottery bowls with holes in the bottom which could have been used as colanders,[37] and some liquids perhaps may have been strained through jelly-bags of muslin or some other similar textile. But when the contents of one pan have to be strained into another, and elaborate cooking operations are in progress, it seems that some of the plainer versions of the bronze strainers must have been used. Probably the small strainers of the type illustrated (Pl. II, No. 6), with their larger holes, belong in the kitchen. Many recipes begin by taking pepper or various herbs, which are put in the mortar and pounded or ground. While stone mortars may have been employed in some cases, the stout pottery bowls known to archæologists as *mortaria* probably did duty in most cases, and these are made with a sprinkling of grit baked into the fabric to help with the grinding process (Pl. IV*b*., No. 1). Stone or wooden pestles were used with them. Among the Coptic kitchen utensils in the Royal

Ontario Museum is a crescent-shaped iron blade with two rings for a wooden handle fixed in its back. This is believed to have been used for mincing meat.[38]

When the food was dished up it was placed on a *discus*—a word which is a general term for all kinds of dishes and plates of circular shape. Large platters and shallow bowls of silver, bronze, or pewter are frequently found in hoards of metal vessels, often decorated with incised patterns or designs in relief. The silver dishes in the Hildesheim treasure are among the most famous examples,[39] as are the numerous bronze bowls found at Pompeii. Fine pottery, particularly the red Samian-ware bowls, with their relief decoration, or the undecorated platters, must also have appeared in the dining-room. One of the more puzzling references made by Apicius is to something he calls a *conchiclar*, a vessel associated with certain dishes in Book V, iv. This may have been some kind of pan, but the existence at Pompeii of some very attractive bronze dishes fluted to resemble a scallop-shell suggests that the name *conchiclar* might refer to a dish of this shape in which the food was served, rather than to the saucepan in which it was cooked.[40] Larger dishes of the same kind could have been used as moulds. In IX, xiii, 1, a recipe for salt fish without fish, Apicius says that the mixture of liver and spices may be made into the shape of a fish or put in a mould if liked, and small moulds in the shape of a pig, a dressed hare, or a ham have actually been found at Pompeii.[41]

[1] W. Koehler, *Die Schule von Tours* (Berlin, 1930–33), Vol. I (text), pp. 288 f., 409. Pls. 114 *d–f*.
[2] Described in De Ricci and Wilson's *Census of the Medieval and Renaissance MSS. in the United States and Canada*, Vol. II, 1937, pp. 1310–1311.
[3] For the history of the two manuscripts in the Renaissance and the Apicius manuscript-tradition in general, see A. Campana, "Contributi alla biblioteca del Poliziano, IV. L'Apicio del Poliziano," *Il Poliziano e il suo tempo, Atti del IV convegno internazionale di*

studi sul Rinascimento (1954), Florence, 1957, pp. 198 ff., esp.
pp. 211 ff., where also previous literature on the subject is cited.
⁴ The following note on the *editio princeps* is contributed by Dr V.
Scholderer.
⁵ E. Brandt, *Untersuchungen zum Römischen Kochbuch* (Philologus,
Supplementband XIX, Heft III), Leipzig, 1927.
⁶ "Studien zu dem römischen Kochbuche des Apicius," *Sitzungs-
berichte der Bayer. Akad. der Wissenschaften*, 1920, 6. Abh.
⁷ On this sauce, see below, p. 21.
⁸ Translation by B. Flower.
⁹ See below, p. 25.
¹⁰ *Corpus Inscriptionum Latinarum* IV, 7110: "liquamen/optimum/
saccatum/Ex officina Umbrici Agathopi." I owe the reference
to the kindness of Miss J. Reynolds.
¹¹ See below, p. 23.
¹² See V. Vikentiev, "Le Silphium et le rite du renouvellement de
la vigeur," *Bull. de l'Institut d'Egypte*, XXXVII, 1 (1954–55),
p. 123 ff.
¹³ L. Richardson, "Pompeii: the Casa Dioscuri and its Painters,"
Memoirs of the American Academy in Rome (1955), p. 71.
¹⁴ J. Liversidge, "Kitchens in Roman Britain," *Archaeological
News Letter*, Vol. VI, No. 4 (1957) p. 83.
¹⁵ Tarbell, *Catalogue of Bronzes etc. in the Field Museum of Natural
History, Chicago* (reproduced from originals in the National
Museum of Naples), Field Museum of Natural History,
Chicago, No. 130, Vol. VII, No. 3 (1909), Fig. 105, p. 118.
¹⁶ *Ibid*, p. 117, Fig. 104.
¹⁷ *Ibid*, p. 116, Figs. 99, 100.
¹⁸ *Antiquité Classique* XXI (1952), p. 42, Fig. 2, No. 7; p. 57.
¹⁹ Espérandieu, *Bas-reliefs de la Gaule romaine*, XI (1938), No. 7762.
²⁰ *Proceedings of the Society of Antiquaries of Scotland* LXXXVII
(1952–53), pp. 12 ff., 24, 26.
²¹ Virgil, *Æneid* I, 211; V, 102, 103.
²² Mau-Kelsey, *Pompeii: its Life and Art* (1902), p. 391.
²³ Daremberg and Saglio, *Dictionnaire des Antiquités grecques et
romaines* I, ii (1887), Fig. 1633, p. 1246.
²⁴ *Bericht d. Röm.-Germ. Kommission* (1912), p. 157, Fig. 76.
²⁵ Radnoti, *Die Römischen Bronzegefässe von Pannonien* (1938),
Pls. XXXII, XXXIII.

[26] The examples illustrated are all in the Cambridge University Museum of Archæology and Ethnology. See also *Antiquaries Journal* XXXI (1951), p. 154 ff., especially p. 156, No. 10, and p. 158, No. 21. I am indebted to Mr B. R. Hartley, M.A., for this reference.

[27] *Yorkshire Philosophical Society Annual Reports* (1935), p. 5; *Antiquaries Journal* XV, p. 198, Pl. 36.

[28] Radnoti, *op. cit.* (above, note 25), Pl. XXXVI, No. 3.

[29] *Proceedings of the Society of Antiquaries of Scotland* (above, note 20), p. 30.

[30] From the Towneley Collection. We are indebted to the Trustees of the British Museum for information about this vessel and the vessels illustrated by Pl. II.

[31] London Museum Catalogue, No. 3, *London in Roman Times* (1930), p. 118, Fig. 41.

[32] *American Journal of Archæology* XXV (1921), p. 44, Fig. 5.

[33] *Ibid.*, p. 47, Figs. 8, 9.

[34] Daremberg and Saglio, *op. cit.* (above, note 23), III, ii, p. 1301 under Lopas.

[35] Mau-Kelsey, *op. cit.* (above, note 22), Fig. 204 r.

[36] Radnoti, *op. cit.* (above, note 25), Pl. XXXVI, No. 2.

[37] T. May, *Pottery found at Silchester* (1916), Pl. L, No. 70.

[38] *American Journal of Archæology* (above, note 32), p. 51, Fig. 12.

[39] Pernice and Winter, *Der Hildesheimer Silberfund* (1901).

[40] Tarbell, *op. cit.* (above, note 15), p. 132, Fig. 203.

[41] Tarbell, *op. cit.* (above, note 15), p. 135, Figs. 224–226.

UNTRANSLATED TERMS

allec: see Introduction, p. 23.
caroenum: wine reduced by boiling, see Introduction, p. 23.
defrutum: must reduced by boiling, see Introduction, p. 23.
garum = *liquamen, q.v.*
hydrogarum: liquamen mixed with water, see Introduction, p. 23.
liquamen: see Introduction, p. 21.
mulsum: see Introduction, p. 25.
oenogarum: liquamen mixed with wine, see Introduction, p. 23.
oxygarum: liquamen mixed with vinegar, see Introduction, p. 23.
passum: see Introduction, p. 24.

MEASURES AND WEIGHTS

acetabulum = $\frac{1}{2}$ gill ($\frac{1}{8}$ pint).
calix = a wineglass-full.
cocleare = $\frac{1}{2}$ *cheme* (about a teaspoon).
cyathus = $\frac{1}{12}$ pint (either untranslated or given in pints).
drachma = $\frac{1}{8}$ oz. (translated: a handful).
hemina = $\frac{1}{2}$ pint.
ligula = spoonful (tablespoon).
quartarius = 1 gill ($\frac{1}{4}$ pint).
scrupulus = 1 scruple ($\frac{1}{24}$ oz.).
sextarius = 1 pint.
uncia = 1 oz.

ABBREVIATIONS

add. = added (by).
Br., Brandt = E. Brandt (*the page numbers refer to the book quoted on p. 12 of the Introduction*).
codd. = consensus of the manuscript tradition.
corr. = corrected (by).
del. = deleted (by).
E = MS. New York, Library of the Academy of Medicine, formerly Cheltenham, Phillipps Collection 275.
F. = B. Flower.
Giarratano = C. Giarratano, in Teubner edition of Apicius.
Guégan = B. Guégan, *Les Dix Livres de Cuisine d'Apicius* (Paris, 1933).
Humelberg = Apicius edition of G. Humelberg (Zürich, 1542).
R. = E. Rosenbaum.
rest. = original text of manuscripts restored (by).
Schuch = Apicius edition of T. Schuch (Heidelberg, 1874).
Teubner = Apicius edition of C. Giarratano and F. Vollmer (Leipzig, Teubner, 1922).
V = MS. Rome, Vatican Library (*Urb. lat.* 1146).
Vehling = J. D. Vehling, *Apicius: Cooking and Dining in Imperial Rome* (Chicago, 1936).
Vollmer = F. Vollmer, in Teubner edition of Apicius.
† = text corrupt.
[   ] = words or passages believed to be interpolations or errors

in the text, or considered to be glosses. If no footnotes are added these parentheses are already in the Teubner edition. These words or passages are as a rule not translated.

⟨ ⟩ = in the Latin text: words or passages added by the present or previous editors. If not stated otherwise in footnotes these additions are already in the Teubner edition.

= in the English text: either corresponding to the Latin text; or words added by the translators for the sake of clarity.

EPIMELES

I. conditum paradoxum. II. conditum melizomum.
III. absinthium Romanum. IV. rosatum et violatium. V. oleum Liburnicum sic facies. VI. vinum ex
atro candidum facies. VII. de liquamine. VIII. ut
carnes sine sale quovis tempore recentes sint. IX. callum porcinum vel bubulum et unguellae coctae ut diu
durent. X. ut carnem salsam dulcem facias. XI. pisces fricti ut diu durent. XII. ostrea ut diu durent.
XIII. ut uncia laseris toto tempore uti possis. XIV. ut
dulcia de melle diu durent. XV. ut mel malum bonum
facias. XVI. mel corruptum ut probes. XVII. uvae
ut diu serventur. XVIII. ut mala et mala granata diu
durent. XIX. ut mala Cydonia diu serventur. XX.
ficum recentem mala pruna pira cerasia ut diu serves.
XXI. citria ut diu durent. XXII. mora ut diu durent.
XXIII. holera ut diu serventur. XXIV. rapae ut diu
serventur. XXV. tubera ut diu serventur. XXVI.
duracina Persica ut diu serventur. XXVII. sales conditos ad multa. XXVIII. olivas virides servare ut quovis
tempore oleum facias. XXIX. cuminatum in ostrea et
conchyliis. XXX. laseratum. XXXI. oenogarum in
tubera. XXXII. oxyporum. XXXIII. hypotrimma.
XXXIV. oxygarum digestibile. XXXV. moretaria.

BOOK I

THE CAREFUL HOUSEKEEPER

I. Spiced wine surprise

1. Spiced wine surprise is made as follows. 15 lb. of
honey are put in a metal vessel into which you have previously
put 2 pints of wine, so as to boil down the wine while cooking
the honey. It is heated over a slow fire of dry wood, stirring
all the while with a stick; when it begins to boil over it is

I. Conditum Paradoxum

1. Conditi paradoxi compositio: mellis pondo XV in
aeneum vas mittuntur, praemissis vini sextariis duobus, ut in
coctura mellis vinum decoquas. quod igni lento et aridis lignis
calefactum, commotum ferula dum coquitur, si effervere
coeperit, vini rore compescitur, praeter quod subtracto igni in
se redit. cum perfrixerit, rursus accenditur. hoc secundo ac
tertio fiet, ac tum demum remotum a foco postridie despumatur.
tum ⟨mittis⟩ piperis uncias IV, iam triti masticis scripulos III,
folii et croci dragmas singulas, dactylorum ossibus torridis
quinque, isdemque dactylis vino mollitis, intercedente prius
suffusione vini de suo modo ac numero, ut tritura lenis habeatur.
his omnibus paratis supermittis vini lenis sextarios XVIII.
carbones perfecto aderunt † duo milia.[1]   (*1*)

2. Conditum melizomum viatorium. Conditum melizomum perpetuum, quod subministratur per viam peregrinanti:
piper tritum cum melle despumato in cupellam mittis conditi
loco, et ad momentum quantum sit bibendum, tantum aut
mellis proferas aut vini misceas. sed suaserit[2] nonnihil vini
melizomo mittas, adiciendum propter mellis exitum solutiorem.

(2)

II. Apsinthium Romanum

Apsinthium Romanum sic facies: conditi Camerini praecep-
tis utique pro apsinthio cessante: in cuius vicem absenti Pontici
purgati terendique unciam, Thebaicam dabis, masticis, folii,
costi scripulos senos, croci scripulos III, vini eiusmodi sextarios
XVIII. carbones amaritudo non exigit.[3]   (*3*)

---

[1] *duo milia* codd., obelized by Br. (p. 24 f.) who thinks it might be
a wrong translation from the Greek.

[2] *suaserit* codd., rest. by Br.

[3] Br. (p. 23 f.) rest. reading of codd., eliminating only *III* after
folii.

checked by adding ⟨cold⟩ wine; it also sinks when removed from the fire. When cool it is heated once more. This must be done a second and third time, and only then is it removed from the fire, and skimmed on the following day. Then take 4 oz. pepper, 3 scruples of pounded mastic, a handful each of aromatic leaf[1] and saffron, 5 roasted date-stones, the dates softened in wine, having previously been soaked in wine of the right kind and quality, so as to produce a soft mash. These preparations completed, pour over 18 pints of sweet wine. In the end add coals, if it is too bitter.[2]

2. SPICED HONEY-WINE FOR TRAVELLERS. Spiced honey wine which keeps for ever is given to people on a journey. Put pounded pepper with skimmed honey in a small vat just as for spiced wine and, when required for drinking, mix part of the honey with some wine. It is advisable to add a little wine to the honey-mixture in order to make the honey run out more freely.

II. ROMAN VERMOUTH

ROMAN VERMOUTH prepare as follows. According to the recipes for Camerinian spiced wine, if you do not have any vermouth: in its stead take 1 oz. cleaned and pounded Pontian vermouth, 1 date, 6 scruples each of mastic, aromatic leaves,[3] and costmary, 3 scruples of saffron, 18 pints of the proper kind of wine. As it should be bitter, you need not add coal.

---

[1] See note (1) to I, xv, 1.
[2] The translation follows Brandt's suggestion; see note to the Latin text. Cp. also the recipe for Roman vermouth, below.
[3] See note (1) to I, xv, 1.

46 EPIMELES

III. ⟨Rosatum et violatium⟩

1. ROSATUM SIC FACIES: folia rosarum, albo sublato, lino inseris et sutilis facias, et vino quam plurimas infundes, ut septem diebus in vino sint. post septem dies rosam de vino tollis, et alias sutiles recentes similiter mittis, ut per dies septem in vino requiescant, et rosam eximis. similiter et tertio facies, et rosam eximis, et vinum colas, et, cum ad bibendum voles uti, addito melle rosatum conficies. sane custodito ut rosam a rore siccam et optimam mittas. Similiter, ut supra, et de ⟨viola⟩ violatium facies, et eodem modo melle temperabis.

(4)

2. ROSATUM SINE ROSA SIC FACIES: folia citri viridia in sportella palmea in dolium musti mittes antequam ferveat, et post quadraginta dies exime. cum necesse fuerit, mel addes et pro rosato utere.

IV

OLEUM LIBURNICUM SIC FACIES: in oleo Hispano mittes helenium et cyperi et folia lauri non vetusta, tunsa omnia et cribellata, ad levissimum pulverem redacta, et sales frictos et tritos, et per triduum vel plus permisce diligenter. post haec aliquanto tempore patere requiescere, et Liburnicum omnes putabunt. (5)

V

VINUM EX ATRO CANDIDUM FACIES: lomentum ex faba factum vel ovorum trium alborem in lagonam mittis et diutissime agitas: alia die erit candidum. et cineres vitis albae idem faciunt.

(6)

III. ⟨Rose wine and violet wine⟩

1. ROSE WINE. Rose wine you will make like this: Thread together rose-leaves from which the white part has been removed, and steep as many as possible in wine for seven days. After seven days take the rose-leaves out of the wine, and in the same way put in other fresh rose-leaves threaded together, to rest seven days in the wine, then take them out. Repeat a third time, take out the rose-leaves, strain the wine, and, when you want to use it for drinking, add honey to make rose wine. But take care to use the best rose-leaves, when the dew has dried off them. Make violet wine in the same way as above, and mix with honey in the same way.

2. ROSE WINE WITHOUT ROSE-LEAVES. Put fresh citron-leaves[1] in a basket made of palm-leaves, into a jar of must before it ferments, and take out after 40 days. When required, add honey and use as rose wine.

IV

LIBURNIAN OIL make as follows. To Spanish oil add helenium[2] and cyperus-root and fresh bay-leaves, all this pounded and sifted until reduced to very fine powder, and dried and pounded salt. Mix these ingredients for three days or longer. After this allow the mixture to rest for some time, and everybody will believe it is Liburnian oil.

V

TO MAKE WHITE WINE OUT OF RED WINE. Put bean-meal or three egg-whites into the flask and stir for a very long time. The next day the wine will be white. The white ashes of vine have the same effect.

[1] See note to I, xii, 5.
[2] calamint?

VI

DE LIQUAMINE EMENDANDO: liquamen si odorem malum fecerit, vas inane inversum fumiga lauro et cupresso, et in hoc liquamen infunde ante ventilatum. si salsum fuerit, mellis sextarium mittis et moves, picas,[1] et emendasti. sed et mustum recens idem praestat.   (7)

VII

1. UT CARNES SINE SALE QUOVIS TEMPORE RECENTES SINT: carnes recentes quales volueris melle tegantur, sed vas pendeat, et, quando volueris, utere. hoc hieme melius fit, aestate paucis diebus durabit.   et in carne cocta itidem facies.   (8)

2. CALLUM PORCINUM VEL BUBULUM ET UNGUELLAE COCTAE UT DIU DURENT: in sinapi ex aceto, sale, melle facta mittis

[1] moves, picas Br., move spicas codd.

VI

HOW TO PURIFY LIQUAMEN. If *liquamen* acquires a bad smell take an empty receptacle, turn over and fumigate with the smoke of burning laurel and cypress, and in this pour the *liquamen* which you have previously exposed to the air. If it is too salty add a pint of honey, stir and season with pitch, and the *liquamen* will be clean again. But fresh must has the same effect.

VII

1. HOW TO KEEP MEAT FRESH AS LONG AS YOU LIKE WITHOUT PICKLING. Cover meat that you wish to keep fresh with honey, but suspend the receptacle, and use when required. This is better in winter; in summer it will keep in this manner only a few days. You can use this method also with cooked meat.

2. HOW TO KEEP PORK OR BEEF SKIN AND COOKED TROTTERS. Put in mustard which is prepared with vinegar,[1] salt, and honey,

---

[1] Preparation of mustard:

1. According to Columella, *De re rustica*, XII, 57:

"Carefully clean mustard seed and sift, then wash in cold water and when well washed leave for two hours in the water. Then remove, press it with your hands and put in a new or a thoroughly cleaned mortar, and pound it with the pestle. When it is pounded put the mash into the middle of the mortar and compress it with the flat of your hand. Next, when you have pressed it, scarify it and after having placed a few glowing coals on it pour water mixed with cooking soda on it, in order to remove all bitterness and paleness. Immediately after lift the mortar so that all moisture may be drained away. After this add strong white vinegar, mix with the pestle and strain. This juice is very good to spice turnips. If, by the way, you want to prepare mustard for use at table, when you have squeezed it out, add pine-kernels which should be as fresh as possible and almonds, pound carefully and pour vinegar on. The rest should be done as directed above. This mustard is not only suitable as sauce, but it is even good to look at, for it is of extreme whiteness when made carefully."

2. According to Palladius, VIII, 9:

"Grind to fine powder 1½ pints of mustard seed, add 5 lb. honey, 1 lb. Spanish oil, 1 pint of strong vinegar, mix carefully and use."

4—R.C.B.

ut tegantur, et, quando volueris, utere: miraberis.   (9)

VIII

UT CARNEM SALSAM DULCEM FACIAS: carnem salsam dulcem
facies, si prius in lacte coquas et postea in aqua.   (10)

IX

1. UT PISCES FRICTI DIU DURENT: eodem momento, quo
friguntur et levantur, ab aceto calido perfunduntur.   (11)
2. OSTREA UT DIU DURENT: lavas ab aceto, aut ex aceto
vasculum picitum lava, et ostrea compone.   (12)

X

UT UNCIA LASERIS TOTO TEMPORE UTARIS: laser in spatiosum
doliolum vitreum mittis et nucleos pineos ut puta viginti,
cumque utendum fuerit lasere, nucleos conteres, et in cibis
miraberis sapores: et tantundem numero nucleorum doliolo
referetur.   (13)

XI

1. UT DULCIA DE MELLE DIU DURENT: accipies quod Graeci
dicunt cnecon et facies farinam et admisces cum melle eo tempore quo dulcia facturus es.   (14)
2. UT MEL MALUM BONUM FACIAS: mel malum bonum facies
ad vendendum, unam partem mali et duas boni si simul
miscueris.   (15)
3. MEL CORRUPTUM UT PROBES: inlunium[1] infundes in melle
et incende: si incorruptum est, lucet.   (16)

---

[1] *inlunium* codd., rest. by Br. (p. 49, n. 63 = ἐλλύχνιον).

so that it is covered, and use when required: you will be surprised.

VIII

To MAKE SALT MEAT SWEET. You make salt meat sweet by cooking it first in milk and then in water.

IX

1. To PRESERVE FRIED FISH. The moment they are fried and taken out of the pan, pour hot vinegar over them.
2. To PRESERVE OYSTERS. Wash them with vinegar, or wash a receptacle treated with pitch with vinegar and place the oysters in it.

X

How TO MAKE ONE OUNCE OF SILPHIUM LAST INDEFINITELY. Put the silphium[1] in a large enough glass jar, together with about 20 pine-kernels. When you have to use the silphium pound some of the pine-kernels, and you will be astonished at the flavour in your food. Replace the number of pine-kernels you have used in the jar.

XI

1. How TO PRESERVE CAKES MADE OF HONEY. Take what the Greeks call safflower, make flour, and mix it with honey at the time you want to make the cakes.
2. How TO MAKE BAD HONEY GOOD. You will make bad honey good for selling as follows: mix one part of bad honey with two parts of good honey.
3. How TO FIND OUT IF HONEY HAS GONE BAD. Put a lamp-wick in the honey and light. If it is good it burns.

[1] See Introduction, p. 28.

XII

1. Uvae ut diu serventur: accipies uvas de vite inlaesas, et aquam pluvialem ad tertias decoques, et mittis in vas, in quo et uvas mittis. vas picari et gypsari facies, et in locum frigidum, ubi sol accessum non habet, reponi facies, et, quando volueris, uvas virides invenies. et ipsam aquam pro hydromelli aegris dabis. et si in hordeo obruas, inlaesas invenies. (*17*)

2. Ut mala et mala granata diu durent: in calidam ferventem merge, et statim leva et suspende. (*18*)

3. Ut mala Cydonia diu serventur: eligis mala sine vitio cum ramulis et foliis, et condes in vas, et suffundes mel et defritum; diu servabis. (*19*)

4. Ficum recentem, mala, pruna, pira, cerasia ut diu serves: omnia cum peciolis diligenter legito et in melle ponito, ne se contingant. (*20*)

5. Citria ut diu durent: in vas citrum[1] mitte, gypsa, suspende. (*21*)

6. Mora ut diu durent: ex moris sucum facito, et cum sapa misce, et in vitreo vase cum mora[2] mitte: custodies multo tempore. (*22*)

7. Holera ut diu serventur: holera electa non satis matura in vas picitum repone. (*23*)

---

[1] *citrum* codd., rest. by Br.
[2] *mora* codd., rest. Br.

XII

1. To KEEP GRAPES FRESH. Take undamaged grapes from the vine, and reduce rain-water to one-third and put it in a receptacle in which you also put the grapes. Treat the receptacle with pitch and seal with gypsum, and store it in a cool place where the sun does not enter, and you will find fresh grapes when required. The water can be given to the sick as honey-water. You will also keep grapes undamaged if you store them in barley.

2. To KEEP APPLES AND POMEGRANATES FRESH. Plunge them in boiling water, take out instantly, and hang up.

3. To KEEP QUINCES FRESH. Choose faultless quinces with their twigs and leaves, and put them in a receptacle, and pour over honey and *defrutum*: you will keep them for a long time.

4. How TO PRESERVE FRESH FIGS, AND APPLES, PLUMS, PEARS, AND CHERRIES. Gather them carefully with their stalks and put them in honey, so that they do not touch each other.

5. To PRESERVE CITRON.[1] Put the fruit in a vessel, seal with gypsum, and hang up.

6. To PRESERVE BLACKBERRIES. Make juice of blackberries, and mix with thickened must,[2] put in a glass vessel together with whole blackberries; you will keep them for a long time.

7. To PRESERVE GREEN VEGETABLES. Choose vegetables that are not fully grown, and put in a receptacle treated with pitch.

---

[1] *citrium, citreum, citrum, citrus*, means here the fruit of the citron-tree (*Citrus medica* Linn.); this appears to be the only variety of citrus fruit known in ancient Italy. The wood was used for expensive furniture, and the leaves, because of their fragrance, were used for various purposes. The juice of the fruit is mentioned mainly in medical contexts, also as a means to strengthen vinegar. But it does not seem to have been eaten. The fruit is oblong, up to about 6 inches long; it can weigh 2–3 lb., has a very thick, coarse skin, which is nowadays candied, and the pips are embedded in the pith, which is leathery and bitter. For the other meaning of the word cp. note to IV, iii, 5.

[2] *sapa*—see Introduction, p. 23.

8. RAPAE UT DIU SERVENTUR: ante accuratas et compositas asperges myrtae bacis cum melle et aceto.

9. ALITER: sinapi tempera melle, aceto, sale, et super compositas rapas infundes.   (*24*)

10. TUBERA UT DIU SERVENTUR: tubera, quae aquae non vexaverint, componis in vas alternis, alternis scobem siccam mittis, cooperis et gypsas, et loco frigido pones.   (*25*)

11. DURACINA PERSICA UT DIU DURENT: eligito optima, et mitte in muriam. postera die exime, et spongiabis diligenter, et collocabis in vas. fundes salem, acetum, satureiam.

                                                   (*26*)

XIII

SALES CONDITOS AD MULTA: Sales conditos ad digestionem, ad ventrem movendum. et omnes morbos et pestilentiam et omnia frigora prohibent generari. sunt autem et suavissimi ultra quam speras: sales communes frictos lib. I, sales Ammonicos frictos lib. II, piperis albi uncias III, gingiber unc. II, ammeos unc. I semis, thymi unc. I semis, apii seminis unc. I semis (si apii semen mittere nolueris, petroselini mittis unc. III), origani unc. III, erucae semen unc. I semis, piperis nigri unc. III, croci unc. I, hysopi Cretici unc. II, folium unc. II, petroselinum unc. II, anethi unc. II.[1]   (*29*)

XIV

OLIVAS VIRIDES SERVARE UT QUOVIS TEMPORE OLEUM FACIAS: olivas de arbore sublatas in illud mittis, et erunt tales quovis tempore quasi mox de arbore demptae. de quibus, si volueris, oleum viride facies.   (*27*)

---

[1] Reading of Br. (p. 40 f.)—rest. from codd.—adopted except for certain spellings.

8. To PRESERVE TURNIPS. First clean and arrange them in a vessel, and then pour on myrtle-berries mixed with honey and vinegar.

9. ANOTHER METHOD. Mix mustard with honey, vinegar, and salt,[1] and pour over the turnips arranged in a vessel.

10. To PRESERVE TRUFFLES. Arrange truffles which are undamaged by water in a receptacle in layers, separated from each other by sawdust, cover with a lid, and seal with gypsum, and keep in a cool place.

11. To PRESERVE PEACHES. Choose the best fruit, and put them in brine. Take them out the following day and sponge carefully, and place them in a receptacle. Pour on salt, vinegar, and savory.

XIII

AROMATIC SALTS TO BE USED FOR MANY THINGS. Aromatic salts are for the digestion, and to move the bowels. They prevent all diseases and the plague, and all colds. Moreover, they are mild, beyond all expectation. Take 1 lb. dried common salt, 2 lb. dried sal ammoniac, 3 oz. white pepper, 2 oz. ginger, 1½ oz. ammi,[2] 1½ oz. thyme, 1½ oz. celery seed (if you do not want to take celery seed take 3 oz. parsley instead), 3 oz. origan, 1½ oz. rocket-seed, 3 oz. black pepper, 1 oz. saffron, 2 oz. hyssop from Crete, 2 oz. aromatic leaves,[3] 2 oz. parsley, 2 oz. dill.

XIV

To PRESERVE GREEN OLIVES SO AS TO MAKE OIL AT ANY TIME YOU WISH. Put the olives gathered from the tree in oil, and they will remain for any length of time as if just gathered from the tree. From these you can make best-quality oil if you wish.

[1] See note to I, vii, 2.
[2] A kind of cumin.
[3] See note (1) to I, xv, 1.

56 EPIMELES

XV

1. CUMINATUM IN OSTREA ET CONCHYLIA: piper, ligusticum, petroselinum, mentam siccam, folium, malabathrum, cuminum plusculum, mel, acetum et liquamen.
2. ALITER: piper, ligusticum, petroselinum, mentam siccam, cuminum plusculum, mel, acetum, liquamen.   (*30*)

XVI

1. LASERATUM: laser Cyrenaicum vel Parthicum tepida dissolvis cum aceto ⟨et⟩ liquamine temperatum, vel piper, petroselinum, mentam siccam, laseris radicem, mel, acetum, liquamen.
2. ALITER: piper, careum, anethum, petroselinum, mentam siccam, silfi, folium, malabathrum, spicam Indicam, costum modicum, mel, acetum, liquamen.   (*31*)

XVII

1. OENOGARUM IN TUBERA: piper, ligusticum, coriandrum, rutam, liquamen, mel, ⟨vinum⟩[1] et oleum modice.
2. ALITER: thymum, satureiam, piper, ligusticum, mel, ⟨vinum⟩,[2] liquamen et oleum.   (*32*)

XVIII

OXYPORUM: cumini unc. II, zingiberis unc. I, rutae viridis unc. I, nitri scripulos VI, dactylorum pinguium scripulos XII,

[1] *vinum* add. Br. (from VII, xvi, 3).
[2] *vinum* add. R.

XV

1. CUMIN SAUCE FOR OYSTERS AND SHELL-FISH. Pepper, lovage, parsley, dry mint, bay-leaf,[1] malabathrum,[2] plenty of cumin,[3] honey, vinegar, and *liquamen.*

2. ANOTHER METHOD. Pepper, lovage, parsley, dry mint, plenty of cumin, honey, vinegar, *liquamen.*

XVI

1. SILPHIUM SAUCE. Dissolve silphium from Cyrenaica or Parthian silphium[4] in luke-warm water and mix with vinegar and liquamen; or mix pepper, parsley, dry mint, silphium-root, honey, vinegar, and *liquamen.*

2. ANOTHER METHOD. Pepper, caraway,[5] dill, parsley, dry mint, silphium, bay-leaf, malabathrum, spikenard, a little costmary, honey, vinegar, *liquamen.*

XVII

1. OENOGARUM FOR TRUFFLES. Pepper, lovage, coriander, rue, *liquamen,* honey, wine, and a little oil.

2. ANOTHER METHOD. Thyme, savory, pepper, lovage, honey, wine, *liquamen,* and oil.

XVIII

OXYPOR(I)UM.[6] 2 oz. cumin, 1 oz. ginger, 1 oz. fresh rue, 6 scruples cooking soda, 12 scruples of juicy dates, 1 oz. pepper,

---

[1] *folium* can be any aromatic leaf; we chose bay-leaf for convenience.
[2] Malabathrum is a shrub from the Far East, the dried leaves of which were imported pressed in bales. An aromatic oil was extracted from these leaves.
[3] *Cuminum cyminum* Linn., similar, but not identical to, caraway (*Carum carvi* Linn.).
[4] *I.e.,* asafœtida.
[5] *Carum carvi* Linn., cp. above, note (3).
[6] = III, xviii, 2 and 3.

piperis unc. I, mellis unc. IX. cuminum aut Aethiopicum aut
Syriacum aut Libycum aceto infundes, sicca et sic tundes.
postea melle comprehendis. cum necesse fuerit, ⟨ex⟩ oxygaro
uteris. *(33)*

XIX

HYPOTRIMMA: piper, ligusticum, mentam aridam, nucleos
pineos, uvam passam, caryotam, caseum dulcem, mel, acetum,
liquamen, oleum, vinum, defritum aut caroenum. *(34)*

XX

1. OXYGARUM DIGESTIBILE: piperis semunciam, silis Gallici
scripulos III, cardamomi scripulos VI, cumini scripulos VI,
folii scripulum I, mentae siccae scripulos VI tunsa cribrataque
melle colligis. cum opus fuerit, liquamen et acetum addis.

2. ALITER: piperis unc. I, petroselini, carei, ligustici unc.
singulas. melle colliguntur. cum opus fuerit, liquamen et
acetum addes. *(35)*

XXI

MORETARIA: mentam, rutam, coriandrum, feniculum, omnia
viridia, ligusticum, piper, mel, liquamen. si opus fuerit,
acetum addes. *(36)*

9 oz. honey. The cumin may be Æthiopian, Syrian, or Libyan. Moisten it with vinegar, dry, and then pound.[1] Then bind everything with the honey. When needed use with vinegar and *liquamen*.

XIX

HYPOTRIMMA. Pepper, lovage, dry mint, pine-kernels, raisins, Jericho date,[2] sweet cheese,[3] honey, vinegar, *liquamen*, oil, wine, *defrutum* or *caroenum*.

XX

1. OXYGARUM, TO PROMOTE THE DIGESTION. ½ oz. pepper, 2 scruples seseli from Gaul, 6 scruples cardamon, 6 scruples cumin, 1 scruple aromatic leaf, 6 scruples dry mint, pound and powder all this and then bind with honey. When needed add *liquamen* and vinegar.

2. ANOTHER METHOD. 1 oz. pepper, 1 oz. each of parsley, caraway, lovage. Pound, bind with honey. When needed, add *liquamen* and vinegar.

XXI

MORETARIA. Mint, rue, coriander, fennel, all fresh, lovage, pepper, honey, *liquamen*. If needed, add vinegar.

---

[1] The version of III, xviii, seems better: pound, and then moisten with vinegar.

[2] Here, and in the following, we have translated *caryota* by 'Jericho date' with reference to Pliny, *Nat. Hist.* XIII, 4, 9 (44 ff.), who states that the *caryotae* were especially good and plentiful in Palestine, especially in the district of Jericho. The *caryotae* are praised as a food and for their juice, from which date-wine is made.

[3] On the subject of cheese-making, see Introduction, p. 26.

SARCOPTES

I. isicia. II. hydrogarum et apothermum et amulatum.
III. vulvulae, botelli. IV. Lucanicae. V. farcimina.

I. Isicia

1. Isicia fiunt marina de cammaris et astacis, de lolligine, de
sepia, de lucusta. isicium condies pipere, liquamine,[1] cumino,
laseris radice. (37)

2. Isicia de lolligine: sublatis crinibus in fulmento tundes,
sicuti adsolet. pulpa et in mortario et in liquamine diligenter
fricatur, et exinde isicia plassantur. (38)

3. Isicia de scillis vel de cammaris amplis: cammari vel
scillae de testa sua eximuntur, et in mortario teruntur cum
pipere et liquamine optimo. pulpa isicia plassantur. (39)

[1] *liquamine* Br. (p. 57), *ligustico* codd.

BOOK II

THE MEAT-MINCER

I. Forcemeat. II. Rissoles with *hydrogarum*; *apothermum*; rissoles in thick sauce. III. Wombs; black pudding. IV. Lucanian sausages. V. Sausages.

I. Forcemeat

1. SEA-FOOD RISSOLES are made from large prawns,[1] or lobsters,[2] from squid, or cuttlefish, or sea-crayfish.[3] You will flavour your rissoles with pepper, *liquamen*, cumin, asafœtida root.

2. RISSOLES OF SQUID. Remove the tentacles and beat it on a board in the usual way. The flesh is carefully pounded in a mortar with *liquamen*, and then formed into rissoles.

3. RISSOLES OF SQUILL[4] OR LARGE PRAWNS. The prawns or squills are taken out of their shells and pounded in a mortar with pepper and best *liquamen*, and rissoles formed from the meat.

[1] *cammarus* is certainly a crustacean, but it is difficult to identify the species. Some Latin sources treat the word as a synonym of *astacus* (see note 2), others as one of *squilla*. We translate the word here and in Book IX by 'large prawn,' having in mind the size of Pacific prawns, but we are aware that, for instance, scampi could be meant just as well. For recipe No. 3 any crustacean, from shrimps to lobsters, could be used.

[2] *astacus* appears to be the Greek word for lobster. Here again there is no certainty as to the variety of lobster the word denotes.

[3] *lucusta*: we translate the word here and in Book IX by sea-crayfish—*i.e.*, the spiny lobster (the French *langouste*), although again one cannot be quite certain whether the word *lucusta* denotes this particular member of the lobster family. Recipe IX, i, 2, however, makes it very probable that this translation is correct.

[4] Squills are stomatopod crustaceans, similar to prawns.

4. OMENTATA ITA FIUNT: assas iecur porcinum et [eum] enervas. ante tamen teres piper, rutam, liquamen, et sic superinmittis iecur et teres et misces[1] sicut[2] pulpa omentata, et singula involvuntur folia lauri, et ad fumum suspenduntur quamdiu voles. cum manducare volueris, tolles de fumo et denuo assas.   (*40*)

5. ⟨ALITER⟩ ISICIUM: adicies in mortarium piper, ligusticum, origanum, fricabis, suffundes liquamen, adicies cerebella cocta, teres diligenter, ne assulas habeat. adicies ova quinque et dissolves diligenter, ut unum corpus efficias. liquamine temperas et in patella aenea exinanies, coques. cum coctum fuerit, versas in tabula munda, tessellas concides. adicies in mortarium piper, ligusticum, origanum, fricabis. in se commisces, ⟨suffundes liquamen, vinum. mittes⟩[3] in caccabum, facies ut ferveat. cum ferbuerit, tractum confringes, obligas, coagitabis, et exinanies in boletari. piper asperges et appones.   (*41*)

6. ISICIA EX SPHONDYLIS: elixatos sphondylos conteres et nervos eorum eximes, deinde cum eis alicam elixatam ⟨et⟩ ova

---

[1] Lacuna to be assumed after *misces*; Br. suggests: ⟨*isicia plassantur et omento teguntur*⟩ . . .
[2] *sicut* codd., rest. by Br. (p. 56).
[3] Lacuna to be assumed after *commisces*; *suffundes . . . mittes* proposed by Br. (p. 56, with another suggestion).

THE MEAT-MINCER 63

4. SAUSAGES. Grill pig's liver and remove the sinews and skin. But first pound pepper, rue, and *liquamen*, then add the liver, pound well, and mix. ⟨Form rissoles and cover with sausage-skin[1]⟩ like meat sausages. Wrap each in bay-leaves and hang to smoke for as long as you please. When you want to eat them take down and grill again.

5. RISSOLES, ANOTHER METHOD. Put in a mortar pepper, lovage, and origan; pound; moisten with *liquamen*, add cooked brains, pound thoroughly to dissolve lumps. Add five eggs and beat well to work all into a smooth paste. Blend with *liquamen*, place in a metal pan, and cook. When it is cooked turn out on a clean board and dice. Put in the mortar pepper, lovage, origan; pound, mix together; pour in *liquamen* and wine, put in a saucepan and bring to the boil. When boiling crumble in pastry to thicken, stir vigorously, and pour in the serving-dish over the diced rissoles; sprinkle with pepper and serve.[2]

6. RISSOLES OF MUSSELS.[3] Boil the mussels, pound and remove sinews, then pound them with boiled spelt-grits[4] and

[1] *omentum*: the translation 'sausage skin' is chosen here and throughout for convenience.
[2] Three halves of pig's brains seem to be the right quantity for five eggs. It sets over a slow fire like soufflé omelette slightly overcooked. Before pounding, the brains are, of course, to be skinned in the usual way.
[3] This recipe occurs again in Book III (xx, 7); cp. note to III, xx, 1.
[4] *alica* (spelt-grits): *alica* is spelt, or German wheat (*Triticum spelta* Linn.), and also a product of this grain, comparable to oat-grits or groats; the process is described by Pliny, *Nat. Hist.* XVIII, ii, 29 (112–116): "*alica* is made of *zea* (=spelt) as we have called the seed. The grain is crushed in a wooden mortar—because a stone one would be too hard, and grind it too finely—with a pestle in the end of which an iron capsule is inserted. The pestles are operated—as is well known—by convicts in chains. When the husks are thus beaten out, the bare core is treated again with the same instruments. In this manner three kinds of *alica* are made: the very fine one; the medium; and the very coarse one which is called *aphaerema*. They have not yet their whiteness by which they are distinguished, yet they are

conteres, ⟨piper, liquamen. isicia ex his facies cum nucleis et⟩[1] pipere. in omento assabis, oenogaro perfundes, et pro isiciis inferes.   (*42*)

7. ISICIA OMENTATA: pulpam concisam teres cum medulla siligine⟨i⟩[2] in vino infusi. piper, liquamen, si velis, et bacam myrtae exenteratam simul conteres. pusilla isicia formabis, intus nucleis et pipere positis. involuta omento subassabis cum caroeno.   (*43*)

II. HYDROGARATUM ET APOTHERMUM ET AMULATUM

1. ISICIA PLENA: accipies adipes fasiani recentes, praeduras et facis ex eo tessellas. cum pipere, liquamine, caroeno in isicio includes, ex hydrogaro coques et inferes.   (*44*)

2. HYDROGARATA ISICIA SIC FACIES: teres piper, ligusticum, pyrethrum minimum, suffundes liquamen; temperas aqua cisternina, dum inducet; exinanies in caccabo, et cum isicio ad vaporem ignis pones, et caleat, et sic sorbendum inferes.   (*45*)

3. IN ISICIA DE PULLO: olei floris lib. I, liquaminis quartarium, piperis semunciam.   (*46*)

4. ALITER DE PULLO: piperis grana XXXI conteres, mittis liquaminis optimi calicem, caroeni tantundem, aquae XI mittes, et ad vaporem ignis pones.   (*47*)

5. ISICIUM SIMPLEX: ad unum liquaminis acetabulum aquae septem mittes, modicum apii viridis, triti piperis cocleare.

---

[1] *piper* . . . *et* add. Br. (p. 56) from III, xx, 7, a repetition of this recipe.
[2] *siligine⟨i⟩* Br. (p. 55), *siligine* codd.

eggs, pepper and *liquamen*. Make rissoles from this with pine-kernels and pepper. Stuff in sausage skin, grill, pour over *oenogarum*, and serve as rissoles.

7. FORCEMEAT SAUSAGES. Chop up meat and pound with white bread without crust which has been steeped in wine. At the same time pound pepper, *liquamen*, and, if you like, seeded myrtle-berry. Make little forcemeat balls, inserting pine-kernels and pepper-corns. Wrap in sausage-skin and cook gently in *caroenum*.

II. RISSOLES WITH HYDROGARUM; APOTHERMUM; RISSOLES IN THICK SAUCE

1. STUFFED RISSOLES. Take fresh pheasant fat, brown, and dice. With pepper, *liquamen*, and *caroenum*, put in rissoles, cook in *hydrogarum*, and serve.

2. RISSOLES IN HYDROGARUM. Make as follows. Pound pepper, lovage, a pinch of pyrethrum; moisten with *liquamen*. Add cistern-water to blend; empty into a saucepan, put in the rissoles, and stand in the steam[1]; heat it up, and serve. The dish should be sipped.

3. TO SERVE WITH CHICKEN RISSOLES. 1 lb. of best oil, 1 gill *liquamen*, ½ oz. pepper.

4. ANOTHER SAUCE FOR CHICKEN ⟨RISSOLES⟩. Pound 31 peppercorns, add 1 wine-glass of best *liquamen*, 1 of *caroenum*, 11 of water, and set it in the steam.

5. SIMPLE RISSOLES. To ½ gill of *liquamen* add 3½ gills of water, a little green celery, and a teaspoonful of ground pepper.

preferable to the Alexandrian variety even so. Then, miraculously, chalk is mixed into it which penetrates the core and gives it colour and delicacy. This chalk is found between Pozzuoli and Naples on a hill called *Leucogaeus* . . ."

[1] *ad vaporem ignis*: this expression might denote that the dish was to be put to simmer on a kind of *vatillum* (see Introduction, section IV, p. 30).

5—R.C.B.

isiciola incoques, et sic ad ventrem solvendum dabis. hydrogaro faeces conditi addes.   (*48*)

6. ISICIA de pavo primum locum habent ita si fricta fuerint
ut callum vincant. Item secundum locum habent de fasianis,
item tertium locum habent de cuniculis, item quartum locum
habent de pullis, item quintum locum habent de porcello
tenero.   (*49*)

7. ISICIA AMULATA AB AHENO SIC FACIES: teres piper, ligusticum, origanum, modicum silfi, zingiber minimum, mellis
modicum; liquamine temperabis, misces; adicies super isicia,
facies ut ferveat.   cum bene bullierit, amulo obligas spisso, et
sorbendum inferes.   (*50*)

8. AMULATUM ALITER: piper teres pridie infusum, cui subinde
liquamen suffundes ita ut bene tritum ac lutulentum facias
piperatum.   cui defritum admisces, quod fit de cotoniis, quod
sole torrente in mellis substantiam cogitur.   quod si non
fuerit, vel Caricarum defritum mittes, quod Romani 'colorem'
vocant.   ac deinceps amulum infusum adicies vel oryzae sucum
et lento igni fervere facias.   (*51*)

9. AMULATUM ALITER: ossucla de pullis exbromas.   deinde
mittis in caccabum porros, anethum, salem.   cum cocta
fuerint, addes piper, apii semen, deinde oryzam infusam teres,
addes liquamen et passum vel defritum.   omnia misces et cum
isiciis inferes.   (*52*)

10. APOTHERMUM SIC FACIES: alicam elixa cum nucleis et
amygdalis depellatis et in aqua infusis et lotis ex creta argen-
taria, ut ad candorem pariter perducantur.   cui ammiscebis
uvam passam, caroenum vel passum, desuper ⟨piper⟩ confractum asparges et in boletari inferes.

III. VULVULAE BOTELLI

1. VULVULAE ISICIATAE SIC FIUNT: piper tritum et cuminum,
capita porrorum brevia duo ad molle purgata, ruta, liquamen.

Cook the rissoles in this, and serve as a laxative. To the *hydrogarum*[1] add lees of spiced wine.

6. RISSOLES. The most prized are peacock rissoles if they are fried so as to make the hard skin tender. Next in order for rissoles comes pheasant, after that rabbit, then chicken, then tender sucking-pig.

7. RISSOLES WITH A THICK SAUCE IN A METAL CASSEROLE. Make as follows. Pound pepper, lovage, origan, a little asafœtida, a pinch of ginger, a little honey; blend with *liquamen*, mix. Pour over the rissoles, bring to the boil. When boiling fast thicken with cornflour and serve. The dish should be sipped.

8. THICK SAUCE, ANOTHER METHOD. Pound pepper soaked overnight, to which you then add *liquamen* to make a well-ground pepper mash of muddy texture. To this add *defrutum* of quinces, further reduced to the consistency of honey by exposure to a hot sun. If you do not have this use *defrutum* of dried figs, which the Romans call 'colouring.' Next add a paste of cornflour and water, or water in which rice has boiled, and bring to the boil over a low fire.

9. THICK SAUCE, ANOTHER METHOD. Boil chicken-bones. ⟨When they have been boiling for some time⟩ add to the saucepan leeks, dill, salt. When they are cooked add pepper and celery seed, then pound steeped rice, add *liquamen* and *passum* or *defrutum*. Mix all this together and serve with rissoles.

10. APOTHERMUM. Make as follows. Boil spelt-grits with pine-kernels and almonds skinned, soaked, and washed with chalk used for cleaning silver, so as to render them equally white. Into this mix raisins, *caroenum* or *passum*, sprinkle ground pepper on top, and serve in a serving-dish (*boletar*).

III. WOMBS; BLACK PUDDING

1. STUFFED WOMBS. Make as follows. Pounded pepper and cumin, two short heads of leek stripped to the soft part, rue,

[1] *I.e.*, the above liquid.

admiscentur pulpae bene tunsae et fricatae denuo, ipso subtrito ita ut commisceri possi⟨n⟩t,[1] mittas piperis grana et
nucleos, et calcabis in materia[2] bene lota. et sic coquuntur
ex aqua, oleo, liquamine, fasciculo porrorum et anetho.   (*54*)

2. BOTELLUM SIC FACIES: sex ovi vitellis coctis, nucleis
pineis concisis cepam, porrum concisum, ius crudum misces,
piper minutum ⟨addes,⟩[3] et sic intestinum farcies. adicies
liquamen et vinum, et sic coques.

IV. LUCANICAE

Lucanicas similiter ut supra scriptum est: [Lucanicarum
confectio] teritur piper, cuminum, satureia, ruta, petroselinum,
condimentum, bacae lauri, liquamen, et admiscetur pulpa bene
tunsa, ita ut denuo bene cum ipso subtrito fricetur. cum
liquamine admixto, pipere integro et abundanti pinguedine et
nucleis inicies in intestinum perquam tenuatim productum, et
sic ad fumum suspenditur.   (*56*)

V. FARCIMINA

1. Ova et cerebella teres, nucleos pineos, piper, liquamen,
laser modicum, et his intestinum implebis. elixas; postea
assas et inferes.   (*57*)

2. ALITER: coctam alicam et tritam cum pulpa concisa et trita
una cum pipere et liquamine et nucleis. farcies intestinum et
elixabis, deinde cum sale assabis et cum sinapi inferes, vel sic
concisum in disco.   (*58*)

3. ALITER: alicam purgas et cum liquamine intestini et
albamine porri concisi minutatim simul elixas. elixa tolles,
pinguedinem concides et copadia pulpae, in se omnia commisces. teres piper, ligusticum, ova tria, haec omnia in

---

[1] *possit* codd.; *possi⟨n⟩t* suggested by Br.
[2] *I.e., vulvula*, Br. (p. 60 f.).
[3] *addes* add. R.; *asparges* add. Giarratano, in Teubner ed.

liquamen. To this pounded mixture add meat well beaten and again pounded, so that it mixes well, further, peppercorns and pine-kernels, and press in the well-washed womb. Cook in water, oil, *liquamen*, with a bouquet of leeks and dill.

2. BLACK PUDDING. Make as follows. With six boiled egg-yolks, and chopped pine-kernels, mix onion, chopped leek, and blood, add finely ground pepper, and with this mixture stuff a sausage-skin. Cook in *liquamen* and wine.

IV. LUCANIAN SAUSAGES

Lucanian sausages are made in a way similar to the above.[1] Pound pepper, cumin, savory, rue, parsley, mixed herbs, laurel-berries, and *liquamen*, and mix with this well-beaten meat, pounding it again with the ground spice mixture. Work in *liquamen*, peppercorns, plenty of fat and pine-kernels, insert into a sausage-skin, drawn out very thinly, and hang in the smoke.

V. SAUSAGES

1. Make a mixture of eggs and brains, pounded pine-kernels, pepper, *liquamen*, a little asafœtida, and with this stuff a sausage-skin. Boil. Afterwards grill and serve.

2. ANOTHER METHOD. Make a mixture of boiled spelt-grits and coarsely minced meat that has been pounded with pepper, *liquamen*, and pine-kernels. Stuff a sausage-skin ⟨with it⟩ and boil. Then grill with salt and serve with mustard, or serve boiled cut up on a round dish.

3. ANOTHER METHOD. Clean spelt-grits and boil with *liquamen*[2] and the finely chopped white part of a leek. When cooked remove. Chop suet and sliced meat and mix all together. Pound pepper, lovage, and three eggs; mix all this

[1] *I.e.*, like stuffed wombs, II, iii, 1.
[2] This passage ("cum liquamine intestini") is not quite clear.

mortario permisces cum nucleis et pipere integro. liquamen suffundes, intestina imples, elixas et subassas, vel elixa tantum: appones.   (59)

4. ALITER CIRCELLOS ISICIATOS: reples intestinum impensa isicii et circellum facies rotundum; fumas. cum miniaverit, subassas, exornas, oenogaro fasiani perfundes, sed cuminum addes.   (60)

in the mortar with pine-kernels and peppercorns. Pour in *liquamen*. Stuff sausage-skins, boil, and grill lightly or serve simply boiled.

4. SAUSAGE RING WITH RISSOLE FILLING. Stuff a sausage-skin with rissole mixture and make a ring of it. Smoke. When it is red grill lightly, arrange on the serving-dish. Pour over *oenogarum* as with pheasant rissoles, but add cumin.

CEPUROS

I. ut omne holus smaragdinum fiat. II. pulmen-
tarium ad ventrem. III. asparagos. IV. cucurbitas.
V. citrium. VI. cucumeres. VII. pepones, melones.
VIII. malvas. IX. cymas et cauliculos. X. porros.
XI. betas. XII. holisera. XIII. rapas sive napos.
XIV. raphanos. XV. holus molle. XVI. herbae rus-
ticae. XVII. urticae. XVIII. intuba et lactucae.
XIX. cardui. XX. [funduli sive] sphongili. XXI.
caroetae.

I. DE HOLERIBUS

UT OMNE HOLUS SMARAGDINUM FIAT: omne holus smaragdinum fit,[1] si cum nitro coquatur.   (*61*)

II. PULMENTARIUM AD VENTREM

1. BETA MINUTAS et porros requietos elixabis, in patina compones. teres piper, cuminum, suffundes liquamen, passum,
ut quaedam dulcedo sit. facias ut ferveat. cum ferbuerit,
inferes.   (*62*)
2. SIMILITER: polypodium in tepidam mittes. ubi mollierit,

[1] *fit* Br. from E; *fiat* Vollmer from V.

72

BOOK III

THE GARDENER

I. To make all vegetables bright green.   II. Broth to be used as a laxative.   III. Asparagus.   IV. Marrow.   V. Pumpkin.   VI. Cucumbers.   VII. Long and round melons.   VIII. Mallows.   IX. Cabbage.   X. Leeks. XI Beets   XII.   Horse-parsley.   XIII. Turnips. XIV. Radishes.   XV. Vegetable purée.   XVI. Wild herbs.   XVII. Stinging nettles.   XVIII. Endive and lettuce   XIX. Artichokes.   XX. Mussels.   XXI. Carrots.

I. On green vegetables

To MAKE ALL VEGETABLES BRIGHT GREEN.   All greens become bright green if boiled with cooking-soda.

II. Broth to be used as a laxative

1. Boil very small beets and leeks from the store, and arrange in a shallow pan.   Pound pepper, cumin; moisten with *liquamen* and *passum* to sweeten.   Bring to the boil, and serve as soon as it has boiled.

2. ANOTHER METHOD.   Put polypody in warm water.   When tender, pass through a sieve and put with pounded pepper and cumin in a pan of boiling water.

3. ANOTHER METHOD.   Make bunches of beetroot; wipe, do not wash.   Sprinkle cooking-soda over them and tie up the separate bunches.   Put in water.   When it cooks put in the pan as seasoning *passum* or *caroenum*, sprinkle on cumin and pepper, and a little oil.   When this boils pound polypody and chopped nuts with *liquamen*, pour into the boiling pan, cover. Take off at once and use.

73

rades, et minutum cum pipere et cumino trito in patinam ferventem mittes et uteris.

3. ALITER AD VENTREM: facies betaciorum fasces; deterge, ne
laves. in eorum medium nitrum asparges et alligas singulos
fasces. mittes in aquam. cum coxeris, condies patinam, cum
eadem passum vel caroenum et cuminum et piper asparges et
oleum modicum. ubi ferbuerit, polypodium et frusta nucum
cum liquamine teres, ⟨in⟩ ferventem patinam fundes, cooperies.
statim depones et uteris.   *(63)*

4. [ALITER BETACIOS VARRONIS. Varro: "betacios, sed nigros,
quorum detersas radices et mulsa decoctas cum sale modico et
oleo vel sale, aqua et oleo in se coctas iusculum facere et potari,
melius etiam si in eo pullus sit decoctus."]   *(64)*

5. ALITER AD VENTREM: apios virides cum suis radicibus
lavabis et siccabis ad solem. deinde albamen et capita porrorum simul elixabis in caccabo novo, ita ut aqua ad tertias
deferveat [id est ut ex tribus eminis aquae una remaneat].
postea teres piper, liquamen et aliquantum mellis humore temperabis, et aquam apiorum decoctorum colabis in mortario, et
superfundes porris.[1] cum simul ferbuerit, appones, et, si
libitum fuerit, apios adicies.   *(65)*

III. ASPARAGOS

Asparagos siccabis, rursum in calidam summittes: callosiores
reddes.   *(66)*

IV. CUCURBITAS

1. GUSTUM DE CUCURBITIS: cucurbitas coctas expressas in
patinam compones. adicies in mortarium piper, cuminum,
silfi modice, [id est laseris radicem], rutae modicum, liquamine
et aceto temperabis, mittes defritum modicum ut coloretur, ius
exinanies in patinam. cum ferbuerint iterum ac tertio, depones
et piper minutum asparges.   *(67)*

[1] *apio* codd.; *porris* F. R.

4. [A GLOSS] BEETROOT, ANOTHER METHOD, FROM VARRO.[1]
Varro writes: "Take beetroot, rub clean and cook in *mulsum*
with a little salt and oil, or boil in water and oil with salt; make
a broth, and drink it. It is even better if a chicken has been
cooked in it first."

5. ANOTHER LAXATIVE. Wash green celery complete with
roots, and dry in the sun. Boil in water. Next boil the heads
and white parts of leeks together in a new saucepan, reducing the
water to one-third. After this mix pounded pepper and
liquamen and blend with a little liquid honey, and strain off the
water in which the celery has cooked into the mortar and pour
over the leeks. Bring to the boil and serve at once, adding the
celery if liked.

III. ASPARAGUS

Dry the asparagus. Plunge again[2] into hot water: this will
prevent them from getting too soft.

IV. MARROW

1. MARROW AS HORS D'ŒUVRES. Cook marrows, drain off
the water, and arrange in a shallow pan. Put in the mortar
pepper, cumin, a little asafœtida, a little rue, and blend with
liquamen and vinegar. Add a little *defrutum* to give colour, and
pour this sauce into the pan. When it has come to the boil
three times take off the fire and sprinkle ground pepper over it.

2. ANOTHER METHOD WITH THE SAUCE FOR TAROS.[3] Boil the
marrows in water as you do taros. Pound pepper, cumin, and
rue, pour in vinegar and *liquamen*, blend. Empty into a
saucepan in which you put a few drops of oil and the chopped

---

[1] Attributed by Humelberg to Varro's satire *Peri edesmaton*.

[2] The *rursum* seems to suggest that the boiling of asparagus is
interrupted—*i.e.*, first they are only blanched, then dried, and put
again into boiling water.

[3] Cp. VII, xvii.

76 CEPUROS

2. ALITER CUCURBITAS IURE COLOCASIORUM: cucurbitas coques ex aqua in modum colocasiorum. teres piper, cuminum, rutam, suffundes acetum, liquamen, temperabis, ⟨mittes⟩ in caccabum, cui adicies ⟨olei guttas⟩[1] et eas cucurbitas incisas, expressas in ius mittes ut ferveant. amulo obligas, piper asparges et inferes. *(68)*

3. ⟨ALITER⟩ CUCURBITAS MORE ALEXANDRINO: elixatas cucurbitas exprimis, sale asparges, in patina compones. teres piper, cuminum, coriandri semen, mentam viridem, laseris radicem, suffundes acetum, adicies caryotam, nucleum, teres, melle, aceto, liquamine, defrito et oleo temperabis, et cucurbitas perfundes. cum ferbuerint, piper asparges et inferes. *(69)*

4. ALITER CUCURBITAS ELIXATAS: ex liquamine, oleo, mero. *(70)*

5. ALITER CUCURBITAS FRICTAS: oenogaro simplici et pipere. *(71)*

6. ALITER CUCURBITAS ELIXATAS ET FRICTAS: in patina compones, cuminatum superfundes; modico oleo super adiecto. fervere facies et inferes. *(72)*

7. ALITER CUCURBITAS FRICTAS TRITAS: piper, ligusticum, cuminum, origanum, cepam, vinum, liquamen et oleum. amulo obligabis in patina, et inferes. *(73)*

8. ALITER CUCURBITAS CUM GALLINA: duracina, tubera, piper, careum, cuminum, silfi, condimenta viridia, mentam, apium, coriandrum, puleium, caroenum,[2] mel, vinum, liquamen, oleum et acetum. *(74)*

V. CITRIUM

Sil montanum, silfi, mentam siccam, acetum, liquamen. *(75)*

VI. CUCUMERES

1. CUCUMERES RASOS: sive ex liquamine, sive ex oenogaro: sine ructu et gravitudine teneriores senties. *(76)*

---

[1] Lacuna indicated in Teubner edition; *olei guttas* add. Br.
[2] *caroenum* R; *caromentam* codd.

and drained marrows, bring to the boil with the sauce. Thicken with cornflour, sprinkle with pepper, and serve.

3. MARROWS, ALEXANDRIAN FASHION. Boil and drain the marrows, sprinkle with salt, arrange in a shallow pan. Pound pepper, cumin, coriander-seed, fresh mint, asafœtida root, moisten with *liquamen*, add Jericho date, pine-kernels, mash well, blend with honey, vinegar, *liquamen*, *defrutum*, and oil, and pour over the marrows. When they have boiled sprinkle with pepper and serve.

4. BOILED MARROWS, ANOTHER METHOD. Serve with *liquamen*, oil, and wine.

5. MARROWS FRIED. Serve with plain *oenogarum* and pepper.

6. MARROWS BOILED AND FRIED. Arrange in a shallow pan; pour on cumin sauce with a little oil added. Bring to the boil and serve.

7. MARROWS FRIED AND MASHED. Pepper, lovage, cumin, origan, onion, wine, *liquamen*, and oil. Thicken with cornflour in the pan and serve.

8. MARROWS WITH FOWL. Peaches, truffles, caraway, cumin, asafœtida, mixed fresh herbs—mint, celery, coriander, and pennyroyal—*caroenum*, honey, wine, *liquamen*, oil, and vinegar.

V. PUMPKIN[1]

⟨Dressing⟩: seseli, asafœtida, dried mint, vinegar, *liquamen*.

VI. CUCUMBERS

1. PEELED CUCUMBERS. Serve with *liquamen* or *oenogarum*: you will find this makes them more tender, and they will not cause flatulence or heaviness.

2. PEELED CUCUMBERS, ANOTHER METHOD. Stew with boiled brains, cumin and a little honey, celery seed, *liquamen*, and oil. Bind with eggs, sprinkle with pepper, and serve.

[1] See note to IV, iii, 5.

2. ALITER CUCUMERES RASOS: elixabis cum cerebellis elixis, cumino et melle modico, ⟨vel⟩ apii semine, liquamine et oleo. ovis obligabis, piper asparges et inferes.   (77)

3. ALITER CUCUMERES: piper, puleium, mel vel passum, liquamen et acetum. interdum et silfi accedit.   (78)

VII. PEPONES ET MELONES

Piper, puleium, mel vel passum, liquamen, acetum: interdum et silfi accedit.   (79)

VIII. MALVAS

Malvas minores ⟨in⟩ oenogaro ex liquamine, oleo, aceto.— Malvas maiores in oenogaro, pipere, liquamine, caroeno vel passo.   (80)

IX. CYMAS ET CAULICULOS

1. CYMAS: cuminum, salem, vinum vetus et oleum. si

3. CUCUMBERS, ANOTHER METHOD. ⟨Dressing for salad:⟩ pepper, pennyroyal, honey or *passum*, *liquamen*, and vinegar. Sometimes asafœtida is added.

VII. LONG AND ROUND MELONS

⟨Dressing:⟩ pepper, pennyroyal, honey or *passum*, *liquamen*, and vinegar. Sometimes asafœtida is added.

VIII. MALLOWS[1]

Serve the round-leaved variety with *oenogarum*, with ⟨more⟩ *liquamen*, oil, and vinegar ⟨added⟩. The wild mallow serve with *oenogarum* with pepper, ⟨more⟩ *liquamen*, *caroenum* or *passum* ⟨added⟩.

IX. CABBAGE

1. YOUNG CABBAGE[2] : (*a*) ⟨Serve with or cook in⟩ cumin, salt,

---

[1] Presumably the mallow-leaves are cooked like spinach before dressing, cp. Sir H. C. Luke, *The Tenth Muse* (London, 1954), No. 215, p. 160, referring to *Malva silvestris = Malva maior* in Cypriot recipes: recommended as alternative for spinach. Recommended by Pliny, *Nat. Hist.*, XX, 21, 84 (222–230), as aphrodisiac and panacea.

[2] We have translated both *cymae* and *cauliculi* simply by 'cabbage,' adding only the distinction 'young' to *cymae*. Pliny gives us very detailed information about cabbage, its varieties, qualities, and cultivation (*Nat. Hist.*, XIX, 8, 41 (136–144)). There are species with broad leaves and a long stalk, others with curly leaves, yet others with very small stalks. The cabbage can be sown all through the year, but sowing is best done at the time of the autumn equinox. When it is sown at that time there will be a young shoot early in the following spring. "This *cyma* is a small shoot (*cauliculus*) growing from the stalk itself, but more delicate and tender. The gourmet Apicius disliked it, so under his influence did Drusus Caesar, not without being reproached for it by his father Tiberius. After the *cyma* the same cabbage produces other shoots in summer and autumn, then in winter, and for a second time *cymae*, for it is a very prolific plant, until it is exhausted by its own fertility." The cabbage can also be sown in spring or mid-summer. Among the varieties named are the cabbage

voles, addes piper et ligusticum, mentam, rutam, coriandrum. folia cauliculorum: liquamen, vinum, oleum.[1]   (*81*)

2. ALITER: cauliculos elixatos mediabis, summa foliorum teres cum coriandro, cepa, cumino, pipere, passo vel caroeno et oleo modico.   (*82*)

3. ALITER: cauliculi elixati in patina compositi condiuntur liquamine, oleo, mero, cumino. piper asparges, porrum, cuminum, coriandrum viride super concides.   (*83*)

4. ALITER: cauliculi conditi ut supra cum elixis porris coquantur.   (*84*)

5. ALITER: cauliculos condies ut supra, admisces olivas virides et simul ferveant.   (*85*)

6. ALITER: cauliculis conditis ut supra superfundes alicam elixam cum nucleis et uva passa; piper asparges.   (*86*)

X. PORROS

1. PORROS MATUROS FIERI: pugnum salis, aquam et oleum: mixtum facies et ibi coques et eximes. cum oleo, liquamine, mero [et] inferes.   (*87*)

2. ALITER PORROS: opertos foliis cauliculorum [et] in prunis coques, ut supra [et][2] inferes.   (*88*)

3. ALITER PORROS: in † baca coctos ut supra inferes.[3]   (*89*)

---

[1] By changing the Teubner edition's punctuation Br. subdivided this paragraph into three short recipes.
[2] [et] R.
[3] See note to the English text.

old wine, and oil. (b) If you wish add pepper and lovage, mint, rue, coriander. (c) Leaves of spring greens: ⟨cook in or serve with⟩ *liquamen*, wine, oil.

2. ANOTHER METHOD. Boil and halve the cabbages, mince the tender parts of the leaves with coriander, onion, cumin, pepper, *passum* or *caroenum*, and a little oil.

3. ANOTHER METHOD. Arrange the boiled cabbages in a shallow pan and dress with *liquamen*, oil, wine, cumin. Sprinkle with pepper, chopped leeks, caraway-seed, and fresh coriander.[1]

4. ANOTHER METHOD. Dress cabbages as above, and heat up with boiled leeks.

5. ANOTHER METHOD. Dress as above, add fresh olives, and allow to come to the boil.

6. ANOTHER METHOD. Dress as above, pour on boiled spelt-grits with pine-kernels and raisins. Sprinkle with pepper.

X. LEEKS

1. FULL-SIZE LEEKS. Make a mixture of a handful of salt, water, and oil, cook in this, and remove. Serve with oil, *liquamen*, and wine.

2. ANOTHER METHOD. Cover the leeks with cabbage-leaves and cook in red-hot coal. Serve as above.

3. ANOTHER METHOD. Cook the leeks with olives[2] and serve as above.

from Cumae, with broad, short leaves and an open, spreading head; that from Aricia, not very high, with many not very tender leaves, and with shoots coming out from under almost every leaf; the cabbage from Pompeii, tall, with a stalk thin at the root, growing thick between the leaves—which does not stand the cold; the Sabellian cabbage, with curly leaves, that are so thick that the stalk itself becomes rather thin.

[1] This could be eaten hot or cold as a kind of coleslaw; it is very good both ways. The next recipe suggests this one to be cold rather than hot.

[2] The interpretation of *in baca* as *cum olivis*, made by Brandt, is accepted. Cp. the cabbage recipe ix, 5, above.

6—R.C.B.

4. ALITER PORROS: ⟨si⟩ in aqua elixati erunt, fabae nondum conditae plurimum admisce conditurae, in qua eos manducaturus es.   (*90*)

XI. BETAS

1. Concides porrum, coriandrum, cuminum, uvam passam † farinam, et omnia in medullam mittes.   ligabis et ita inferes ex liquamine, oleo et aceto.[1]   (*91*)

2. ALITER BETAS ELIXAS: ex sinapi, oleo modico et aceto bene inferuntur.   (*92*)

XII. HOLISERA

Holisera in fasciculum redacta ⟨a⟩ manu ex liquamine, oleo et mero bene inferuntur, vel cum piscibus assis.   (*93*)

XIII. RAPAS SIVE NAPOS

1. RAPAS SIVE NAPOS: elixatos exprimes, deinde teres cumi-

---

[1] See note to the English text.

4. ANOTHER METHOD. If the leeks are boiled in water add to the sauce in which you want to eat them a large quantity of beans, cooked but not yet dressed.

XI. BEETS

1. Chop leeks, coriander, cumin, raisins, add flour, and add all this to the pith ⟨of the incised beets⟩.[1] Thicken, and serve with *liquamen*, oil, and vinegar.

2. BOILED BEETS, ANOTHER METHOD.[2] They are good served with a dressing of mustard, a little oil, and vinegar.

XII. HORSE-PARSLEY OR ALEXANDERS[3]

Make up into bunches. They are good eaten raw with *liquamen*, oil, and wine, or you can eat them with grilled fish.

XIII. TURNIPS

1. Boil the turnips, drain. Then pound together plenty of

[1] Brandt interprets *medulla* as *medulla betae incisae*, with reference to a Columella recipe (XII, 56, 1), and so keeps the reading of the codd. Vollmer sees in *farina* a corruption; Schuch emends *Varianam*, which would be a certain kind of raisin. We had thought at first '*medulla*' would be *medulla siliginis—i.e.*, flour—and *farina* a gloss. But then the wording *omnia in medullam mittes* would be very strange. But, in any case, the recipe is not quite clear.

[2] This is probably beetroot salad. The Romans knew two kinds of beets, the white and the 'black,' the latter being our beetroot. The above recipes do not show which kind is meant, but No. 2 suggests our beetroot.

[3] *olisera* codd.; *Thesaurus Linguae Latinae s.v. holus atrum—olisatrum* —considers it a variant of *Holus atrum*. This is an umbelliferous plant, *Smyrnium olusatrum*, Greek *hipposelinon*, formerly used in England as celery—see 'Alexanders' in the O.E.D. Pliny, *Nat. Hist.*, XX, 11, 46 (117), recommends a decoction of the root in wine for calculus and the bite of mad dogs. Columella, XII, 7 and 58, gives recipes for preserving the root.

num plurimum, rutam minus, laser parthicum, mel, acetum,
liquamen, defritum et oleum modice.   fervere facies et inferes.
                                                                    (94)
2. ALITER RAPAS SIVE NAPOS: elixas, inferes.   oleum superstillabis; si voles, acetum adde.   (95)

XIV. RAFANOS

Rafanos cum piperato, ita ut piper cum liquamine teras.

XV. HOLUS MOLLE

1. HOLUS MOLLE EX HOLISATRO: coctum ex aqua nitrata
expressum concides minutatim, et teres piper, ligusticum,
satureiam siccam cum cepa sicca, liquamen, oleum et vinum.
                                                                    (97)
2. ALITER HOLUS MOLLE: apium coques ex aqua nitrata,
exprimes et concides minutatim. in mortario teres piper,
ligusticum, origanum, cepam, vinum, liquamen et oleum.
coques in pultario, et sic apium commisces.   (98)
3. ALITER HOLUS MOLLE EX FOLIIS LACTUCARUM CUM CEPIS:
coques ex aqua nitrata, expressum concides minutatim. in
mortario teres piper, ligusticum, apii semen, mentam siccam,
cepam, liquamen, oleum et vinum.
[Aliter] holus molle ne arescat, summa quaeque ampu-
tantur, et purgamenta et caules madefactos in aqua apsinthi
contegito.   (99) (100)

XVI. HERBAE RUSTICAE

Liquamine, oleo, aceto a manu vel in patina pipere, cumino,
bacis lentisci.   (101)

cumin, somewhat less rue, asafœtida; add honey, vinegar, *liquamen, defrutum,* and a little oil. Bring to the boil and serve with the turnips.

2. ANOTHER METHOD. Boil the turnips, serve sprinkled with oil; adding vinegar if liked.

XIV. RADISHES

Serve with pepper-sauce made by pounding pepper with *liquamen.*

XV. VEGETABLE PURÉES

1. HORSE-PARSLEY PURÉE. Boil in water with cooking-soda, drain, and chop finely. Pound pepper, lovage, dried savory, and dried onion, add *liquamen,* oil, and wine. ⟨Mix with the horse-parsley and serve.⟩

2. ANOTHER VEGETABLE PUREE. Boil celery in water with cooking soda, drain, and chop finely. Pound in the mortar pepper, lovage, origan, and onion, add wine, *liquamen,* and oil. Cook in a saucepan and mix with the celery.

3. PURÉE OF LETTUCE-LEAVES WITH ONIONS. Boil in water with cooking-soda; drain; chop finely. Pound in the mortar pepper, lovage, celery seed, dried mint, and onion, add *liquamen,* oil, and wine. ⟨Mix with the lettuce and onions and serve.⟩

To prevent vegetable purée from getting dry cut off the ends of the leaves ⟨of the vegetables you are going to use⟩ and cover the washed trimmings and the stalks which have been soaked in absinth water.

XVI. WILD HERBS

Can be eaten as they are, dipped in a dressing of *liquamen,* oil, and vinegar, or cooked in a shallow pan with pepper, cumin, mastic berries.

XVII. Urticae

Urticam feminam, sole in ariete posito, adversus aegritudinem sumes, si voles. (*102*)

XVIII. Intuba et lactucae

1. Intuba ex liquamine, oleo modico, † medere[1] cepa concisa. pro lactucis vero hieme intuba ex embammate vel melle et aceto acri. (*103*)
2. Lactucas cum oxyporio et aceto et modico liquamine. (*104*)
3. Ad digestionem et inflationem et ne lactucae laedant: cumini unc. II, zingiberis unc. I, rutae viridis unc. I, dactylorum pinguium scripulos XII, piperis unc. I, mellis unc. IX; cuminum aut Aethiopicum aut Syriacum aut Libycum. tundes cuminum et postea infundes in aceto. cum siccaverit, postea melle omnia comprehendes. cum necesse fuerit, dimidium cocleare cum aceto et liquamine modico misces aut post cenam dimidium cocleare accipies. (*105*)

XIX. Cardui

1. Carduos: liquamine, oleo et ovis concisis.

---

[1] *mero* suggested by Br.

XVII. STINGING NETTLES

Take the wild nettle, when the sun is in the sign of Aries, against illness, if you wish.

XVIII. ENDIVE AND LETTUCE

1. ENDIVES.[1] (*a*) Dress with *liquamen*, a little oil, wine, and chopped onion.

(*b*) In winter use endives instead of lettuce with a dressing or with honey and strong vinegar.

2–3. DRESS LETTUCES with *oxypor(i)um*,[2] vinegar, and a little *liquamen*, to make them more easily digestible, to prevent flatulence, and so that the lettuces cannot harm your system: 2 oz. cumin, 1 oz. ginger, 1 oz. fresh rue, 12 scruples ($=\frac{1}{2}$ oz.) juicy dates, 1 oz. pepper, 9 oz. honey; the cumin may be Æthiopian, Syrian, or Libyan. Pound the cumin, and afterwards moisten with vinegar. When it has become dry bind everything with the honey. When needed mix half a teaspoonful with vinegar and a little *liquamen*, or take half a teaspoonful after the meal.

XIX. ARTICHOKES

1. ⟨Boil and serve⟩ with *liquamen*, oil, and chopped hard-boiled eggs.[3]

---

[1] This could be endive or chicory.

[2] Cp. the Oxypor(i)um recipe with I, xviii. Brandt suggested that 2 and 3 should be taken as one recipe, and this suggestion is certainly right. He also thinks that the Oxypor(i)um recipe given here is the more correct version of the two.

[3] Or: cook them in this mixture; or: stuff with the eggs and cook in oil and *liquamen*; compare the Basque recipe "œufs Maritchu," E. David, *French Country Cooking* (London 1951), p. 82: the artichokes are boiled and stripped of their outer leaves and then sauté-ed; a sauce is prepared separately; the artichokes are served in this sauce with scrambled egg on top.

2. ALITER CARDUOS: rutam, mentam, coriandrum, feniculum, omnia viridia teres.   addes piper, ligusticum, mel, liquamen et oleum.

3. ALITER CARDUOS ELIXOS: piper, cuminum, liquamen et oleum.   (*106*)

XX. SPHONDYLI [vel fundili]

1. SPHONDYLI FRICTI ex oenogaro simplici.

2. ALITER: SPHONDYLI ELIXI ex sale, oleo, mero, coriandro viridi conciso et pipere integro.   (*107*)

3. ALITER: SPHONDYLOS ELIXOS perfundes amulato infra scripto: apii semen, rutam, mel, piper teres, passum, liquamen et oleum modice.   amulo obligas, piper asperges et inferes.

(*108*)

2. ARTICHOKES, ANOTHER METHOD. Rue, mint, coriander, fennel, all fresh; pound. Add pepper, lovage, honey, *liquamen*, and oil. ⟨Cook the artichokes in this.⟩

3. BOILED ARTICHOKES. Dress with pepper, cumin, *liquamen*, and oil.

XX. MUSSELS

1. FRIED MUSSELS.[1] Serve with plain *oenogarum*.

2. ANOTHER METHOD. Serve mussels boiled with salt, oil, wine, chopped fresh coriander, and peppercorns.

3. BOILED MUSSELS, ANOTHER METHOD. Pour over the following thick sauce: celery-seed, rue, honey, pepper; pound; add *passum*, *liquamen*, and a little oil. Thicken with cornflour, sprinkle with pepper, and serve.

[1] *Sphondyli*—basic meaning 'vertebra'—can mean either artichokes or a kind of mussel. Guégan takes it to mean *fonds d'artichauts*, though it is not clear how he arrives at this. If artichokes it means the head—*i.e.*, just the whole of it. Brandt also interprets the word as artichokes, except in two recipes: No. 4, because of its close relationship to the recipes IX, xiii, and No. 7, which is a literal repetition of II, i, 6, and in these he takes it to be mussels. The compiler of our cookery-book, in Brandt's opinion, gave these two recipes here by mistake, because of the identical name for the two very different things. Now, *sphondyli* occur again in V, ii, 1, cooked with lentils. Guégan translates this too as 'artichoke bottom.' With the lentils mussels are much more likely than artichokes. The *sphondyli* occur also in IX, xiv, in a sauce made of oysters, *sphondyli*, and various herbs; in this case nobody doubts that mussels are meant. In the recipes below there is at least one (apart from 4 and 7) that would be quite impossible with artichokes, No. 6. It seems more likely, then, that the compiler found the entire *sphondyli* chapter in the book on sea-food. He placed one of them in the *isicia* section of Book II— forgetting later to eliminate it in its original context—and transferred the whole chapter to the book on vegetables, because he did not know enough about cooking to see from the recipes which kind of *sphondyli* was meant. If this assumption is correct *sphondyli* denoted only mussels with Apicius, for all the recipes in which *sphondyli* occur belong to Apicius' original recipes. Vehling reads *sphondylia*, and translates 'cow-parsnips.'

4. ALITER SPHONDYLOS: teres cuminum, rutam, liquamen, caroenum modice, oleum, coriandrum viride et porrum. et sphondylos inferes pro salso.   (*109*)

5. ALITER: SPHONDYLOS ELIXATOS praedurabis, mittes in caccabum oleum, liquamen, piper. passo colorabis et obligas.
(*110*)

6. ALITER: SPHONDYLOS oleo, liquamine complebis, vel oleo et sale assabis. piper asparges et inferes.   (*111*)

7. [ALITER: SPHONDYLOS ELIXATOS conteres et nervos eorum eximes. deinde cum eis alicam elixatam et ova conteres, liquamen, piper. isicia ex his facies cum nucleis et pipere. in omento[1] assabis, oenogaro continges et pro isiciis inferes].
(*112*)

XXI. CAROETAE SEU PASTINACAE

1. CAROETAE FRICTAE oenogaro inferuntur.
2. ALITER CAROETAS: sale, oleo puro et aceto.

3. ALITER: CAROETAS ELIXATAS concisas in cuminato oleo modico coques et inferes. cuminatum coli⟨cul⟩orum[2] facies.
(*113*)

[1] Punctuation according to Br.
[2] *coliorum* codd., corr. by Br.

4. MUSSELS, ANOTHER METHOD. Pound cumin, rue, *liqua-men*, a little *caroenum*, oil, fresh coriander, and leek. Serve the mussels ⟨in this sauce⟩ instead of salt fish.

5. ANOTHER METHOD. Lightly brown boiled mussels. Put in a saucepan oil, *liquamen*, pepper, colour with *passum*, and thicken. ⟨Serve with the mussels.⟩

6. ANOTHER METHOD. Fill the mussels with oil and *liqua-men*, or fry in oil and salt. Sprinkle with pepper and serve.

7. = II, i, 6.

XXI. CARROTS OR PARSNIPS

1. FRIED CARROTS. Serve with *oenogarum*.

2. ANOTHER METHOD. ⟨Serve raw ?⟩ with salt, pure oil, and vinegar.

3. ANOTHER METHOD. Boil the carrots, and chop. Then cook in cumin-sauce with a little oil, and serve. Make the cumin-sauce as for cabbage.

LIBER IV

PANDECTER

I. sala cattabia. II. patinae piscium holerum pomorum.
III. minutal de piscibus vel esiciis. IV. tisana vel
sucum. V. gustum.

I. Sala cattabia (?)

1. Sala cattabia: piper, mentam, apium, puleium aridum,
caseum, nucleos pineos, mel, acetum, liquamen, ovorum vitella,
aquam recentem. panem ex posca maceratum exprimes,
caseum bubulum, cucumeres in caccabulo compones, inter-
positis nucleis. mittes concisi capparis minuti . . . iocusculis
gallinarum. ius perfundes, super frigidam collocabis et sic
appones.   (*116*)

2. Aliter sala cattabia Apiciana: adicies in mortario apii
semen, puleium aridum, mentam aridam, zingiber, coriandrum
viride, uvam passam enucleatam, mel, acetum, oleum et
vinum conteres. adicies in caccabulo panis Picentini frusta,
interpones pulpas pulli, glandulas haedinas, caseum Vestinum,
nucleos pineos, cucumeres, cepas aridas minute concisas. ius
supra perfundes. insuper nivem sub ora asparges et inferes.

92

BOOK IV

MANY INGREDIENTS

I. Sala cattabia. II. Patinae of fish, green vegetables, and fruit. III. Fricassee of fish. IV. Barley soup or broth. V. Vegetable and fruit stews.

I. Sala Cattabia

1. SALA CATTABIA. Pepper, mint, celery (-seed?), dried pennyroyal, cheese, pine-kernels, honey, vinegar, *liquamen*, yolks of egg, fresh water. ⟨Pound, mix.⟩ Have ready some pieces of bread soaked in water mixed with vinegar. Squeeze out the moisture, and arrange in a mould, followed by layers of cow's milk cheese, cucumbers, alternating with pine-kernels. Add finely chopped capers . . . [*text corrupt; editors assume gap*], alternating with ⟨previously cooked⟩ chicken liver. Pour on the dressing, place over cold water ⟨to cool⟩, and serve.[1]

2. SALA CATTABIA A LA APICIUS. Put in the mortar celery-seed, dried pennyroyal, dried mint, ginger, fresh coriander, stoned raisins, honey, vinegar, oil, and wine. Pound and mix together. Place in a mould pieces of Picentine[2] bread, and arrange in alternating layers chicken meat, goat's sweetbreads,

---

[1] In this and the two following recipes it is not clear whether the ingredients are to be pre-cooked, or whether, before cooling, the contents of the mould should be cooked. The latter is assumed by Guégan. We tried out No. 2 with the ingredients pre-cooked, and it was extremely successful; it would in this way be a salad on the principle of herring salad and the like.

[2] Picentine bread. According to Pliny (XVIII, 11, 27 (106)) this bread—invented by the people of Picenum—was made of spelt-grits. The spelt-grits were left to soak for nine days, and on the tenth day were made into dough by mixing them with raisin juice. The dough was put into earthenware pots and baked hard in the oven. The pots

3. ALITER SALA CATTABIA: panem Alexandrinum excavabis, in posca macerabis. adicies in mortarium piper, mel, mentam, alium, coriandrum viride, caseum bubulum sale conditum, aquam, oleum. insuper nivem, et inferes. (*118*)

II. PATINAE PISCIUM HOLERUM POMORUM

1. PATINA COTIDIANA: cerebella elixata teres cum pipere. cuminum, laser cum liquamine, caroeno, lacte et ovis. ad ignem lenem vel ad aquam calidam coques. (*121*)

2. ALITER PATINA VERSATILIS: nucleos, nuces fractas; torres eas et teres cum melle, pipere, liquamine, lacte et ovis. olei modicum. (*122*)

3. ALITER PATINA: thyrsum lactucae teres cum pipere, liquamine, caroeno, aqua, oleo. coques, ovis obligabis; piper asparges et inferes. (*123*)

4. ALITER PATINA FUSILIS: accipies holisatra, purgas, lavas, coques, refrigerabis, restringes. accipies cerebella IV, enervabis, coques. adicies in mortario piperis scripulos VI, suffundes liquamen, fricabis. postea adicies cerebella, fricabis iterum. adicies holisatra et simul conteres. postea franges ova VIII, adicias cyathum liquaminis, vini cyathum, passi cyathum,

Vestine[1] cheese, pine-kernels, cucumbers, finely chopped dried onions. Pour the dressing over it. Cool in snow and serve.

3. SALA CATTABIA, ANOTHER METHOD. Hollow out an Alexandrian[2] loaf, soak ⟨the soft part⟩ in water mixed with vinegar. Put in the mortar pepper, honey, mint, garlic, fresh coriander, salted cow's-milk cheese, water, and oil. ⟨Arrange similar ingredients as in the two previous recipes, squeezing out the moisture from the soaked bread⟩, cool in snow, and serve.

II. PATINAE OF FISH, GREEN VEGETABLES, AND FRUIT

1. EVERYDAY PATINA. Pound boiled brains with pepper. ⟨Make into a mixture with⟩ cumin, asafœtida, *liquamen, caroenum*, milk, and eggs. Cook over a low fire or in a *bain-marie*.[3]

2. TURNOVER.[4] Toast pine-kernels and chopped nuts, pound with honey, pepper, *liquamen*, milk, and eggs. ⟨Cook in⟩ a little oil.

3. ANOTHER PATINA. Pound the stalks ⟨and ribs?⟩ of lettuce with pepper, *liquamen, caroenum*, water, oil. Cook. Thicken with eggs. Sprinkle with pepper and serve.

4. CREAM OF HORSE-PARSLEY. Take horse-parsley, clean, wash, cook, let it cool and drain. Take 4 brains, skin and remove stringy parts, cook. Put in the mortar 6 scruples of pepper, moisten with *liquamen*, and pound. Then add the brains, pound again. Add the horse-parsley and pound all together. Next break 8 eggs, add 1 cyathus each of *liquamen*,

were supposed to break in the process. This bread was only eaten in a moistened state, usually dipped in milk and honey. We used for Picentine bread the coarsest wholemeal bread available.

[1] See Introduction, p. 26; we used Cheddar instead of Vestine cheese; any hard farm-house cheese would do.

[2] Alexandrian bread was presumably a bread invented by the people of Alexandria, possibly made of grain from there. It contained, according to Pliny (*Nat. Hist.*, XX, 15, 58 (163)), cumin.

[3] See Introduction, section IV (p. 30), under *vatillum* and water-heaters in general.

[4] = IV, ii, 16.

contrita simul temperabis. patinam perunges, impones in thermospodio. postea cum coctum fuerit, piper asparges et inferes.   (*124*)

5. ALITER PATINA DE ASPARAGIS FRIGIDA: accipies asparagos purgatos, in mortario fricabis, aqua suffundes, perfricabis, per colum colabis. Et mittes ⟨in caccabum⟩ ficedulas curatas. teres in mortario piperis scripulos VI, adicies liquamen, fricabis, ⟨postea adicies⟩ vini cyathum unum, passi cyathum unum, mittes in caccabum olei uncias III. illic ferveant. perunges patinam, in ea ova VI cum oenogaro misces, cum suco asparagi impones cineri calido, mittes impensam supra scriptam. tunc ficedulas compones. coques, piper asperges et inferes.
(*125*)

6. ALITER PATINA DE ASPARAGIS: adicies in mortario asparagorum praecisuras, quae proiciuntur, teres, suffundes vinum, colas. teres piper, ligusticum, coriandrum viride, satureiam, cepam, vinum, liquamen et oleum. sucum transferes in patellam perunctam, et, si volueris, ova dissolves ad ignem, ut obliget. piper minutum asperges ⟨et inferes⟩.   (*126*)

7. PATINAM EX RUSTICIS, SIVE TAMNIS SIVE SINAPI VIRIDI SIVE CUCUMERE SIVE CAULICULIS: item facies: si volueris, substernes pulpas piscium vel pullorum.   (*127*)

8. [ALITER] PATINA DE SABUCO CALIDA ET FRIGIDA: accipies semen de sabuco, purgabis, ex aqua decoques, paulum exsiccabis, patinam perunges et in patinam compones ad surcellum. adicies piperis scripulos VI, suffundes liquamen, ⟨fricabis⟩, postea adicies liquaminis cyathum unum, vini cyathum, passi cyathum, teres, tandem in patinam mittes olei unc. IV, pones in thermospodio et facies ut ferveat. cum ferbuerit, franges postea ova VI, agitabis et patinam sic obligabis. cum obligaveris, piper asparges et inferes.   (*128*)

9. PATINAM DE ROSIS: accipies rosas et exfoliabis: album

wine, *passum*, beat well, and blend together. Grease a shallow pan ⟨put in your mixture⟩ and place in the hot ashes. When it is cooked sprinkle with pepper and serve.

5. COLD ASPARAGUS PATINA. Take cleaned asparagus, pound in the mortar, add water, beat thoroughly and pass through a sieve. Next put in a saucepan fig-peckers which you have prepared for cooking. Pound in the mortar 6 scruples of pepper, moisten with *liquamen*, grind well, add 1 cyathus each of wine and *passum*, put in a saucepan 3 oz. of oil, and bring the mixture to the boil. Grease a shallow pan, and mix in it 6 eggs with *oenogarum*, add the asparagus purée, pour on the mixture described above, and arrange the birds ⟨on top⟩. Place in the hot ashes, cook, ⟨let it cool⟩, sprinkle with pepper, and serve.

6. ASPARAGUS PATINA, ANOTHER METHOD. Put in the mortar asparagus tips,[1] pound, add wine, pass through the sieve. Pound pepper, lovage, fresh coriander, savory, onion, wine, *liquamen*, and oil. Put purée and spices into a greased shallow pan, and if you wish break eggs over it when it is on the fire, so that the mixture sets. Sprinkle finely ground pepper over it and serve.

7. PATINA OF WILD HERBS, BLACK BRYONY, MUSTARD PLANT, CUCUMBER, OR CABBAGE. Prepare in the same way ⟨*i.e.*, as IV, ii, 19⟩,[2] and if you wish add fish fillets or chicken meat.

8. HOT OR COLD PATINA OF ELDERBERRIES. Take elderberries, clean them, and boil in water. Dry slightly and arrange in a greased shallow pan with a small stick. Add 6 scruples of pepper, moisten with *liquamen*, then add 1 cyathus each of *liquamen*, wine, and *passum*, mix well; finally put in the pan 4 oz. of oil, place in the hot ashes, and bring to the boil. When the mixture is boiling break 6 eggs over it, stir well, and so bind it. When it has set sprinkle with pepper and serve ⟨hot or cold⟩.

9. PATINA OF ROSES. Take roses and strip off the petals.

[1] Probably green.
[2] Brandt's idea that IV, ii, 19, should precede this recipe is certainly correct.

7—R.C.B.

tolles, mittes in mortarium, suffundes liquamen, fricabis. postea mittes liquaminis cyathum unum semis, et sucum per colum colabis. accipies cerebella IV, enervabis et teres piperis scripulos VIII. suffundes ex suco, fricabis. postea ova VIII frangis, ⟨mittis⟩ vini cyathum unum semis et passi cyathum unum, olei modicum. postea patinam perunges et eam impones cineri calido, et sic impensam supra scriptam mittes. cum cocta fuerit in thermospodio, piperis pulverem super asperges et inferes. (*129*)

10. PATINA DE CUCURBITIS: cucurbitas elixas et frictas in patina compones, cuminatum superfundes, modico oleo super adiecto. fervere facias et inferes. (*130*)

11. PATINA DE APUA: apuam lavas, ex oleo maceras, in Cumana compones, adicies oleum, liquamen, vinum. alligas fasciculos rutae et origani, et subinde fasciculos apa † babtidiabis.[1] cum cocta fuerit, proicies fasciculos. et piper asperges et inferes. (*131*)

12. PATINA DE APUA SINE APUA: pulpas piscis assi vel elixi minutatim facies ita abundanter, ut patinam qualem voles implere possis. teres piper et modicum rutae, suffundes liquamen quod satis erit, sic et ova cruda confracta[2] et olei modicum, et commisces in patina cum pulpis ut unum corpus fiat. desuper leniter compones urticas marinas, ut non cum ovis misceantur. impones ad vaporem, ut cum ovis ire non possint, et, cum siccaverint, super aspergis piper tritum et inferes. ad mensam nemo agnoscet quid manducet. (*132*)

13. PATINAM EX LACTE: nucleos infundes et siccas. echinos recentes inpreparatos[3] habebis: accipies patinam, et in eam compones singula infra scripta: mediana malvarum et betarum et porros maturos, apios, holus molle et viridia elixa, pullum carptum ex iure coctum, cerebella elixa, Lucanicas, ova dura per medium incisa. mittes longaones porcinos ex iure Terentino

---

[1] Br. (p. 149) proposes to accept this reading as a rendering of *apobaptizabis.*
[2] *sic . . . confracta* after *pulpis* codd., transferred by Br.
[3] *inpreparatos* codd., rest. by Br.

Lift out the white part ⟨of the petals⟩ and put in the mortar, moisten with *liquamen*, and pound. Next put 1½ cyathi of *liquamen*, and strain the juice through a sieve. Take 4 brains, skin and remove the stringy parts, and pound 8 scruples of pepper; add some of the juice; pound. Then break 8 eggs, add 1½ cyathi of wine, 1 cyathus of *passum*, and a little oil. Grease a shallow pan and place it in hot ashes, and put the above mixture in it. When it has cooked in the ashes sprinkle with finely ground pepper and serve.

10. PATINA OF VEGETABLE MARROWS. Boil the marrows, then fry and arrange in a shallow pan. Pour over cumin-sauce with a little oil added. Bring to the boil and serve.

11. PATINA OF ANCHOVY. Wash the anchovy, and steep it in oil. Arrange in an earthenware saucepan, add oil, *liquamen*, wine. Make a bouquet of rue and origan, and put it in. When cooked remove the bouquet. Sprinkle with pepper and serve.

12. PATINA OF ANCHOVY WITHOUT ANCHOVY. Take fillets of grilled or boiled fish and mince enough to fill a pan of the size you wish. Pound pepper and a little rue, add sufficient *liquamen*, break eggs and stir in, add a little oil, and mix everything in the pan with the fish, so that it forms a smooth mixture. On top of this you place jellyfish, taking care that they do not mix with the eggs. Cook in the steam so that the jellyfish cannot combine with the eggs, and when they are dry sprinkle with ground pepper and serve. At table no one will know what he is eating.

13. PATINA WITH MILK. Soak pine-kernels and let them dry. Have ready fresh, unprepared sea-urchins. Take a shallow pan and arrange in it the following ingredients: hearts of mallows and beets; fully grown leeks; celery sticks; vegetable purée; boiled greens; pieces of chicken cooked in broth; boiled brains; Lucanian[1] sausages; hard-boiled eggs cut in halves; pork sausages stuffed with Terentian sauce[2] cooked and

---

[1] See recipe II, iv.   [2] Cp. VIII, i, 10.

farsos, coctos, concisos, iecinera pullorum, pulpas piscis aselli
fricti, urticas marinas, pulpas ostreorum, caseos recentes.
alternis compones, nucleos et piper integrum asparges. ius
tale perfundes: piper, ligusticum, apii semen, silfi. coques.
at ubi cocta fuerit, lacte colas, cui cruda ova commisces, ut
unum corpus fiat, et super illa omnia perfundes. cum cocta
fuerit, ⟨addes⟩ echinos recentiores, piper asperges et inferes.

(133)

14. PATINAM APICIANAM SIC FACIES:[1] frusta suminis cocti,
pulpas piscium, pulpas pulli, ficedulas vel pectora turdorum
cocta et quaecumque optima fuerint; haec omnia concides
diligenter praeter ficedulas. ova vero cruda cum oleo dissolvis.
teres piper, ligusticum, suffundes liquamen, vinum, passum,
et in caccabum mittis ut calefiat, et amulo obligas. antea
tamen pulpas concisas universas illuc mittes, et sic bulliat. at,
ubi coctum fuerit, levabis cum iure suo et in patellam alternis
de trulla refundes cum piperis granis integris et nucleis pineis,
ita ut per singula coria substernas diploidem, in[2] laganum similiter; quotquot lagana posueris, tot trullas impensae desuper
adicies. unum vero laganum fistula percuties et super impones. piper asparges. ante tamen illas pulpas ovis confractis
obligabis, et sic in caccabum mittes cum impensa. patellam
aeneam qualem debes habere infra ostenditur. *(134)*

15. PATINA COTIDIANA: accipies frusta suminis cocti, pulpas
piscium coctas, pulpas pulli coctas. haec omnia concides
diligenter. accipias patellam aeneam, ova confringes in
caccabum et dissolves. adicies in mortarium piper, ligusticum,

---

[1] ⟨*accipies*⟩ inserted here by Vollmer.
[2] *in* codd., rest. by Br.

chopped; chicken liver; fried fillets of hake; jellyfish; oysters without their shells; fresh cheese. Arrange all this in layers. Add the pine-kernels and peppercorns on top and pour over the following sauce: pepper, lovage, celery-seed, asafœtida. Cook. When it is done strain milk into which you mix raw eggs to a smooth mixture. Pour it over the dish. When it has set garnish with the fresh sea-urchins, sprinkle with pepper, and serve.

14. PATINA À LA APICIUS. Make in the following way. Pieces of cooked sow's udder, fillets of fish, chicken meat, fig-peckers, cooked breasts of turtle-dove, and whatever other good things you can think of. Chop all this, apart from the fig-peckers, carefully. Then stir raw eggs into oil. Pound pepper, lovage, moisten with *liquamen*, wine, and *passum*, put in a saucepan, heat, and thicken with cornflour. But first add all the different meats and let them cook. When cooked transfer with the sauce, using a ladle, into a pan in layers, having added peppercorns and pine-kernels. Place under each layer as a base an oil-cake, and put on each oil-cake one ladleful of the meat mixture. Finally pierce one oil-cake with a reed stalk and place this on top. Sprinkle with pepper. Before you put all these meats with the sauce into the saucepan you should have bound them with the eggs. What kind of metal pan you need is shown below.[1]

15. EVERYDAY PATINA.[2] Take pieces of cooked sow's udder, cooked fillets of fish, cooked chicken meat. Chop all this finely. Take a metal pan. Break eggs into a saucepan and beat. Put in the mortar pepper, lovage, pound, moisten

[1] This sentence certainly refers to an illustration. Cp. Brandt, p. 126.

[2] This recipe is a shortened and simplified version of the preceding one, omitting some of the costlier ingredients. It is therefore to be assumed that the method of preparation is to be the same as before— *i.e.*, the meat to be bound with the eggs and put into the sauce before cooking and thickening. The text is slightly corrupt, and there is a gap between *diploides* and *patinam aeneam*. The translation is adapted to the procedure in the preceding recipe.

fricabis, suffundes liquamen, vinum, passum, oleum modice, reexinanies in caccabum, facies ut ferveat. cum ferbuerit [et]¹ obligas. pulpas, quas subcultrasti, in ius mittis. substerne diploides . . . patinam aeneam, et trullam plenam pulpae, et disparges oleum, ⟨et⟩ laganum pones similiter. quotquot lagana posueris, tot trullas impensae adicies. unum laganum fistula percuties, a superficie insuper[ficiem]² pones. piper asperges et inferes. (*135*)

16. PATINA VERSATILIS VICE DULCIS: nucleos pineos, nuces fractas et purgatas, attorrebis eas, teres cum melle, pipere, liquamine, lacte, ovis, modico mero et oleo, versas in discum.³ (*136*)

17. PATELLAM TYROTARICHAM EX QUOCUMQUE SALSO VOLUERIS: coques ex oleo, exossabis. et cerebella cocta, pulpas piscium, iocuscula pullorum, ova dura, caseum mollem excaldatum, haec omnia calefacies in patella. teres piper, ligusticum, origanum, rutae bacam, vinum, mulsum, oleum. ⟨in⟩ patella ad lentum ignem ⟨pones⟩ ut coquatur. ovis crudis obligabis, adornabis, cuminum minutum asparges et inferes. (*137*)

18. PATELLAM SICCAM⁴: ISICIA DE THURSIONE: enervabis, concides minutatim. teres piper, ligusticum, origanum, petroselinum, coriandrum, cuminum, rutae bacam, mentam siccam, ipsum thursionem. isicia deformabis. ⟨adicies⟩ vinum, liquamen, oleum. coques. coctum in patellam collocabis. ius in ea facies: piper, ligusticum, satureiam, cepam, vinum, liquamen, oleum. ⟨in⟩ patellam pone sut coquatur. ovis obligabis, piper asparges et inferes. (*138*)

19. PATELLAM EX HOLISATRO: elixas ex aqua nitrata, exprimis in patellam. teres piper, ligusticum, coriandrum, satureiam, cepam, vinum, liquamen, acetum, oleum. transferes in patel-

---

¹ *et* codd., del. R.
² *versas in discum in superficiem* E, *insuper insup(er)ficiem* V; Br. transferred *versas in discum* to the end of the following recipe and suggested *insuper[ficiem]*.
³ See No. 15, n. 2 above.   ⁴ See note to the English text.

with *liquamen*, wine, *passum*, a little oil, pour into the saucepan, bring to the boil, and thicken. Put the chopped meats into the sauce. Put at the bottom of the metal pan an oil-cake as a coating, then a ladleful of the meat mixture, sprinkle with oil, then add another oil-cake, and so forth, putting on each oil-cake one ladleful of meat. Pierce one cake with a reed-stalk and place on top. Sprinkle with pepper and serve.

16. TURNOVER AS A SWEET.[1] Toast pine-kernels and broken and clean nuts, and pound with honey, pepper, *liquamen*, milk, eggs, a little wine and oil. ⟨Cook in a shallow pan⟩ and turn out on to a round serving-dish.

17. PATELLA WITH CHEESE AND SALT FISH. Make it with any salt fish you like. Cook in oil; bone. Take cooked brains, the boned fish, chicken's liver, hard-boiled eggs, soft cheese washed in warm water. Heat all this up in a shallow pan. Next pound pepper, lovage, origan, rue-berries, wine, *mulsum*, oil, put in the pan, and allow to cook gently over a low fire. Bind with raw eggs, garnish, sprinkle with finely ground cumin, and serve.

18. DRY[2] PATELLA: RISSOLES OF PORPOISE. Remove skin and bones of the fish, and chop finely. Pound pepper, lovage, origan, parsley, coriander, cumin, rue-berries, dried mint, and the porpoise. Shape into rissoles. Put wine, *liquamen*, and oil ⟨into a pan⟩ and cook. When cooked arrange in a shallow pan. Make the following sauce for it: take pepper, lovage, savory, onion, wine, *liquamen*, and oil. Put in the pan and cook. Bind with eggs, sprinkle with pepper, and serve.

19. PATELLA WITH HORSE-PARSLEY.[3] Boil in water to which cooking-soda has been added, squeeze out moisture, and place in a shallow pan. Pound pepper, lovage, coriander, savory,

[1] = IV, ii, 2.
[2] The title seems corrupt, as there is nothing dry about this *patella*. Vollmer suggested an adjective like *Siculam* instead of *siccam*.
[3] This recipe should precede No. 7.

lam, coques, amulo obligas. thymum et piper minutum
asparges. et de quacumque herba, si volueris, facies ut supra.

20. PATINA DE APUA FRICTA: apuam lavas, ova confringes et
cum apua commisces. adicies liquamen, vinum, oleum, facies
ut ferveat, et cum ferbuerit, mittes apuam. cum duxerit,
subtiliter versas. facies ut coloret, oenogarum simplex perfundes. piper asparges et inferes. (*140*.)

21. PATINA EX LAGITIS ET CEREBELLIS: friges ova dura, cerebella elixas et enervas, gigeria pullorum coques. haec omnia
divides praeter piscem, compones in patina praemixta salsum
coctum in medio pones. teres piper, ligusticum, suffundes
⟨passum⟩, ut dulce sit. piperatum mittes in patinam, facies ut
ferveat. cum ferbuerit, ramo rutae agitabis et amulo obligabis.
(*141*)

22. PATINA MULLORUM LOCO SALSI: mullos rades, in patina
munda compones, adicies ⟨olei quod satis est et salsum interpones. facies⟩ ut ferveat. cum ferbuerit, mulsum mittes
aut passum. piper asparges et inferes. (*142*)

23. PATINA PISCIUM LOCO SALSI: pisces qualeslibet curatos
friges, in patinam compones, adicies olei quod satis est et salsum
interpones. facies ut ferveat. cum ferbuerit, mittes mulsam
et ius agitabis. (*143*)

24. PATINA PISCIUM: pisces qualeslibet rades et curatos
mittes. cepas siccas Ascalonias vel alterius generis concides in
patinam et pisces super compones. adicies liquamen, oleum.
cum coctum fuerit, salsum coctum in medio pones. addendum
acetum. asparges et coronam bubulam. (*144*)

onion, wine, *liquamen*, vinegar, oil. Put this mixture in the pan, cook, and thicken with cornflour. Sprinkle with powdered thyme and pepper. You can make this dish with any herb you like.

20. PATINA OF FRIED ANCHOVY.[1] Wash the anchovy, break eggs, and roll the fish in them. Take *liquamen*, wine, oil, and bring to the boil. When boiling put the anchovy in. When it sets turn carefully on to the other side; let them colour. Pour over them *oenogarum*, sprinkle with pepper, and serve.

21. PATINA OF ⟨SALT⟩ LAGITA-FISH[2] AND BRAINS. Fry eggs until hard. Boil brains, skin, and remove stringy parts. Cook chicken giblets. Chop all this up, apart from the fish. Mix together and arrange in a shallow pan, and place the cooked salt fish in the middle. Pound pepper, lovage; add *passum* to sweeten. Put this pepper-sauce in the pan, and bring to the boil. When boiling stir with a sprig of rue, and thicken with cornflour.

22. PATINA OF RED MULLETS INSTEAD OF SALT FISH. Scale the mullets, arrange in a clean, shallow pan. Add sufficient oil, and intersperse with salt fish. Bring to the boil. When boiling add *passum* or *mulsum*. Sprinkle with pepper, and serve.

23. PATINA OF FISH INSTEAD OF SALT FISH. Prepare any fish you like, and fry. Place in a shallow pan, add sufficient oil, and intersperse with salt fish. Bring to the boil. When boiling add honey-water, and stir.

24. PATINA OF FISH. Take any fish you like, scale, and prepare. Chop dried shallots or other onions into the pan and place the fish on top. Add liquamen and oil, and cook. Put cooked salt fish in the centre. Add vinegar. Sprinkle also with *corona bubula*.[3]

[1] This is a very good and simple dish, and could be made with any smallish fish—*e.g.*, herring; for medium-sized herring take one small egg to each fish.

[2] Guégan treats *lagita* as if it was the same as *lacerta*: horse-mackerel.

[3] Perhaps a kind of origan—like *Cunila bubula*, Pliny, *Nat. Hist.*, XIX, 8, 50 (165).

25. PATELLAM LUCRETIANAM: cepas pallachanas purgas (viridia earum proicies), in patinam concides. liquaminis modicum, oleum et aquam. dum coquitur, salsum crudum in medium ponis. at ubi cum salso prope cocta fuerit, mellis cocleare asparges, aceti et defriti pusillum. gustas. si fatuum fuerit, liquamen adicies, si salsum, mellis modicum. et coronam bubulam aspergis, et bulliat.   (*145*)

26. PATINAM DE LAGITIS: lagitas rades, lavas, ova confringis et cum lagitis commisces. adicies liquamen, vinum, oleum, facies ut ferveat. cum ferbuerit, oenogarum simplex perfundis. piper asperges et inferes.   (*146*)

27. PATINA ZOMOTEGANON: a crudo quoslibet pisces lavas, in patina compones. adicies oleum, liquamen, vinum, [coctum]¹ fasciculum porri, coriandri. dum coquitur, teres piper, ligustici, origani, fasciculum ⟨coctum⟩.² de suo sibi fricabis, suffundes ius de suo sibi, ova cruda dissolves, temperas. exinanies in patinam, facies ut obligetur. cum tenuerit, piper asparges et inferes.   (*147*)

28. PATINA SOLEARUM: soleas battues et curatas compones in patina. adicies oleum, liquamen, vinum. dum coquitur, teres piper, ligusticum, origanum, fricabis, suffundes ius, ova cruda et unum corpus facies. super soleas refundes, lento igni coques. cum duxerit, piper asparges et inferes.   (*148*)

29. PATINA DE PISCIBUS: piperis unciam, caroeni heminam, conditi heminam, olei unc. II.   (*149*)

30. PATINA DE PISCICULIS: uvam passam, piper, ligusticum, origanum, cepam, vinum, liquamen, oleum. transferes in

¹ *coctum* codd., transferred to next line by Br.
² *ligustici, origani* codd., rest. by Br.

25. PATELLA À LA LUCRETIUS.[1]   Clean spring onions, throwing away their green, and chop into a shallow pan.   Add a little *liquamen*, oil, and water.   While it cooks put raw salt fish in the centre.   But as soon as it is all nearly cooked add a teaspoonful of honey, and very little vinegar and *defrutum*. Taste.   If it is too insipid add *liquamen*; if too salty a little honey.   Sprinkle also with *corona bubula*,[2] and let it bubble.

26. PATINA OF LAGITA-FISH.[3]   Scale and wash the fish. Break eggs, and roll the fish in these.   Add *liquamen*, wine, oil, bring to the boil.   When it boils pour over plain *oenogarum*. Sprinkle with pepper and serve.

27. PATINA ZOMOTEGANON (*i.e.*, with broth).   Wash any raw fish you like and place in a shallow pan.   Add oil, *liquamen*, wine, a bouquet of leek and coriander.   While this is cooking pound pepper, lovage, origan, and the cooked bouquet.   Pound by itself, add some of the fish stock, stir in raw eggs, blend. Pour into the pan, allow to set.   When set sprinkle with pepper and serve.

28. PATINA OF SOLES.   Beat and clean the soles and place in a shallow pan.[4]   Add oil, *liquamen*, and wine.   While the fish is cooking pound pepper, lovage, origan, grind well; pour on some of the fish stock, add raw eggs, and work into a smooth mixture.   Pour over the soles and cook over a low fire.   When the mixture has set sprinkle with pepper and serve.

29. PATINA OF FISH.   1 oz. pepper, ½ pint each of *caroenum* and spiced wine, 2 oz. oil.[5]

30. PATINA OF SMALL FISH.   Raisins, pepper, lovage, origan, onion, wine, *liquamen*, oil.   ⟨Pound and mix.⟩   Transfer into

[1] The identity of this Lucretius has not been established.
[2] See preceding recipe.
[3] See note to No. 21.
[4] This very commendable dish seems best made from fillets of sole. Take enough eggs to cover the fish.   Allow about ten minutes for the egg-mixture to set, after the fish itself is cooked.
[5] This is only the sauce; the rest has to be inferred from other fish *patinae*.

patellam. cum cocta fuerit, adicies in ipsam pisciculos coctos.
amulo obligas et inferes.   (*150*)

31. PATINA DE PISCIBUS DENTICE, AURATA ET MUGILE: accipies
pisces, curatos subassabis, postea eos in pulpas carpes. deinde
ostrea curabis. adicies in mortarium piperis scripulos VI,
suffundes liquamen, fricabis. postea adicies liquaminis cyathum unum, vini cyathum unum, mittes in caccabum et olei
unc. III et ostrea. oenogarum facies fervere. cum ferbuerit,
patinam perunges et in ⟨eam⟩[1] pulpam supra scriptam mittes
et [in][2] condituram de ostreis. facies ut ferveat. cum ferbuerit, franges ova XI, infundes super ostrea. cum strinxerint,
piper asparges et inferes.   (*151*)

32. PATINA DE PISCE LUPO: teres piper, cuminum, petroselinum, rutam, cepam, mel, liquamen, passum, olei guttas.

(*152*)

33. PATINA DE SORBIS CALIDA ET FRIGIDA: accipies sorba,
purgas, in mortario fricabis, per colum colabis. cerebella
enervabis IV cocta, mittes in mortario piperis scripulos VIII,
suffundes liquamen, fricabis. adicies sorba, in se contempera-
bis, franges ova VIII, adicies cyathum liquaminis unum.
patinam mundam perunges et in thermospodio pones, et sic
eam impensam mittes, ac subtus supra thermospodium habeat.[3]
cum cocta fuerit, piper minutum asparges et inferes.

(*166*)

34. PATINA DE PERSICIS: Persica duriora purgabis, frustatim
concides, elixas, in patina compones, olei modicum superstillabis et cum cuminato inferes.   (*167*)

35. PATINA DE PIRIS: pira elixa et purgata e medio teres cum
pipere, cumino, melle, passo, liquamine, oleo modico. ovis
missis patinam facies, piper super asparges et inferes.

(*168*)

---

[1] add. R.
[2] del. R.
[3] *thermospodium habeat* codd., rest. by Br.

a shallow pan. When cooked add the small fish, which have been previously cooked. Thicken with cornflour and serve.

31. PATINA OF DENTEX, GOLD-BREAM, AND GREY MULLET. Take the fish, clean, and slightly grill, then mince. Next clean oysters. Put in the mortar 6 scruples of pepper, moisten with *liquamen* and wine, put into a saucepan with 3 oz. of oil and the oysters. Bring the ⟨above⟩ *oenogarum* to the boil. When it boils grease a shallow pan and put in the minced fish and the oyster sauce. Bring to the boil. When boiling break 11 eggs[1] over the oysters ⟨and fish mixture⟩. When set sprinkle with pepper and serve.

32. PATINA OF SEA-PERCH.[2] Pound pepper, cumin, parsley, rue, onion, honey, *liquamen*, *passum*, a few drops of oil.

33. HOT OR COLD PATINA OF SORB-APPLES. Take sorb-apples, clean, pound in the mortar, and pass through a sieve. Skin and remove stringy parts of 4 cooked brains. Put in the mortar 8 scruples of pepper, moisten with *liquamen*, and pound. Add the sorb-apples and mix thoroughly; break 8 eggs, add 1 cyathus of *liquamen*. Grease a clean, shallow pan, place in the ashes, and fill with your mixture; it should have the ashes below and above. When it is cooked sprinkle with ground pepper and serve ⟨hot or cold⟩.

34. PATINA OF PEACHES. Clean firm peaches, cut them into pieces, and boil. Arrange in a shallow pan, sprinkle with a little oil, and serve with cumin-sauce.

35. PATINA OF PEARS. Boil and core pears, pound with pepper, cumin, honey, *passum*, *liquamen*, and a little oil. Add eggs to make a *patina*-mixture, sprinkle with pepper, and serve.

---

[1] 11 *eggs*: the manuscripts have 40; 11 is suggested by Schuch; Vollmer refers to IV, ii, 8, where 6 eggs are mentioned. 40 is certainly too many, and could very well be a scribe's error for 11 (XL = XI); on the other hand, the quantity of eggs must depend on the quantity of fish and oysters used. So 11 seems all right if only one fish of each kind is taken.   [2] This is again only the sauce.

36. Patina urticarum calida et frigida: urticam accipies, lavas, colas per colum, exsiccabis in tabula, eam concides. teres piperis scripulos X, suffundes liquamen, fricabis. postea adicies liquaminis cyathos II, olei uncias VI. caccabus ferveat. cum ferbuerit, coctum tolles ut refrigescat. postea patinam mundam perunges, franges ova VIII et agitabis. perfundes, subtus supra cinerem calidam habeat. ⟨cum⟩ cocta ⟨fuerit⟩, piper minutum asparges et inferes.   (*169*)

37. Patina de Cydoneis: mala Cydonia cum porris, melle, liquamine, oleo, defrito coques et inferes, vel elixata ex melle.
(*170*)

III. Minutal de piscibus vel isiciis

1. Minutal marinum: ⟨pones⟩ pisces in caccabum, adicies liquamen, oleum, vinum, cocturam. porros capitatos, coriandrum minutatim concides, isiciola de pisce minuta facies et pulpas piscis cocti concerpis, urticas marinas bene lotas mittes. haec omnia cum cocta fuerint, teres piper, ligusticum, origanum, fricabis, liquamen suffundes, ius de suo sibi, exinanies in caccabum. cum ferbuerit, tractam confringes, obligas, coagitas. piper asparges et inferes.   (*171*)

2. Minutal Terentinum: concides in caccabum albamen de porris minutatim, adicies oleum, liquamen, cocturam, isiciola valde minuta, et sic temperas ut tenerum sit. isicium Terentinum facies: inter isicia confectionem invenies. ius tale

36. HOT OR COLD PATINA OF STINGING NETTLES. Take the nettles, wash, drain in the colander, dry on a board, and chop. Pound 10 scruples of pepper, moisten with *liquamen*, and pound. Then add 2 cyathi of *liquamen*, and 6 oz. of oil, put in a saucepan, and bring to the boil. When it is cooked take out and cool. Well grease a shallow pan. Break 8 eggs, and stir. Pour your mixture into ⟨the pan⟩; place in the ashes so that it is covered above and below. When it is cooked sprinkle with ground pepper and serve ⟨hot or cold⟩.

37. PATINA OF QUINCES. Stew quinces with leeks in honey, *liquamen*, oil, and *defrutum* and serve; or boil ⟨and serve⟩ with honey.[1]

III. FRICASSEE OF FISH OR FORCEMEAT

1. FRICASSEE OF SEA FOOD. Put fish in a saucepan, add *liquamen*, oil, wine, stock. Finely chop leeks with their heads ⟨*i.e.*, green and white parts⟩ and coriander, make tiny fish-balls, and chop up fillets of cooked fish, and add sea-urchins, having washed them well. When all this is cooked crush pepper, lovage, origan, pound thoroughly, moisten with *liquamen*, and some of the cooking liquor, and put into the saucepan. When it bubbles crumble pastry into it to bind, and stir well. Sprinkle with pepper and serve.

2. FRICASSEE À LA TERENTIUS.[2] Finely chop into a saucepan the white of leeks, add oil, *liquamen*, stock, very small meatballs. Mix well into a creamy mixture. Now make a force-

---

[1] The second part could also be interpreted: boil the quinces, and afterwards stew them in honey; we tried this—*i.e.*, stewed the quinces in a little water, and afterwards very slowly in honey; the result is a thickish quince-sauce, the taste excellent.

[2] Terentius seems to have been a writer on culinary matters. He may be identified with a certain Tarantinos mentioned in the *Geoponica*. Cp. Brandt, p. 92 ff.

facies: piper, ligusticum, origanum, fricabis, suffundes liquamen, ius de suo sibi, vino et passo temperabis. mittes ⟨in⟩ caccabum. cum ferbuerit, tractam confringes, obligas. piper asparges et inferes.   (*172*)

3. MINUTAL APICIANUM: oleum, liquamen, vinum, porrum capitatum, mentam, pisciculos, isiciola minuta, testiculos caponum, glandulas porcellinas.   haec omnia in se coquantur. teres piper, ligusticum, coriandrum viride vel semen, suffundis liquamen, adicies mellis modicum et ius de suo sibi, vino et melle temperabis facies ut ferveat. cum ferbuerit, tractam confringes, obligas, coagitas.   piper asparges et inferes.

(*173*)

4. MINUTAL MATIANUM: adicies in caccabum oleum, liquamen, cocturam, concides porrum, coriandrum, isicia minuta. spatulam porcinam coctam tessellatim concides cum sua sibi tergilla.   facies ut simul coquantur. media coctura mala Matiana purgata intrinsecus, concisa tessellatim mittes. dum coquitur, teres piper, cuminum, coriandrum viride vel semen, mentam, laseris radicem, suffundes acetum, mel, liquamen, defritum modice et ius de sui sibi, aceto modico temperabis. facies ut ferveat.   cum ferbuerit, tractam confringes et ex ea obligas.   piper asparges et inferes.   (*174*)

5. MINUTAL DULCE EX CITRIIS: adicies in caccabo oleum,

meat *à la* Terentius[1]: the recipe for which you will find among
the force-meat recipes. Then make the following sauce:
pound pepper, lovage, origan; moisten with *liquamen*, and some
of the above broth, mix in wine and *passum*. Put into the
saucepan. When it bubbles crumble pastry into it to bind.
Sprinkle with pepper and serve.

3. FRICASSEE À LA APICIUS. Oil, *liquamen*, wine, leeks with
their white part, mint, small fish, tiny meat-balls, testicles of
capons, sweetbread of sucking-pig. Let all this cook together.
Pound pepper, lovage, fresh coriander or coriander seed,
moisten with *liquamen*, add a little honey and some of the cooking liquor, blend with wine and honey, bring to the boil.
When it boils crumble pastry into it to bind. Stir well.
Sprinkle with pepper and serve.

4. FRICASSEE À LA MATIUS.[2] Put in the saucepan oil,
liquamen, stock. Chop up leek, coriander, and tiny meat-balls.
Dice, with the crackling left on, a shoulder of pork which has
been previously cooked. Cook all together. Half-way through
the cooking add Matian apples, cored and diced. While this
is cooking pound together pepper, cumin, fresh coriander or
coriander seed, mint, and asafœtida root, pour in vinegar,
honey, *liquamen*, a little *defrutum*, and some of the cooking-
liquor, mix with a little vinegar. Bring to the boil. When it
boils crumble pastry and bind the sauce with this. Sprinkle
with pepper and serve.

5. SWEET FRICASSEE OF PUMPKIN.[3] Put in the saucepan oil,

---

[1] The recipe for the forcemeat *à la* Terentius is not contained in our
compilation. It is to be assumed that the forcemeat is to be cooked
in the mixture first described, and then the sauce added.

[2] Matius was a friend of Julius Caesar who wrote a book on domestic
science.
For 3–4 lb. shoulder of pork take about ½–¾ lb. meat-balls (pre-
cooked) and 1 lb. of good cooking-apples.

[3] *Citrium* here cannot be the *Citrus medica* (see note to I, xii, 5),
although the relevant articles in Pauly-Wissowa's *Realenzyklopädie*,
the *Thesaurus Linguae Latinae*, and also Brandt take it to mean this
fruit. The word must here have the meaning *citrullus*, pumpkin

liquamen, cocturam, porrum capitatum, concides coriandrum minutatim, spatulam porcinam coctam et isiciola minuta. dum coquitur, teres piper, cuminum, coriandrum ⟨viride⟩ vel semen, rutam viridem, laseris radicem, suffundis acetum, defritum, ius de suo sibi, aceto temperabis. facies ut ferveat. cum ferbuerit, citrium purgatum intro foras, tessellatim concisum et elixatum in caccabum mittes. tractam confringes et ex ea obligas. piper asparges et inferes.   (*175*)

6. MINUTAL EX PRAECOQUIS: adicies in caccabum oleum, liquamen, vinum, concides cepam Ascaloniam aridam, spatulam porcinam coctam tessellatim concides. his omnibus coctis teres piper, cuminum, mentam siccam. anethum, suffundis mel, liquamen, passum, acetum modice, ius de suo sibi, temperabis. praecoqua enucleata mittis. facies ut ferveant, donec percoquantur. tractam confringes, ex ea obligas. piper asparges et inferes.   (*176*)

7. A. MINUTAL EX IECINERIBUS ET PULMONIBUS LEPORIS: invenies inter lepores quemadmodum facies.

7. B. ⟨ALITER MINUTAL DULCE⟩[1]: adicies ⟨in⟩ caccabum liquamen, vinum, oleum, cocturam, porrum et coriandrum concisum, isicia minuta, spatulam porcinam coctam tessellatim concisam, et in eundem caccabum inmittes. dum coquitur, teres piper, ligusticum, origanum, ius de suo sibi, vino et passo temperabis. facies ut ferveat. cum ferbuerit, tractam confringes et ex ea obligas. piper asparges et inferes.   (*177*)

[1] add. Br.

liquamen, stock, coriander, shoulder of pork cooked previously, and tiny meat-balls. While this is cooking pound pepper, cumin, coriander—fresh or seed—fresh rue, asafœtida root, moisten with vinegar, *defrutum*, and some of the cooking liquor, blend with vinegar, bring to the boil. When it is boiling put in the saucepan pumpkin cleaned inside and outside, diced, and boiled. Crumble pastry, and bind with this. Sprinkle with pepper and serve.

6. FRICASSEE WITH APRICOTS. Put in the saucepan oil, *liquamen*, wine, chop in dry shallot, add diced shoulder of pork cooked previously. When all this is cooked pound pepper, cumin, dried mint, and dill, moisten with honey, *liquamen*, *passum*, a little vinegar, and some of the cooking-liquor; mix well. Add the stoned apricots. Bring to the boil, and let it boil until done. Crumble pastry to bind. Sprinkle with pepper and serve.

7 (*a*). FRICASSEE WITH LIVER AND LIGHTS OF HARE. You will find the recipe for this under Hare ⟨VIII, viii, 5⟩.

7 (*b*). ⟨SWEET FRICASSEE, ANOTHER METHOD.⟩ Put in the saucepan *liquamen*, wine, oil, stock, chopped leek and coriander, tiny meat-balls, and diced shoulder of pork cooked previously. Put all this in the same saucepan. While it is cooking pound pepper, lovage, origan, some of the cooking-liquor, and blend with wine and *passum*.[1] Bring to the boil. When it boils crumble pastry to bind. Sprinkle with pepper and serve.

(*i.e.*, No. 4 in the article "citrium" of the *Thesaurus*). Guégan translated it correctly by *citrouille*; his argument, however, that it must be a large variety of the gourd family is not valid: he thinks it should be large because the word is used in the recipe in the singular. But this is a practice that is fairly normal in a cookery-book, and it occurs quite often in Apicius—*e.g.*, dactyl*um*, caryot*am*, clearly used collectively, and not to denote one single date. Nevertheless, the recipe makes it quite clear that a kind of gourd is meant, be it a large or small one. The cleaning inside and outside, and the dicing and boiling, would make no sense with a citron.

[1] As this recipe is entitled "sweet fricassee," a rather large quantity of *passum* should be taken.

8. Minutal ex rosis: eodem iure supra scripto, sed passum plus adicies.   (*178*)

IV. Tisanam vel sucum

1. Tisanam sic facies: tisanam lavando fricas, quam ante diem infundes. impones supra ignem [calidum]. cum bullierit, mittes olei satis et anethi modicum fasciculum, cepam siccam, satureiam et coloefium, ut ibi coquantur propter sucum. mittes coriandrum viride et salem simul tritum et facies ut ferveat. cum bene ferbuerit, tolles fasciculum et transferes in alterum caccabum tisanam sic, ne fundum tangat propter combusturam. lias ⟨bene⟩ et colas in caccabulo super acronem coloefium ut bene tegatur.[1] teres piper, ligusticum, pulei aridi modicum, cuminum et sil[2] frictum. suffundis ⟨mel⟩, acetum, defritum, liquamen, refundis in caccabum super coloefium acronem. facies ut ferveat super ignem lentum.   (*179*)

2. Tisanam barricam: infundis cicer, lenticulam, pisam. defricas tisanam et cum leguminibus elixas. ubi bene bullierit, olei satis mittis et super viridia concidis porrum, coriandrum, anethum, feniculum, betam, malvam, cauliculum mollem. haec viridia minutatim concisa in caccabum mittis. cauliculos elixas et teres feniculi semen satis, origanum, silfi, ligusticum. postquam triveris, liquamine temperabis, et super legumina refundis et agitas. cauliculorum minutas super concidis.
     (*180*)

8. FRICASSEE WITH ROSES. Make with the preceding sauce, but take more *passum*.

IV. BARLEY SOUP OR BROTH

1. BARLEY SOUP. Wash and crush barley which has been soaking since the previous day. Put on the fire. When it boils add sufficient oil, a small bouquet of dill, dry onion, savory, and leg of pork.[1] Let all this cook with the barley for flavour. Add fresh coriander and salt pounded together, and bring to the boil. When it has boiled well remove the bouquet and transfer the barley to another saucepan, taking care that it does not stick to the pan and burn. Cream well, and strain into a pan over the leg of pork so that it is well covered. Pound pepper, lovage, a little dried pennyroyal, cumin, and dried seseli. Moisten with honey, vinegar, *defrutum*, and *liquamen*, and pour into the pan over the leg of pork. Cook over a slow fire.

2. BARLEY SOUP WITH DRIED VEGETABLES. Soak chick-peas, lentils, and peas. Crush barley, and boil with the dried vegetables. When it has boiled long enough add sufficient oil, and chop the following greens: leeks, coriander, dill, fennel, beet, mallow, and tender cabbage. Put all these finely chopped greens into the saucepan. Boil cabbage, pound a generous quantity of fennel-seed, origan, asafœtida, lovage, and after pounding blend with *liquamen*. Pour ⟨this mixture⟩ over the dried vegetables ⟨and barley⟩ and stir. Put chopped cabbage leaves on top.

V. VEGETABLE AND FRUIT STEWS ⟨to be served with the first course⟩

1. TURNOVER STEW. Boil small white beets, leeks that have

[1] Or top part of pig's trotters?

apios, bulbos, cocleas elixas, gigeria pullorum ⟨et⟩ ascellas, isicia coques ex iure. perungis patinam et folia malvarum substernis et praemixta holera componis sic ut laxa⟨mentum habeant⟩, permisces bulbos † inversos,[1] Damascena, cocleas, isicia, Lucanicas breves concidis, liquamine, oleo, vino, aceto ponis ut ferveat. cum ferbuerit, teres piper, ligusticum, zingiber, pyrethrum modicum, fricabis, suffundis et facies ut bulliat patina. ova complura confringis et ius mortarii reliquum commoves, commisces, patinam obligabis. dum ducit, oenogarum ad eam sic facies: teres piper, ligusticum, fricabis, suffundis liquamen et vinum, passo temperabis vel vino dulci. temperabis in caccabulo, mittis olei modicum, facies ut ferveat. cum ferbuerit, amulo obligas. patinam versas in lancem, folia malvarum ante tollis, oenogaro perfundis, insuper piper aspargis et inferes.   (*181*)

2. GUSTUM DE HOLERIBUS. condies bulbos liquamine, oleo et vino. cum cocti fuerint, iecinera porcelli et gallinarum et ungellas et ascellas divisas ⟨adicies⟩. haec omnia cum bulbis ferveant. cum ferbuerint, teres piper, ligusticum, suffundis

---

[1] *inversos*, obelized by R.; Brandt, in unpublished notes to Apicius, tentatively suggested *immersos* (I owe this information to the kindness of Dr W. Ehlers, general editor of the *Thesaurus Linguae Latinae*, Munich).

been stored, celery, bulbs,[1] snails; stew giblets and wings of chicken and meat-balls.   Grease a shallow pan and line with mallow leaves, and place in it the green vegetables, which you have mixed before ⟨with the meat⟩, so that they have room; mix in the bulbs[2]; chop damsons, the snails, the meat-balls, and small Lucanian sausages, and put everything with wine, oil, and vinegar on to the fire and bring to the boil.   When boiling crush pepper, lovage, ginger, and a little pyrethrum, pound well, ⟨moisten⟩; pour in ⟨part of it⟩ and let the stew come to the boil again.   Break several eggs, mix them with the remainder of the liquid left in the mortar, and add to the stew to bind.   While it is setting prepare the following *oenogarum* to serve with it: crush pepper and lovage, pound well, moisten with *liquamen* and wine, blend with *passum* or sweet wine.   Stir it in a saucepan, add a little oil, bring to the boil.   When it boils bind with cornflour.   Turn the stew out into a serving-dish (*lanx*), remove the mallow leaves, pour the *oenogarum* over, sprinkle with pepper, and serve.

2. VEGETABLE STEW.   Cook bulbs[3] in *liquamen*, oil, and wine. When they are cooked add pig's liver and legs and wings of chicken, cut up.   Let all this cook with the bulbs.   When it is done pound pepper, lovage, moisten with *liquamen*, wine, and

---

[1] *Bulbs:* The Greeks and Romans ate the bulbous roots of various plants which are nowadays only cultivated for their flowers—for instance, the bulbs of gladiolus or asphodel.   The latter were, according to Pliny, *Nat. Hist.*, XXI, 17, 67–68 (107–111), baked in the ashes and eaten with salt and oil, or pounded with figs.   Most highly praised by the Romans were the Megarean bulbs.   The bulbs vary in size, shape, bitterness, and colour.   They grew wild, but they were also cultivated.   (Cp. Pliny, XIX, 5, 30 (93–97)).   They were considered a very powerful aphrodisiac (Cp., *e.g.*, Columella, X, lines 105–106, and the Varro fragment added after VII, xiv, 3).

[2] The words *bulbos inversos* are obscure.

[3] See note (1) to the preceding recipe.   This recipe is very good with Spanish onions; take a fairly large quantity of wine to provide enough liquid, and about one large glass of sweet wine instead of *passum*.   About 5–6 large onions with legs and wings of one chicken and about ½ lb. of pig's liver will serve 4–5 people.

liquamen, vinum et passum, ut dulce sit, ius de suo sibi suffundis, revocas in bulbos.   cum ferbuerint, ad momentum amulo
obligas.   (*182*)

3. GUSTUM DE CUCURBITIS FARSILIBUS: cucurbitas a latere
subtiliter ad modum tessellae oblongae decidis et excavas et
mittis in frigidam.   impensam ad eas sic facies: teres piper,
ligusticum, origanum, suffundis liquamen, cerebella cocta teres,
ova cruda dissolves et mittes ut unum corpus efficias; liquamine
temperabis.   et cucurbitas supra scriptas non plene coctas ex
ea impensa imples, de tessella sua recludis, surclas et coctas
eximis et frigis.   oenogarum sic facies: teres piper, ligusticum,
suffundis vinum et liquamen, passo temperabis, olei modicum
mittis in caccabum et facies ut ferveat.   cum ferbuerit, amulo
obligas, et cucurbitas frictas oenogaro perfundis et piper aspargis
et inferes.   (*183*)

4. GUSTUM DE PRAECOQUIS: [duracina primotina] pusilla
praecoquia[1] purgas, enucleas, in frigidam mittis, in patina componis.   teres piper, mentam siccam, suffundis liquamen,
adicies mel, passum, vinum et acetum.   refundis in patinam
super praecoqua, olei modicum mittis et lento igni ferveat.
cum ferbuerit, amulo obligas.   piper aspargis et inferes.

(*184*)

---

[1] *dureina* (*-acina*) *primotica* codd., considered as gloss by Br.;
pusilla praecoquia considered as gloss by Vollmer—Giarratano, rest,
by Br. as belonging to the text,

passum to sweeten; add some of the cooking-liquor. Pour this back on the bulbs. As soon as they boil thicken with cornflour.

3. STUFFED MARROWS. Carefully cut out oblong pieces from the sides of the marrows, hollow the marrows, and put them in cold water. Then make the following mixture: pound pepper, lovage, origan, moisten with *liquamen*, mince cooked brains, beat raw eggs, and work all this to a smooth mixture. Blend with *liquamen*. Fill the marrows—which you have meanwhile partly cooked—with this mixture, replace the cut-out pieces, tie them up, boil until done, then take them out of the water and fry. Make the following *oenogarum* ⟨to serve with the marrows⟩: pound pepper, lovage; moisten with wine and *liquamen*; blend with *passum*, add a little oil, put in a saucepan, and bring to the boil. When boiling thicken with cornflour. Pour it over the fried marrows, sprinkle with pepper, and serve.

4. STEW OF APRICOTS. Take small apricots, clean, stone, and plunge in cold water, then arrange in a shallow pan. Pound pepper, dried mint, moisten with *liquamen*, add honey, *passum*, wine, and vinegar. Pour in the pan over the apricots, add a little oil, and cook over a low fire. When it is boiling thicken with cornflour. Sprinkle with pepper and serve,

OSPREON

I. pultes.   II. lenticula.   III. pisa.   IV. concicla.
V. tisana et alica.   VI. fabaciae virides et Baianae.
VII. faenum Graecum.   VIII. faseoli et cicer.

I. PULTES

1. PULTES IULIANAE SIC COQUUNTUR: alicam purgatam infundis, coques, facies ut ferveat.   cum ferbuerit, oleum mittis,
cum spissaverit, lias diligenter.   adicies cerebella duo cocta et
selibram pulpae quasi ad isicia liatae, cum cerebellis teres et in
caccabum mittis. teres piper, ligusticum, feniculi semen,
suffundis liquamen et vinum modice, mittis in caccabum supra
cerebella et pulpam.   ubi satis ferbuerit, cum iure misces.   ex
hoc paulatim alicam condies, et ad trullam permisces et lias, ut
quasi sucus videatur.   (*186*)
2. PULTES CUM IURE OENOCOCTI[1]: pultes oenococti iure
condies, copadia, similam sive alicam coctam hoc iure condies,
et cum copadiis porcinis apponis oenococti[2] iure conditis.

(*187*)

[1] = *aenococti*, cp. Br., p. 114.   [2] *oeno cocti* codd.

BOOK V

PULSE

I. Pottages. II. Lentils. III. Dried peas. IV. *Con-chicla*. V. Barley and spelt-grits. VI. Green beans and beans from Baiae. VII. Fenugreek. VIII. French beans and chick-peas.

I. POTTAGES

1. JULIAN POTTAGE is made in the following way. Soak hulled spelt, cook, bring to the boil. When boiling add oil. When it thickens stir to a creamy consistency. Take two brains previously cooked and half a pound of meat, minced as for rissoles, pound together with the brains, and put into a saucepan. Then pound pepper, lovage, fennel-seed, moisten with *liquamen* and a little wine, and put into the saucepan over the brains and the meat. When this has cooked enough mix it with stock. Add this mixture gradually to the spelt, mixing it in by the ladleful, and stir until smooth, to the consistency of thick soup.

2. POTTAGE WITH SAUCE FOR SUCKING-PIG IN A (METAL) CASSEROLE. Mix the pottage with a sauce as for sucking-pig cooked in a metal casserole.[1] That is to say, mix chopped-up meat and cooked fine wheat flour or spelt-grits with this sauce and serve with chopped pork cooked in a similar sauce.

3 (*a*). POTTAGE WITH PASTRY AND MILK. Put a pint of milk and a little water in a new saucepan and bring to the boil over a slow fire. Dry three slices of pastry, crumble these, and put the crumbs into the milk. Stir to prevent it from burning, adding water. When it is cooked pour it over lamb ⟨and serve⟩.

[1] Cp. VIII, vii, 11.

123

3. A. PULTES TRACTOGALATAE: lactis sextarium et aquae modicum mittes in caccabo novo et lento igni ferveat. tres orbiculos tractae siccas et confringis et partibus in lac summittis. ne uratur, aquam miscendo agitabis. cum cocta fuerit, ut est, super agninam mittis.[1]   (*188*)

3. B. ex melle et musteis cum lacte similiter facies, salem et oleum minus mittis.   (*189*)

4. PULTES: alicam purgatam infundis, coques. cum fer-buerit, oleum mittis. cum spissaverit, adicies cerebella duo cocta et selibram pulpae quasi ad isicia liatae, cum cerebellis teres et in caccabum mittes. teres piper, ligusticum, feniculi semen, suffundis liquamen et meri modicum, et mittis in caccabum supra cerebella et pulpam. ubi satis ferbuerit, cum iure misces. ex hoc paulatim alicam condies, et lias ut quasi sucus videatur.   (*185*)

II. LENTICULA

1. LENTICULA EX SFONDYLIS [sive fondilis]: accipies caccabum mundum, ⟨mittes, coques⟩. adicies in mortarium piper, cuminum, semen coriandri, mentam, rutam,[2] puleium, fricabis, suffundis acetum, adicies mel, liquamen et defritum, aceto temperabis, reexinanies in caccabo. sfondylos elixatos teres et mittis ut ferveant. cum bene ferbuerint, obligas. adicies in boletari oleum viride.   (*190*)

2. LENTICULAM DE CASTANEIS: accipies caccabum novum, et castaneas purgatas diligenter mittis. adicies aquam et nitrum modice, facies ut coquatur. cum coquitur, mittis in mortario

---

[1] Lacuna, containing at least one recipe—cp. Br., p. 85.
[2] *menta, rutae* codd., *mentam, rutam* R.

3 (*b*).[1] You can make it in a similar manner with honey and sweet-wine cake[2] and milk, taking less salt and oil.

4. POTTAGE.[3] Soak hulled spelt, cook. When boiling add oil. When it thickens take two brains cooked previously and half a pound of meat minced as for rissoles, pound with the brains, and put into a saucepan. Then pound pepper, lovage, fennel-seed, moisten with *liquamen* and a little wine, and put into the saucepan over the brains and the meat. When this has cooked enough mix it with stock. Add this mixture gradually to the spelt, and stir until creamy, to the consistency of a thick soup.

II. LENTILS

1. LENTILS WITH MUSSELS.[4] Take a clean saucepan, ⟨put in the lentils, and cook⟩. Put in a mortar pepper, cumin, coriander-seed, mint, rue, pennyroyal; pound, moisten with vinegar; add honey, *liquamen*, and *defrutum*, blend with vinegar, pour into the saucepan. Pound boiled mussels, add ⟨to the lentils⟩, and bring to the boil. When they boil, bind. Sprinkle with best oil in the serving-dish.

2. LENTILS WITH CHESTNUTS.[5] ⟨Boil the lentils.⟩ Take a new saucepan and put in the carefully cleaned chestnuts. Add water and a little cooking-soda. Put on the fire to cook.

---

[1] At least one recipe is missing here, as the following remark cannot refer to the previous recipe, which does not mention either salt or oil.

[2] See note to VII, x.

[3] This is the same recipe as No. 1 of this chapter. According to Brandt (p. 130, n. 201), this might perhaps be explained as follows: the '*Julianae*' of No. 1 could refer to the emperor Julian the Apostate (if it refers to an emperor at all). The compiler of our Apicius edition chose a simple recipe and gave it the name of the Emperor, who was renowned for his simple tastes, but he then forgot to remove the recipe from the original place, a thing that happens in other places of the edition too—*e.g.*, IV, iv, 1 and 2, and V, v, 1 and 2.

[4] See note to III, xx.

[5] $\frac{3}{4}$ lb. lentils and $\frac{1}{2}$ lb. chestnuts will serve 4–5 people.

piper, cuminum, semen coriandri, mentam, rutam,[1] laseris
radicem, puleium, fricabis. suffundis acetum, ⟨adicies⟩ mel,
liquamen, aceto temperabis, et super castaneas coctas refundis.
adicies oleum, facies ut ferveat. cum bene ferbuerit, tudiclabis
[ut in mortario teres]. gustas: si quid deest, addes. cum in
boletar miseris, addes oleum viride.   (*191*)

3. ALITER LENTICULAM: coquis. cum despumaverit, porrum
et coriandrum viride supermittis. ⟨teres⟩ coriandri semen,
puleium, laseris radicem, semen mentae et rutae,[2] suffundis
acetum, adicies mel, liquamine, aceto, defrito temperabis,
adicies oleum, agitabis. si quid opus fuerit, mittis. amulo
obligas, insuper oleum viride mittis, piper aspargis et inferes.
                                                      (*192*)

III. Pisa

1. Pisam coques. cum despumaverit, porrum, coriandrum
et cuminum supra mittis. teres piper, ligusticum, [careum hoc
est caravita] careum, anethum, ocimum viride, suffundis liquamen, vino et liquamine temperabis, facies ut ferveat. cum
ferbuerit, agitabis. si quid defuerit, mittis et inferes. (*193*)

2. PISAM FARSILEM: coques. cui oleum mittis. ⟨accipies⟩
abdomen, et mittis in caccabum liquamen et porrum capitatum,
coriandrum viride. imponis ut coquatur. isicia minuta facies
quadrata, et coques simul turdos vel aucellas vel de pullo
concisa et cerebella prope cocta cum iuscello coques. Lucanicas assas, petasonem elixas, porros ex aqua coques, nucleorum
heminam frigis. teres piper, ligusticum, origanum, zingiber,
ius abdominis fundis, lias. angularem accipies, qui versari
potest, et omentis tegis. oleo perfundis, deinde nucleos aspargis et supra pisam mittis ut tegas fundum angularis, et sic
componis supra petasonis pulpas, porros, Lucanicas concisas.

---

[1] *mentae, rutae* E, *menta(m), rutae* V, *mentam, rutam* R.
[2] *semen mentae et rutae* codd., R. would rather read *mentam et rutam*
and eliminate *semen*.

When cooked put in the mortar pepper, cumin, coriander-seed, mint, rue, asafœtida root, and pennyroyal; pound. Moisten with vinegar, add honey and *liquamen*, blend with vinegar, and pour over the cooked chestnuts. Add oil, bring to the boil. When it is boiling well, stir. ⟨Mix with the lentils.⟩ Taste: if something is missing, add it. When you have put it in the serving-dish add best oil.

3. LENTILS, ANOTHER METHOD. Boil ⟨the lentils⟩; when you have skimmed off the froth put in leeks and green coriander. Pound coriander-seed, pennyroyal, asafœtida root, mint, and rue, moisten with vinegar, add honey, blend with *liquamen*, vinegar, and *defrutum*. ⟨Pour over the lentils⟩, add oil, stir. ⟨Taste⟩: if something is wanting, add it. Thicken with corn-flour, pour on best oil, sprinkle with pepper, and serve.

III. DRIED PEAS

1. Boil the peas. When the froth has been skimmed off put in leeks, coriander, and cumin. Pound pepper, lovage, caraway, dill, fresh basil, moisten with *liquamen*, blend with wine and *liquamen* ⟨add to the peas⟩, bring to the boil. When it boils stir. If something is wanting, add, and then serve.

2. PEASE MOULD. Cook the peas, add oil. Take belly of pork, put in a saucepan ⟨together with⟩ *liquamen*; leeks including the white; fresh coriander. Set on the fire to cook. Make small cubes of minced meat and cook, together with thrushes or other small birds, or pieces of chicken, and cook brains that have been parboiled previously in stock. Grill Lucanian sausages; boil a shoulder of pork; boil leeks in water; toast 1 lb. of pine-kernels. Pound pepper, lovage, origan, ginger; add the stock from the belly of pork; thicken. Take a mould which can be turned out, and line with sausage casing.[1] Grease with oil, put in the pine-kernels, and some of the peas

---

[1] As a substitute for *omentum* tin-foil or grease-proof paper or "Cellophane" can be used.

iterum pisam supermittis. item alternis aptabis obsonia, quousque impleatur angularis. novissime pisam mittis, ut intus omnia contineat. coques in furno vel lento igni imponis, ut ducat ad se deorsum. ova dura facies, vitella eicies, in mortario mittis cum pipere albo, nucleis, melle, vino candido et liquamine modico. teres et mittis in vas ut ferveat. cum ferbuerit, pisam mittis in lancem, et hoc iure perfundis. hoc ius candidum appellatur.   (*194*)

3. PISAM INDICAM: pisam coques. cum despumaverit, porrum et coriandrum concidis et mittis in caccabum ut ferveat. et accipies sepias minutas, sic quomodo sunt cum atramento suo, ut simul coquantur. adicies oleum, liquamen et vinum. fasciculum porri et coriandri. facies ut coquantur. cum coctum fuerit, teres piper, ligusticum, origanum, carei modicum, suffundis ius de suo sibi, vino et passo temperabis. sepias minutatim concidis et in pisam mittis. piper asparges ⟨et inferes⟩.   (*195*)

on top, so that the bottom of the mould is covered.   Place over it the meat of the shoulder of pork, the leeks, the diced sausages, next a layer of peas.   In the same way arrange the other ingredients in alternating layers until the mould is filled, finishing with a layer of peas.   Cook in the oven or over a slow fire so that it sets.   Hard-boil eggs, remove the yolks, put the whites in the mortar, and pound with white pepper and pine-kernels; moisten with honey, add white wine and a little *liquamen*. Put in a saucepan and bring to the boil.   When boiling turn the pease-mould out on to a serving-dish and pour this sauce over.   This sauce is called white sauce.[1]

3. PEAS, INDIAN MANNER.   Boil the peas.   When the froth has been skimmed off chop leek and coriander, put into the saucepan, and bring to the boil.   Take very small cuttle-fish with their ink and let them cook like this ⟨*i.e.*, with the ink⟩. Add oil, *liquamen*, and wine, and a bouquet of leek and coriander.   Let it cook.   When cooked pound pepper, lovage, origan, and a little caraway, moisten with some of the broth from the cuttlefish, blend with wine and *passum*.   Chop the cuttlefish finely and add to the peas.   ⟨Mix with the sauce, cook again.⟩   Sprinkle with pepper and serve.

---

[1] This recipe—although complicated and rather laborious—is well worth trying.   Approximate quantities for 6 people: 1 lb. peas (split or whole), 1 lb. or a little more of belly of pork, 1 lb. or a little over of shoulder of pork, 1 small chicken, 1 brain (=2 halves), 1 head of leek to be boiled with the belly of pork, 2 heads of leek for the main dish, ½ lb. of minced meat, ½ lb. of pork chipolatas (in order to avoid the additional trouble of making Lucanian sausages).   If these quantities are taken about 6 oz. pine-kernels (cashew-nuts are a good substitute if pine-kernels prove too expensive) are enough to line well the bottom of the mould instead of the 1 lb. mentioned in the recipe.   Quantities for the white sauce: the white of 6 eggs, about 6 oz. pine-kernels, 1 small glass of white wine (or less, just enough to make it runny), honey and *liquamen* (or salt) to taste.   Arrange the prepared ingredients in a deep baking tin; the first sauce should be added after each layer of meat, just giving sufficient moisture to the otherwise quite dry filling.   Bake in a slow oven for just over an hour, by which time it should have set and be ready for turning out.

4. ⟨ALITER:⟩ pisam coques, agitabis et mittis in frigidam.
cum refrigeraverit, denuo agitabis. concidis cepam minutatim
et albamentum ovi, oleo et sale condies. aceti modicum adicies. in boletari vitellum ovi cocti colas, insuper oleum viride
mittis et inferes.   (*196*)

5. PISAM VITELLIANAM SIVE FABAM: pisam coques, lias. teres
piper, ligusticum, zingiber, et super condimenta mittis vitella
ovorum, quae dura coxeris, mellis unc. III, liquamen, vinum et
acetum. haec omnia mittis in caccabum et condimenta quae
trivisti. adiecto oleo ponis ut ferveat. condies pisam, lias,
si aspera fuerit. mel mittis et inferes.   (*197*)

6. ALITER PISAM SIVE FABAM: ubi despumaverit, teres mel,
liquamen, caroenum, cuminum, rutam, apii semen, oleum et
vinum. tudiclabis. cum pipere trito et cum isiciis inferes.
(*198*)

7. ALITER PISAM SIVE FABAM: despumatam subtrito lasere
Parthico, liquamine et caroeno condies. oleum modice
superfundis et inferes.   (*199*)

8. PISAM ADULTERAM VERSATILEM: coques pisam. cerebella
vel aucellas vel turdos exossatos a pectore, Lucanicas, iecinera,
gigeria pullorum in caccabum mittis, liquamen, oleum. fasciculos porri capitati, coriandrum viride concidis, et cum cerebellis coques. teres piper, ligusticum et liquamen.   (*200*)

4. ⟨Peas, another method.⟩ Boil the peas, stir, and let them cool. When they are cold stir again. Finely chop an onion and boiled egg-white, and season with oil and salt; add a little vinegar. ⟨Mix with the peas, and turn everything into the serving-dish⟩, pass yolk of egg through a sieve on to the peas, add some best oil, and serve.

5. Peas or beans à la Vitellius.[1] Boil the peas ⟨or beans⟩, stir until smooth. Pound pepper, lovage, ginger; and over the spices put yolks of hard-boiled eggs, 3 oz. honey, *liquamen*, wine, and vinegar. Put all this, including the spices which you have pounded, in the saucepan. Add oil, and bring to the boil. Season the peas with this. Stir until smooth if lumpy. Add honey and serve.

6. Peas or beans, another method. ⟨Boil the peas or beans.⟩ When the froth has been skimmed off pound honey, *liquamen*, *caroenum*, cumin, rue, celery seed, oil, and wine; stir ⟨and mix with the peas⟩. ⟨Cook until done.⟩ Serve with ground pepper and meat balls.

7. Peas and beans, another method. ⟨Boil the peas or beans⟩, skim off the froth. Season with pounded asafœtida, *liquamen*, and *caroenum*. Pour over a little oil, and serve.

8. Pease turnover. Boil the peas. Put brains, small birds or thrushes boned from the breast, Lucanian sausages, liver, and chicken giblets into a saucepan, add *liquamen* and oil. Chop up leeks with their white part and green coriander and cook with the brains ⟨or birds, as the case may be⟩. Pound pepper, lovage and *liquamen* . . . [*the remainder is missing, but can be restored from No. 2.*][2]: ⟨and some of the cooking liquor to make a sauce. Line a mould with sausage-casing, grease, and arrange peas and the other ingredients in alternating layers, finishing off with a layer of peas. Cook in the oven or over a low fire, until it sets. Turn out on to a serving-dish and serve.⟩

[1] The Emperor (A.D. 69). See Tacitus, *Hist.*, II, 62, and Suetonius, *Vit.*, 13.

[2] As this is a simplified version of No. 2, the egg sauce may have been omitted; there could, of course, have been a sauce,

9. Pisam sive fabam Vitellianam: pisam sive fabam coques. cum despumaverit, mittis porrum, coriandrum et flores malvarum. dum coquitur, teres piper, ligusticum, origanum, feniculi semen, suffundis liquamen et vinum, ⟨mittis⟩ in caccabum, adicies oleum. cum ferbuerit, agitas. oleum viride insuper mittis et inferes.   (*201*)

IV. Conchicla

1. ⟨Conchiclam⟩ cum faba: coques. teres piper, ligusticum, cuminum, coriandrum viride, suffundis liquamen, vino et liquamine temperabis, mittis in caccabum, adicies oleum. lento igni ferveat et inferes.   (*202*)

9. PEAS OR BEANS À LA VITELLIUS.   Boil the peas or beans.
When the froth has been skimmed off add leeks, coriander, and
flowers of mallow.   While this is cooking pound pepper, lovage,
origan, fennel seed, moisten with *liquamen* and wine, put in the
saucepan ⟨to the peas or beans⟩, add oil.   When it boils
⟨again⟩, stir.   Pour over best oil and serve.

IV. CONCHICLA[1]

1. CONCHICLA WITH BEANS.   Boil the beans.   Pound pepper,
lovage, cumin, fresh coriander, moisten with *liquamen*, blend
with wine and *liquamen*, put into the saucepan ⟨with the beans⟩,
add oil.   Cook over a low fire, and serve.

[1] *Conchicla*, a contraction of *conchicula*, is, according to the *Thesaurus
linguae latinae* and the current Latin dictionaries, a diminutive of
conchis, which means a bean with its pod.   But it seems impossible
that *conchicla* can have this meaning in our recipes.   Only No. 1 is
made with beans; the other five recipes of this chapter have peas as
their main vegetable ingredient.   Further, the direction to skim off
the froth only makes sense with dried peas, beans, lentils, and so forth,
but not with peas or beans in their pods, and it is given in precisely
the same manner in the preceding recipes for peas, beans, and lentils.
Moreover, the title *conchicla de pisa simplici* of No. 3, worded like
most of the *patina* titles, suggests that *conchicla* is the name of the dish.
Since *patina* as the name for the dish is derived from the name of the
vessel in which it is cooked and served, *conchicla* could also be derived
from the name of a vessel, in this case the serving-dish only, the
saucepans mentioned for the actual cooking—being the *cumana*, an
operculum (covered pan), or the *conchiclar(is)*, otherwise apparently an
unknown word.   If this is so *conchicla* would be a diminutive of
concha, which in Cato, Horace, and other authors can mean a vessel
in the shape of a *concha*.   The passages quoted in the *Thesaurus*
mention *conchae* for oil, salt, as drinking-vessels, and for water.   A
number of such *conchae* of various sizes have been preserved (see
Introduction, section IV).   If our assumption is correct the *con-
chiclae*, which belong to the dishes eaten with the first course of a
dinner, would have been served up in shell-shaped dishes.   As to the
conchiclar or *conchiclaris* mentioned in No. 5, the word could be a
derivative of *conchicla* (meaning this time the prepared dish only, and
not the serving-dish) and would then be a special vessel in which to
prepare *conchicla*.

2. CONCHICLAM APICIANAM: accipies Cumanam mundam, ubi coques pisam, cui mittis Lucanicas concisas, isiciola porcina, pulpas, petasonem. teres piper, ligusticum, origanum, anethum, cepam siccam, coriandrum viride, suffundis liquamen, vino et liquamine temperabis. mittis in Cumanam, cui adicies oleum, pungis ubique, ut combibat oleum. igni lento coques ita ut ferveat et inferes. (*203*)

3. CONCHICLAM DE PISA SIMPLICI: pisam coques. cum despumaverit, fasciculum porri et coriandri mittis. dum coquitur teres piper, ligusticum, origanum, fasciculum, de suo sibi fricabis, suffundis ⟨liquamen, vino et⟩ liquamine temperabis, mittis ⟨in Cumanam⟩. super adicies oleum, et lento igni ferveat, et inferes. (*204*)

4. CONCHICLA COMMODIANA: pisam coques. cum despumaverit, teres piper, ligusticum, anethum, cepam siccam, suffundis liquamen, vino et liquamine temperabis. mittis in caccabum ut combibat. deinde ova quattuor solves, in sextarium pisae mittis, agitas, mittis in Cumanam, ad ignem ponis, ut ducat, et inferes. (*205*)

5. ALITER CONCHICLAM SIC FACIES: concidis pullum minutatim, liquamine, oleo et vino ferveat. concidis cepam, coriandrum minutum, cerebella enervata, mittes in eundem pullum. cum coctus fuerit, levas et exossas. concides minutatim cepam et coriandrum, colas ibi pisam coctam non conditam. accipies conchiclarem pro modo. componis varie. deinde teres piper, cuminum, suffundis ius de suo sibi. item in mortario ova duo dissolves, temperas. ius de suo sibi suffundis pisae integre

2. CONCHICLA À LA APICIUS. Take a clean earthenware saucepan in which you cook dried peas; add cut-up Lucanian sausages, tiny pork meat-balls, various meats, shoulder of pork.[1] Pound pepper, lovage, origan, dill, dried onion, fresh coriander, moisten with *liquamen*, blend with wine and *liquamen*. Put in the saucepan, add oil. Prick ⟨the meats and peas⟩ all over, so that the oil is absorbed. Cook over a low fire, and serve.

3. CONCHICLA OF PLAIN PEAS. Boil the peas. When the froth has been skimmed off add a bouquet of leeks and coriander. While it is cooking crush pepper, lovage, origan, the bouquet, pound altogether, moisten with *liquamen*, blend with wine and *liquamen*, put into the earthenware saucepan ⟨with the peas⟩. Pour oil over, cook over a low fire, and serve.

4. CONCHICLA À LA COMMODUS.[2] Boil the peas. When the froth has been skimmed off pound pepper, lovage, dill, dried onion; moisten with *liquamen*; blend with wine and *liquamen*. Put into the saucepan ⟨with the peas⟩ until it is absorbed. Then break four eggs to each pint of peas, add, stir. Put everything into an earthenware saucepan, place over a low fire to allow it to set, and serve.

5. CONCHICLA, ANOTHER METHOD. Cut a chicken into small pieces, cook in *liquamen*, oil, and wine. Add to the chicken chopped onion, finely chopped coriander, and skinned brains. When it is cooked take out and bone. Chop an onion and coriander finely, and strain over this the cooked peas, not yet seasoned. Take a suitable saucepan (*conchiclar*), arrange ⟨your ingredients⟩ all mixed together. Then crush pepper, cumin, add some of the chicken stock. Likewise break in the mortar two eggs and mix ⟨with the other things⟩. Pour the remaining stock from the chicken over whole boiled peas,[3] and

---

[1] Possibly the shoulder of pork is supposed to be precooked, but the recipe would work also if the meat were raw; it would only take longer.   [2] The Emperor.

[3] *I.e.*, before the peas are sieved keep some whole—enough to cover the pan.

elixae, vel nucleis adornabis, et lento igni fervere facies et inferes. (206)

6. ALITER CONCHICLATUS PULLUS VEL PORCELLUS: exossas pullum a pectore, femora eius iungis in porrectum, surculo alligas, et impensam [concicla farsilis] paras. et farcies alternis pisam lotam,[1] cerebella, Lucanicas et cetera. teres ⟨piper⟩, ligusticum, origanum et zingiber, liquamen suffundis, passo et vino temperabis. facies ut ferveat, et, cum ferbuerit, mittis modice. et impensam cum condieris, alternis in pullo componis, omento tegis et in operculo deponis et in furnum mittis, ut coquantur paulatim, et inferes. (207)

V. TISANAM ET ALICAM

1. ALICAM VEL SUCUM TISANAE SIC FACIES[2]: tisanam vel alicam lavando fricas, quam ante diem infundis. imponis supra ignem. cum bullierit, mittis olei satis et anethi modicum fasciculum, cepam siccam, satureiam et coloefium, ut ibi coquantur propter sucum. mittis coriandrum viride et salem simul tritum et facies ut ferveat. cum bene ferbuerit, tollis fasciculum et transferes in alterum caccabum tisanam, sic ne fundum tangat propter combusturam. lias bene et colas in caccabo super acronem coloefium ut bene tegatur. teres piper, ligusticum, pulei aridi modicum, cuminum ⟨et⟩ sil[3] frictum. suffundis mel, acetum, defritum, liquamen, refundis in caccabum super coloefium acronem. facies ut ferveat super ignem lentum. (208)

2. ALITER TISANAM: infundis cicer, lenticulam, pisam, defricas tisanam et cum leguminibus elixas. ubi bene bullierit, olei satis mittis et super viridia concidis porrum, coriandrum, anethum, feniculum, ⟨betam, malvam cauliculum⟩ mollem. haec viridia minutatim concisa in caccabum mittis. cauliculos

---

[1] One expects *coctam.*
[2] Changes in punctuation and text made according to IV, iv, 1, which is the same recipe.   [3] *sil* codd. here; cp. IV, iv, 1, note 2.

garnish with these or pine-kernels, cook over a low fire, and serve.

6. CHICKEN OR SUCKING-PIG STUFFED WITH CONCHICLA. Bone a chicken from the breast, join its legs, stretching them, skewer. Prepare the stuffing: cooked peas, brains, Lucanian sausages, and all the other usual things. Pound pepper, lovage, origan, and ginger, moisten with *liquamen*, blend with *passum* and wine. Bring to the boil, and when it has boiled add a little ⟨to the stuffing⟩. And when you have made your stuffing arrange everything in alternating layers in the chicken, wrap it in sausage-casing, place in a casserole, put in the oven, and cook gently. Serve.

V. BARLEY AND SPELT-GRITS

1. SPELT-GRITS OR BARLEY SOUP. Make in the following way. Wash and crush barley or spelt-grits which have been soaking since the previous day. (*The remainder of the recipe* = *IV, iv*, 1.)

2. BARLEY SOUP, ANOTHER METHOD. = IV, iv, 2.

elixas et teres feniculi semen satis, origanum, silfi, ligusticum. postquam triveris, liquamine temperas et super legumina refundis. agitas. cauliculorum minutas super concidis.

(209)

VI. FABACIAE VIRIDES ET BAIANAE

1. FABACIAE VIRIDES ex liquamine, oleo, coriandro viridi, cumino et porro conciso coctae inferuntur.

2. ALITER FABACIAE: frictae ex liquamine inferuntur.[1]

3. ALITER FABACIAE: ex sinapi trito, melle, nucleis, ruta, cumino et aceto inferuntur.[2]

4. BAIANAS: elixas, minutatim concidis. ruta, apio viridi, porro, aceto, oleo, liquamine, caroeno vel passo modico inferes.[3]

(210)

VII. FAENUM GRAECUM

FAENUM GRAECUM ex liquamine, oleo et vino.   (211)

VIII. FASEOLI ET CICER

1. FASEOLI VIRIDES ET CICER ex sale, cumino, oleo et mero modico inferuntur.

2. ALITER FASEOLUS SIVE CICER: frictos ex oenogaro et pipere. gustabis. et elixati, sumpto semine; cum ovis in patella, feniculo viridi, pipere, liquamine et caroeno modico pro salso inferuntur. vel simpliciter, ut solet.[4]

---

[1] Punctuation by Br.
[2] Punctuation by Br.
[3] Punctuation by Br.
[4] Punctuation by Br., who sees three short recipes here.

VI. GREEN BEANS AND BEANS FROM BAIAE

1. GREEN BEANS are served cooked with *liquamen*, oil, fresh coriander, cumin, and chopped leek.

2. ANOTHER METHOD. Fried, served with *liquamen*.

3. ANOTHER METHOD. ⟨Boiled⟩, served with ground mustard, honey, pine-kernels, rue, cumin, and vinegar.

4. BEANS FROM BAIAE. Boil, chop finely. Serve with rue, green celery, leeks, oil, *liquamen*, a little *caroenum* or *passum*.

VII. FENUGREEK

FENUGREEK. With *liquamen*, oil, and wine.

VIII. FRENCH BEANS AND CHICK-PEAS

1. FRESH FRENCH BEANS AND CHICK-PEAS are served with salt, cumin, oil, and a little wine.

2. FRENCH BEANS OR CHICK-PEAS, ANOTHER METHOD.

(*a*) You can eat them fried with *oenogarum* and pepper.

(*b*) They are also served instead of salt fish, boiled, using their seed, with eggs in a dish, and green fennel, pepper, *liquamen*, and a little *caroenum*.

(*c*) Or serve them plain, as is customary.

LIBER VI

AEROPETES

I. In struthione.   II. In grue vel anate perdice turture
palumbo columbo et diversis avibus.   III. In turdis.
IV. In ficedulis.   V. In pavo.   VI. In fasiano.   VI. In
ansere.   VIII. In pullo.

I. IN STRUTHIONE

1. IN STRUTHIONE ELIXO: piper, mentam, cuminum assum,
apii semen, dactylos vel caryotas, mel, acetum, passum, liquamen et oleum modice, et in caccabo facies ut bulliat.   amulo
obligas, et sic partes struthionis in lance perfundis, et desuper
piper aspargis. si autem in condituram coquere volueris, alicam
addis.

2. ALITER ⟨IN⟩ STRUTHIONE ELIXO: piper, ligusticum, thymum aut satureiam, mel, sinape, acetum, liquamen et oleum.

(*212*)

II. IN GRUE VEL ANATE PERDICE TURTURE PALUMBO
COLUMBO ET DIVERSIS AVIBUS

1. Gruem vel anatem lavas et ornas et includis in olla.
adicies aquam, salem, anethum, dimidia coctura decoques, dum

140

BOOK VI

BIRDS

I. Sauces for ostrich. II. Crane, duck, partridge,
turtle-dove, wood-pigeon, pigeon, and various other
birds. III. Thrushes. IV. Fig-peckers. V. Peacock. VI. Pheasant. VII. Goose. VIII. Chicken.

I. Sauces for Ostrich

1. Sauce for boiled ostrich. Take pepper, mint, grilled
cumin, celery-seed, dates or Jericho dates, honey, vinegar,
passum, *liquamen*, and a little oil, and bring to the boil in a
saucepan. Thicken with cornflour and pour this sauce over
the pieces of ostrich in the serving-dish, and sprinkle with
pepper. But if you wish to cook the ostrich in the sauce add
spelt-grits.

2. Another sauce for boiled ostrich. Pepper, lovage,
thyme or savory, honey, mustard, vinegar, *liquamen*, and oil.

II. Crane, Duck, Partridge, Turtle-dove, Wood-pigeon, Pigeon, and various other birds

1. Wash the crane or duck, truss, and put in a large saucepan.
Add water, salt, dill, and cook until half done. When it gets
firm take it out and put it into another pan with oil and *liquamen*, a bouquet of origan and coriander. When it is nearly
done add a little *defrutum* to give it colour. Then pound pepper, add some of the cooking-liquor, blend with vinegar.
Put into a saucepan, bring to the boil, thicken with cornflour.
Place the bird in a serving-dish and pour the sauce over it.

2. (a) For crane, duck, or chicken. Take pepper, dried

obduretur, levas et iterum in caccabum mittis cum oleo et
liquamine, cum fasciculo origani et coriandri.   prope cocturam
defritum modice mittis, ut coloret.   teres piper, ligusticum,
cuminum, coriandrum, laseris radicem, rutam, caroenum, mel,
suffundis ius de suo sibi, aceto temperas.   in caccabo reexinanies
ut calefiat, amulo obligabis.   imponis in lance et ius perfundis.

(213)

2. IN GRUE ⟨VEL⟩ IN ANATE VEL IN PULLO: piper, cepam
siccam, ligusticum, cuminum, apii semen, pruna [vel] Damascena enucleata, mulsum, acetum,[1] liquamen, defritum, oleum et
coques.

gruem[2] cum coquis, caput eius aqua quam non contingat,
sed sit foris ab aqua.   cum cocta fuerit, de sabano calido
involves gruem et caput eius trahe: cum nervis sequetur, ut
pulpae vel ossa remaneant; cum nervis enim manducare non
potes.   (<i>214</i>) (<i>215</i>)

3. GRUEM VEL ANATEM EX RAPIS: lavas, ornas et in olla
elixabis cum aqua, sale et anetho dimidia coctura.   rapas
coque, ut exbromari possint.   levabis de olla, et iterum lavabis, et in caccabum mittis anatem cum oleo et liquamine et
fasciculo porri et coriandri.   rapam lotam et minutatim concisam desuper mittis, facies ut coquatur.   modica coctura mittis
defritum ut coloret. ius tale parabis: piper, cuminum,
coriandrum, laseris radicem, suffundis acetum et ius de suo
sibi, reexinanies super anatem ut ferveat.   cum ferbuerit,
amulo obligabis, et super rapas adicies.   piper aspargis et
adponis.   (<i>216</i>)

4. ALITER IN GRUEM VEL ANATEM ELIXAM: piper, ligusticum,
cuminum, coriandrum siccum, mentam, origanum, nucleos,
caryotam, liquamen, oleum, mel, sinape et vinum.   (<i>217</i>)

5. ALITER GRUEM VEL ANATEM ASSAM: eas de hoc iure perfundis: teres piper, ligusticum, origanum, liquamen, mel,
aceti modicum et olei.   ferveat bene.   Mittis amulum et supra
ius rotulas cucurbitae elixae vel colocasiae ut bulliant.   si sunt,

---

[1] *acetumi* in Teubner ed. is a misprint.   [2] Punctuation by Br.

onion, lovage, cumin, celery-seed, stoned damsons, *mulsum*,
vinegar, *liquamen*, *defrutum*, and oil.   Cook.

(*b*) When you cook a crane see to it that the head does not
touch the water, but is outside it.   When the crane is cooked
wrap it in a warm cloth and pull its head: it will come off with
the sinews, so that only the meat and the bones remain.   ⟨This
is necessary⟩ because one cannot eat it with the sinews.

3. CRANE OR DUCK WITH TURNIPS.[1]   Wash and truss the
bird and boil it in a large saucepan in water, salt, and dill,
until half done.   Cook the turnips so that they lose their
pungency.   Remove the duck from the pan, wash again, and
put into another saucepan with oil, *liquamen*, and a bouquet of
leek and coriander.   Put over it one washed and finely chopped
⟨uncooked⟩ turnip, and braise.   When it has been cooking for
a while add *defrutum* to give it colour.   Then prepare the following sauce: pepper, cumin, coriander, asafœtida root, add
vinegar, and some of the cooking-liquor; pour over the duck
and bring to the boil.   When it boils thicken with cornflour
and add to the turnips.   Sprinkle with pepper and serve.

4. ANOTHER SAUCE FOR BOILED CRANE OR DUCK.   Pepper,
lovage, cumin, dried coriander, mint, origan, pine-kernels,
Jericho dates, *liquamen*, oil, honey, mustard, and wine.

5. SAUCE FOR ROAST CRANE OR DUCK.   Make the following
sauce and pour over the roast bird: pound pepper, lovage,
origan, *liquamen*, honey, a little vinegar, and a little oil.   Cook
well.   Add cornflour ⟨to bind⟩ and put into the sauce slices of
boiled cucumber or taro.[2]   Boil.   If available, add also cooked

---

[1] This dish seems to be a predecessor of *canard aux navets*.   The
recipe for this given by E. David (*French Country Cooking*, p. 138)
differs mainly in that the bird is not parboiled before being braised,
and that the bed on which it is braised contains onions, carrots, a stick
of celery, and bacon instead of our oil, and after 10–15 minutes wine
and stock are added.   The turnips are cooked separately, and afterwards placed round the duck.   This parallel makes it unnecessary to
assume with Guégan—who also refers to the *canard aux navets*—
that the turnips are boiled together with the duck.

[2] See note to VII, xvii.

et ungellas coques et iecinera pullorum. in boletari piper
minutum aspargis et inferes.   (*218*)

6. ALITER IN GRUE VEL ANATE ELIXA: piper, ligusticum, apii
semen, erucam vel coriandrum, mentam, caryotam, mel,
acetum, liquamen, defritum et sinape. idem facies et si in
caccabo assas.   (*219*)

III. IN PERDICE ET ATTAGENA ET IN TURTURE ELIXIS

1. piper,[1] ligusticum, apii semen, mentam, myrtae bacas vel
uvam passam, mel, vinum, acetum, liquamen et oleum.
uteris frigido.   (*220*)

2. perdicem[2] cum pluma sua elixabis et madefactam depilabis.
[perdices coctura]. occisa perdix potest ex iure coqui, ne
indurescat; si † dierum fuerit, elixa coqui debet.   (*221*)

3. IN PERDICE ET ATTAGENA ET IN TURTURE: piper, ligusticum,
mentam, rutae semen, liquamen, merum et oleum.   calefacies.
                                                       (*222*)

IV. IN PALUMBIS COLUMBIS [AVIBUS IN ALTILE ET IN
FENICOPTERO]

1. IN ASSIS: piper, ligusticum, coriandrum, careum, cepam
siccam, mentam, ovi vitellum, caryotam, mel, acetum, liquamen,
oleum et vinum.   (*223*)

2. ALITER ⟨IN⟩ ELIXIS: piper, careum, apii semen, petroselinum, condimenta moretaria, caryotam, mel, acetum, vinum,
oleum et sinape. (*224*)

3. ALITER: piper, ligusticum, petroselinum, apii semen,
rutam, nucleos, caryotam, mel, acetum, liquamen, sinape et
oleum modice.   (*225*)

4. ALITER: piper, ligusticum, laser vivum, suffundis liqua-

---

[1] Vollmer's addition removed by Br.
[2] Vollmer's addition removed and punctuation changed by Br.

pig's trotters and chicken livers.   Sprinkle in the serving-dish with ground pepper, and serve.

6. SAUCE FOR BOILED CRANE OR DUCK.   Pepper, lovage, celery-seed, rocket or coriander, mint, Jericho date, honey, vinegar, *liquamen*, *defrutum*, and mustard.   You can also braise the bird in this sauce in a pan.

III. FOR BOILED PARTRIDGE, HAZEL-HEN, OR TURTLE-DOVE

1. Pepper, lovage, celery-seed, mint, myrtle-berries or raisins, honey, wine, vinegar, *liquamen*, and oil.   Use this as a cold dressing.

2. Boil a partridge with its feathers on and pluck while wet. The partridge when ⟨just⟩ killed can be braised in a sauce so that it does not get tough; if ⟨killed⟩ days ⟨before⟩ it should be boiled in water first.

3. FOR PARTRIDGE, HAZEL-HEN, OR TURTLE-DOVE.   Pepper, lovage, mint, seed of rue, *liquamen*, wine, and oil.   Heat up.

IV. FOR WOOD-PIGEONS AND PIGEONS

1. ROAST.   Pepper, lovage, coriander, caraway, dried onion, mint, yolk of egg, Jericho date, honey, vinegar, *liquamen*, oil, and wine.[1]

2. BOILED.   Pepper, caraway, celery-seed, parsley, the spices you use for *moretum*,[2] Jericho date, honey, vinegar, wine, oil, and mustard.

3. ANOTHER SAUCE.   Pepper, lovage, parsley, celery-seed, rue, pine-kernels, Jericho date, honey, vinegar, *liquamen*, mustard, and a little oil.

4. ANOTHER SAUCE.   Pepper, lovage, fresh asafœtida, moisten

---

[1] It is not clear whether this sauce is to be cold or hot; it looks rather like a liquid mayonnaise.

[2] See I, xxi.   This recipe seems also to be one for a cold dressing.

10—R.C.B.

men, vino et liquamine temperabis, et mittis super columbum
vel palumbum.   pipere aspersum inferes.   *(226)*

V

1. IUS IN DIVERSIS AVIBUS: piper, cuminum frictum,
ligusticam, mentam, uvam passam enucleatam aut Damascena,
mel modice.   vino myrteo temperabis, aceto, liquamine et
oleo.   calefacies et agitabis apio et satureia.   *(227)*

2. ALITER IUS IN AVIBUS: piper, petroselinum, ligusticum,
mentam siccam, cneci flos, vino suffundis, adicies Ponticam vel
amygdala tosta, mel modicum ⟨cum⟩ vino et aceto, liquamine
temperabis.   oleum in pultarium super ius mittis, calefacies,
ius agitabis apio viridi et nepeta.   incaraxas et perfundis. *(228)*

3. IUS CANDIDUM IN AVEM ELIXAM: piper, ligusticum,
cuminum, apii semen, Ponticam vel amygdala tosta vel nuces
depellatas, mel modicum, liquamen, acetum et oleum.   *(229)*

4. IUS VIRIDE IN AVIBUS: piper, careum, spicam Indicam,
cuminum, folium, condimenta viridia omne genus, dactylum,
mel, acetum, vinum modice, liquamen et oleum.   *(230)*

5. IUS CANDIDUM IN ANSERE ELIXO: piper, careum, cuminum,
apii semen, thymum, cepam, laseris radicem, nucleos tostos,
mel, acetum, liquamen et oleum.   *(231)*

6. AD AVES HIRCOSAS OMNI GENERE: piper, ligusticum,
thymum, mentam aridam, calvam, caryotam, mel, acetum,
vinum, liquamen, oleum, defritum, sinape.   avem sapidiorem
et altiliorem facies et ei pinguedinem servabis, si eam farina
oleo subacta contextam in furnum miseris.   *(232)*

with *liquamen*, blend with wine and *liquamen*, and pour over the wood-pigeon or pigeon. Sprinkle with pepper and serve.

V

1. SAUCE FOR VARIOUS BIRDS. Pepper, grilled cumin, lovage, mint, stoned raisins or damsons, a little honey; blend with myrtle-wine,[1] vinegar, *liquamen*, and oil. Heat up and stir with celery and savory.

2. ANOTHER SAUCE FOR BIRDS. Pepper, parsley, lovage, dried mint, safflower; moisten with wine, add hazel-nuts or toasted almonds, and a little honey with wine and vinegar, and blend with *liquamen*. Put this mixture into a deep pan, add oil, and heat. Stir with green celery and catmint. Make incisions in the birds and pour the sauce over them.

3. WHITE SAUCE WITH A BOILED BIRD. Pepper, lovage, cumin, celery-seed, toasted hazel-nuts or almonds or shelled walnuts, a little honey, *liquamen*, vinegar, and oil.

4. GREEN SAUCE WITH BIRDS. Pepper, caraway, Indian nard, cumin, aromatic leaf, green herbs of any kind you like, dates, honey, vinegar, a little wine, *liquamen*, and oil.

5. WHITE SAUCE WITH BOILED GOOSE. Pepper, caraway, cumin, celery-seed, thyme, onion, asafœtida root, toasted pine-kernels, honey, vinegar, *liquamen*, and oil.

6. (*a*) FOR 'HIGH' BIRDS OF ANY KIND. Pepper, lovage, thyme, dried mint, filbert nut, Jericho date, honey, vinegar, wine, *liquamen*, oil, *defrutum*, mustard.

(*b*) You give a bird a greater flavour and make it more nourishing, and keep all the fat in, if you wrap it in pastry made of oil and flour and cook it in the oven.

[1] A recipe for myrtle-wine recommended as a remedy for indigestion and pain in the side and abdomen is given by Cato (*De Agricultura*, 125): "Make myrtle-wine as follows: dry black myrtle-berries in the shade. When they are shrivelled up keep them until the time of the vintage, crush ½ peck of myrtle-berries in 3 gallons of must, seal the vessel. When the must has ceased to ferment remove the myrtle-berries."

7. ALITER AVEM: in ventrem eius fractas olivas novas mittis et consutam sic elixabis. deinde coctas olivas eximes. *(233)*

VI

1. IN PHOENICOPTERO. phoenicopterum eliberas, lavas, ornas, includis in caccabum, adicies aquam, salem, anethum et aceti modicum. dimidia coctura alligas fasciculum porri et coriandri, et coquatur. prope cocturam defritum mittis, coloras. adicies in mortarium piper, cuminum, coriandrum, laseris radicem, mentam, rutam, fricabis, suffundis acetum, adicies caryotam, ius de suo sibi perfundis. reexinanies in eundem caccabum, amulo obligas, ius perfundis et inferes. idem facies et in psittaco.   *(234)*

2. ALITER: assas avem, teres piper, ligusticum, apii semen, sesamum frictum, petroselinum, mentam, cepam siccam, caryotam; melle, vino, liquamine, aceto, oleo et defrito temperabis.   *(235)*

VII

AVES OMNES NE LIQUESCANT: cum plumis elixare omnibus melius erit. prius tamen exenterantur per guttur vel a navi † as sublata.[1]   *(236)*

VIII. ⟨IN ANSERE⟩

ANSEREM ELIXUM CALIDUM EX IURE FRIGIDO APICIANO: teres piper, ligusticum, coriandri semen, mentam, rutam, refundis liquamen et oleum modice, temperas. anserem elixum ferventem sabano mundo exsiccabis, ius perfundis et inferes.

(237)

---

[1] Br. suggests: *vel e navi assublatae.*

7. ANOTHER WAY TO COOK A BIRD. Stuff the bird with chopped fresh olives, sew it up, and boil. Afterwards remove the cooked olives.

VI

1. FLAMINGO. Pluck the flamingo, wash, truss, and put it in a saucepan; add water, dill, and a little vinegar. Half-way through the cooking make a bouquet of leek and coriander and let it cook ⟨with the bird⟩. When it is nearly done add *defrutum* to give it colour. Put in a mortar pepper, caraway, coriander, asafoetida root, mint, rue; pound; moisten with vinegar, add Jericho dates, pour over some of the cooking-liquor. Put it in the same saucepan, thicken with cornflour, pour the sauce over the bird, and serve. The same recipe can also be used for parrot.

2. ANOTHER METHOD. Roast the bird. Pound pepper, lovage, celery-seed, grilled sesame, parsley, mint, dried onion, Jericho date. Blend with honey, wine, *liquamen*, vinegar, oil, and *defrutum*.

VII

To prevent birds from going bad it is advisable to boil them ⟨for a while⟩ with their feathers on. But before this they should be drawn, either through the gullet or from the rear end while held up.[1]

VIII. ⟨GOOSE⟩

HOT BOILED GOOSE WITH COLD SAUCE À LA APICIUS. ⟨Boil the bird.⟩ Pound pepper, lovage, coriander seed, mint, rue, add *liquamen* and a little oil. Mix. Dry the hot boiled goose with a clean cloth, pour the sauce over, and serve.

---

[1] The text is corrupt. It is translated here according to Brandt's suggestion.

IX. ⟨IN PULLO⟩

1 A.   IN PULLO ELIXO IUS CRUDUM: adicies in mortarium anethi semen, mentam siccam, laseris radicem, suffundis acetum, adicies caryotam, refundis liquamen, sinapis modicum et oleo ⟨et⟩ defrito temperas et sic mittis.   (*238*)

B.   ⟨ALITER⟩   PULLUM[1]: anethatum mellis modico ⟨et⟩ liquamine temperabis.   levas pullum coctum et sabano mundo siccas, caraxas et ius scissuris infundis, ut combibat, et cum combiberit, assabis et suo sibi iure pinnis[2] tangis.   pipere aspersum inferes.   (*239*)

2.   PULLUM PARTHICUM: pullum aperies a navi et in quadrato ornas.   teres piper, ligusticum, carei modicum; suffunde liquamen; vino temperas.   componis in Cumana pullum et condituram super pullum facies.   laser [et] vivum in tepida dissolvis, et in pullum mittis simul, et coques.   pipere aspersum inferes.   (*240*)

3.   PULLUM OXYZOMUM: olei acetabulum maius, ⟨laseris⟩ satis modice, liquaminis acetabulum minus, aceti acetabulum perquam minus, piperis scripulos sex, petroselini scripulum, porri fasciculum.   (*241*)

4.   PULLUM NUMIDICUM: pullum curas, elixas, levas,[3] lasere ac pipere ⟨aspergis⟩ et assas.   teres piper, cuminum, coriandri semen, laseris radicem, rutam, caryotam, nucleos, suffundis acetum, mel, liquamen et oleum, temperabis.   cum ferbuerit, amulo obligas, pullum perfundis, piper aspergis et inferes.

(*242*)

5.   PULLUM LASERATUM: pullum aperies a navi, lavabis, ornabis et ⟨in⟩ Cumana ponis.   teres piper, ligusticum, laser vivum, suffundis liquamen, vino et liquamine temperabis, et mittis pullo.   coctus si fuerit, pipere aspersum inferes. (*243*)

---

[1] Codd. begins new recipe here; *Aliter* add. by Br.
[2] *pinnis* codd., rest. by Br.
[3] *lavas* codd., corr. by R.

IX. ⟨Chicken⟩

1. (*a*) Cold (uncooked) sauce for boiled chicken. Put in a mortar dill-seed, dried mint, asafœtida root, moisten with vinegar, add Jericho date, pour in *liquamen*, a little mustard, and mix with oil and *defrutum*, and so serve.

(*b*) Chicken, another method. Mix the above dill sauce with a little honey and *liquamen*. Lift out the boiled chicken and dry with a clean cloth, make criss-cross incisions in the skin, and pour the sauce into them so that it soaks in; and, when it has soaked in, roast, and with the feathers brush it with its own broth. Sprinkle with pepper and serve.

2. Chicken in the Parthian way. Open the chicken at the rear end and truss it on a square board. Pound pepper, lovage, a little caraway; moisten with *liquamen*, blend with wine. Put the chicken in an earthenware pot and pour the sauce over it. Dissolve some fresh asafœtida in lukewarm water, put it over the chicken, and let it cook. Sprinkle with pepper and serve.

3. Chicken with a sauce piquante. A good ½ gill of oil, a little asafœtida, just under ½ gill of *liquamen*, the same amount of vinegar, 6 scruples of pepper, 1 scruple of parsley, and a bunch of leeks.

4. Chicken in the Numidian way. Prepare the chicken, boil, take out ⟨of the water⟩, sprinkle with asafœtida and pepper, and roast. Pound pepper, cumin, coriander seed, asafœtida root, rue, Jericho date, pine-kernels; moisten with vinegar, honey, *liquamen*, and oil. Mix well. When it boils thicken with cornflour, pour over the chicken, sprinkle with pepper, and serve.

5. Chicken with asafœtida. Open the chicken at the rear end. Wash, truss, and put it in an earthenware pot. Pound pepper, lovage, fresh asafœtida, moisten with *liquamen*, blend with wine and *liquamen*, and pour over the chicken. When it is cooked sprinkle with pepper and serve.

6. PULLUM PAROPTUM: laseris modicum, piperis scripulos sex, olei acetabulum, liquaminis acetabulum, petroselini modice. (*244*)

7. PULLUM ELIXUM EX IURE SUO: teres piper, cuminum, thymi modicum, feniculi semen, mentam, rutam, laseris radicem, suffundis acetum, adicies caryotam et teres; melle, aceto, liquamine et oleo temperabis ⟨et in⟩ pullum refrigeratum et siccatum mittis; quem perfusum inferes. (*245*)

8. PULLUM ELIXUM CUM CUCURBITIS ELIXIS: iure supra scripto, addito sinapi, perfundis et inferes. (*246*)

9 A. PULLUM ELIXUM CUM COLOCASIIS ELIXIS: supra scripto iure perfundis et inferes.

B. ⟨idem⟩ facis et in elixum cum olivis columbadibus. (*247*)

10. ... non valde, ita ut laxamentum habeat, ne dissiliat dum coquitur in olla, submissis in sportella. cum bullierit, frequenter levas et ponis ne dissiliat. (*248*)

11. PULLUS VARIANUS[1]: pullum coques iure hoc: liquamine, oleo, vino, ⟨cui mittis⟩ fasciculum porri, coriandri, satureiae. cum coctus fuerit, teres piper, nucleos, ⟨liquaminis⟩ cyathos duos et ius de suo sibi suffundis et fasciculos proicies. lacte temperas, et reexinanies mortarium supra pullum, ut ferveat. obligas eundem albamentis ovorum tritis, ponis in lance et iure supra scripto perfundis.   hoc ius candidum appellatur. (*249*)

12. PULLUM FRONTONIANUM: pullum praedura, condies

---

[1] *Varianus* Humelberg, accepted by Br.; *vardanus* codd.

6. ROAST CHICKEN. ⟨Serve with a cold sauce of⟩ a little asafœtida, 6 scruples of pepper, ½ gill each of oil and *liquamen*, a little parsley.

7. BOILED CHICKEN. Prepare the following sauce. Pound pepper, cumin, a little thyme, fennel seed, mint, rue, asafœtida root; moisten with vinegar, add Jericho date, and pound this too. Blend with honey, vinegar, *liquamen*, and oil. Pour over the cooled and dried chicken and serve.

8. BOILED CHICKEN WITH BOILED MARROWS. Make the preceding sauce, add mustard, pour over the chicken, and serve.

9. (*a*) BOILED CHICKEN WITH BOILED TAROS.[1] Pour the preceding sauce over, and serve.

(*b*) The same sauce can also be made for boiled chicken with salted olives.

10. [*Beginning is missing*] . . . not much, so that a little room is left and it does not disintegrate while cooking in the pot, the chicken having been put in a basket. While it is boiling lift out frequently, and put back so that it does not disintegrate.

11. CHICKEN À LA VARIUS.[2] Cook the chicken in the following liquor: *liquamen*, oil, wine, to which you add a bouquet of leek, coriander, savory. When it is done pound pepper, pine-kernels, pour on two cyathi ⟨=⅙ pint⟩ of *liquamen* and some of the cooking-liquor from which you have removed the bouquet. Blend with milk and pour the contents of the mortar over the chicken. Bring to the boil. Pour in beaten eggwhite to bind. Put the chicken on a serving-dish and pour the sauce over. This is known as white sauce.

12. CHICKEN À LA FRONTO.[3] Brown the chicken, put in a

---

[1] See note to VII, xvii.

[2] If one accepts Humelberg's emendation *Varianus* this refers probably to the Emperor Varius Heliogabalus (A.D. 218–222), who is reputed to have invented dishes; cp. Brandt, p. 94.

[3] The name refers probably to an author of agricultural writings, mentioned in the *Geoponica*; cp. Brandt, p. 92.

liquamine oleo mixto, cui mittis fasciculum anethi, porri,
satureiae et coriandri viridis, et coques. ubi coctus fuerit,
levabis eum, in lance defrito perunges, piper aspargis et inferes.
(*250*)

13. PULLUS TRACTOGALATUS: pullum coques liquamine, oleo,
vino, cui mittis fasciculum coriandri, cepam. deinde, cum
coctus fuerit, levabis eum de iure suo et mittis in caccabum
novum lac et salem modicum, mel et aquae minimum. [id est
tertiam partem.][1] ponis ad ignem lentum ut tepescat, tractum
confringis et mittis paulatim, assidue agitas, ne uratur. pullum
illic mittis integrum vel carptum, versabis in lancem, perfundis
ius tale: piper, ligusticum, origanum, suffundis mel et defritum
modicum, et ius de suo sibi, temperas. in caccabulo facies ut
bulliat. cum bullierit, amulo obligas et inferes.   (*251*)

14. PULLUS FARSILIS: pullum sicuti liquaminatum a cervice
expedies. teres piper, ligusticum, zingiber, pulpam caesam,
alicam elixam, teres cerebellum ex iure coctum, ova confringis
et commisces, ut unum corpus efficias. liquamine temperas et
oleum modice mittis, piper integrum, nucleos abundanter.
fac impensam et imples pullum vel porcellum, ita ut laxamentum habeat. similiter in capo facies. ossibus eiectis coques.
(*253*)

15. PULLUS LEUCOZOMUS: accipies pullum et ornas ut supra.
aperies illum a pectore. accipiat aquam et oleum Hispanum
abundans. agitatur ut ex se ambulet[2] et humorem consumat.
postea, cum coctus fuerit, quodcumque porro remanserit inde
levas. piper aspargis et inferes.   (*254*)

---

[1] Recognized as gloss by Br.
[2] *ambulet* codd.; rest. by Br.

mixture of *liquamen* and oil to which you add a bouquet of dill, leek, savory, and green coriander; and braise. When it is done take it out, place on a serving-dish, sprinkle generously with *defrutum*, powder with pepper, and serve.

13. CHICKEN WITH MILK AND PASTRY SAUCE. Braise the chicken in *liquamen*, oil, and wine, to which you add a bouquet of fresh coriander and onions. Then, when done, lift it from its stock and put into a new saucepan milk and a little salt, honey, and very little water. Set by a slow fire to warm, crumble pastry, and add gradually, stirring continually to prevent burning. Put in the chicken whole or in pieces, turn out on a serving-dish, and pour over the following sauce: pepper, lovage, origan, add honey and a little *defrutum* and cooking-liquor. Mix well. Bring to the boil in a saucepan. When it boils thicken with cornflour and serve.

14. STUFFED CHICKEN. Draw the chicken—as for chicken in *liquamen*—from the neck. Pound pepper, lovage, ginger, chopped meat, boiled spelt-grits; pound a brain cooked in stock, break eggs into it, and work all this into a smooth mixture. Blend with *liquamen* and add a little oil, whole peppercorns, and plenty of pine-kernels. Stuff with this mixture a chicken or a sucking-pig, leaving a little room. You can use the same stuffing also for a capon. Cook it with the bones removed.

15. CHICKEN WITH WHITE SAUCE.[1] Take a chicken and truss as above. Open it at the breast. Fill it with water and plenty of Spanish oil. ⟨While cooking⟩ move it ⟨frequently⟩, so that it gives off its juice and absorbs the liquid. When done take it out of whatever is left of the liquid, sprinkle with pepper, and serve.

[1] The title does not make sense unless some white sauce is to be added.

LIBER VII

POLYTELES

I. Vulvae steriles, callum, libelli, coticulae et ungellae.
II. sumen. III. ficatum. IV. ofellae. V. assaturae.
VI. in elixam et in copadiis. VII. ventricula. VIII.
lumbuli et renes. IX. perna. X. iocinera sive
pulmones. XI. dulcia domestica et melce. XII. bulbi.
XIII. fungi farnei vel boleti. XIV. tubera. XV. in
colocasia. XVI. cocleas. XVII. ova.

I. Vulvae steriles, callum, libelli, coticulae et
ungellae

1. Vulvae steriles: lasere Cyrenaico vel Parthico, aceto et
liquamine temperato appones.　　　*(258)*

2. In vulva [et] sterili: piper, apii semen, mentam siccam,
laseris radicem, mel, acetum et liquamen.

3. Vulvae [et] steriles: pipere,[1] liquamine, cum lasere
Parthico apponis.

4. Vulvae steriles: pipere, liquamine et condito modico
apponis.

5. Callum, libelli, coticulae, ungellae: cum pipere,
liquamine, lasere apponis.　　　*(259)*

---

[1] *piper et liquamine* codd., corr. by Br.

156

BOOK VII

THE GOURMET

I. Wombs from sterile sows, skin, fillets, ribs, and
trotters. II. Sow's udder. III. Pig's liver. IV.
Ofellae. V. Roasts. VI. Sauces for boiled meat and
meat slices. VII. Pig's stomach. VIII. Kidneys.
IX. Ham. X. Liver and lights. XI. Home-made
sweets and *melcae*. XII. Bulbs. XIII. Tree fungi
and mushrooms. XIV. Truffles. XV. Sauce for taro.
XVI. Snails. XVII. Eggs.

I. WOMBS FROM STERILE SOWS, SKIN, FILLETS, RIBS, AND TROTTERS

1. WOMBS FROM STERILE SOWS.[1] Serve with Cyrenaican
silphium or asafœtida, blended with vinegar and *liquamen*.

2. SAUCE FOR STERILE WOMB. Pepper, celery-seed, dried
mint, asafœtida root, honey, vinegar, and *liquamen*.

3. STERILE WOMBS. Serve with pepper and *liquamen* and
asafœtida.

4. STERILE WOMBS. Serve with pepper, *liquamen*, and spiced
wine.

5. SKIN, FILLETS, RIBS, AND TROTTERS. Serve with pepper,
liquamen, and asafœtida.

6. GRILLED WOMB. Roll in bran, and afterwards soak in
brine, then cook.

II. SOW'S UDDER

1. Boil the udder, bind together with reed, sprinkle with

---

[1] Pliny mentions the spaying of sows—*Nat. Hist.*, VIII, 51, 77 (209):
"The females (*scil.*, of pigs) are also spayed like those of camels, so
that they are suspended by their forelegs after two days without
food, and their womb is cut out. They grow fatter in this way."

6. VULVAM UT TOSTAM FACIAS, in cantabro involve et postea in muriam mitte et sic coque.   (260)

II. SUMEN

1. Sumen elixas, de cannis surclas, sale aspargis et in furnum mittis vel in craticulam. subassas. teres piper, ligusticum, liquamen, mero et passo ⟨temperabis⟩, amulo obligas et sumen perfundis.   (261)

2. SUMEN PLENUM: teritur piper, careum, echinus salsus. consuitur et sic coquitur. manducatur cum allece ⟨et⟩ sinapi.
(262)

III. FICATUM

1. IN FICATO OENOGARUM: piper, thymum, ligusticum, liquamen, vinum modice, oleum.   (263)

2. ALITER: ficatum praecidis ad cannam, infundis in liquamine, piper, ligusticum, bacas lauri duas. involves in omento et in craticula assas et inferes.   (264)

IV. OFELLAE

1. OFELLAS OSTIENSES. [in ofillam] designas ofellas in cute, ita ut cutis sic remaneat. teres piper, ligusticum, anethum, cuminum, silfium, bacam lauri unam, suffundis liquamen, fricas, in angularem refundis simul cum ofellis. ubi requieverint in condimentis biduo vel triduo, promis, surclas decussatim, et in furnum mittis. cum coxeris, ofellas, quas designaveras, separabis et teres piper, ligusticum, suffundis liquamen et passum modicum, ut dulce fiat. cum ferbuerit, ius amulo obligas. ofellas satias et inferes.   (265)

2. OFELLAS APICIANAS: ofellas exossas, in rotundum complicas, surclas, ad furnum admoves. postea praeduras, levas et, ⟨ut⟩ humorem exspuant, in craticula igni lento exsiccabis, ita ne urantur. teres piper, ligusticum, cyperi, cuminum; liqua-

pepper, and put in the oven or on the gridiron.   Half roast.
Pound pepper, lovage, *liquamen*, blend with wine and *passum*,
thicken with cornflour, and pour over the udder.

2. STUFFED UDDER.   Pound pepper, caraway, and salted
sea-urchin.   ⟨Stuff the udder⟩, sew up, and thus cook.   You
eat it with *allec* and mustard.

III. PIG'S LIVER

1. OENOGARUM FOR PIG'S LIVER.[1]   Pepper, thyme, lovage,
liquamen, a little wine, oil.

2. ANOTHER RECIPE FOR PIG'S LIVER.   Make incisions in the
liver with a reed, steep in *liquamen*, pepper, lovage, and two
laurel berries.   Wrap in sausage-casing, grill, and serve.

IV. OFELLAE (PIECES OF MEAT)

1. RAGOUT IN THE MANNER OF OSTIA.   Mark out the meat
on the skin, taking care that the skin remains intact.   Crush
pepper, lovage, dill, cumin, asafœtida, one laurel berry, moisten
with *liquamen*, pound.   Pour into an angular pan, together
with the meat.   Let it marinade for about two or three days,
then take it out.   Bind crosswise and put in the oven.   When
cooked separate the marked-out pieces and pound pepper and
lovage, moisten with *liquamen*, and add a little *passum* to sweeten.
When this boils thicken with cornflour.   Saturate the meat
with this sauce and serve.

2. MEAT PIECES À LA APICIUS.   Bone the meat pieces, roll
them up, bind together, and put in the oven.   Then brown
them, take them out, and in order to make them give forth
their juice dry them out on the grill with a slow fire, taking care

---

[1] *Ficatum*, liver of pigs fed on figs.   Pliny writes (VIII, 51,
77 (209)): "A method is also employed to treat the liver of sows like
that of geese, a method invented by Marcus Apicius.   They are
stuffed with dried figs, and when they are full they are killed directly
after having been given a drink of *mulsum*."

mine et passo temperabis. cum hoc iure ofellas in caccabum mittis. cum coctae fuerint, levas et siccas, sine iure, pipere asperso, et inferes. si pingues fuerint, cum surclas, tollis cutem. potes et de abdomine huiusmodi ofellas facere.   (*266*)

3. OFELLAE APRUGINEO MORE: ex oleo ⟨et⟩ liquamine condiuntur, et mittitur eis condimentum, cum coctae fuerint. et super adicitur his, cum in foco sunt, conditura, et denuo bulliunt. piper tritum, condimentum, mel, liquamen, amulum, cum iam bulliunt. et sine liquamine et oleo elixantur, coquuntur et sic pipere perfunduntur. ⟨mittis⟩ ius supra scriptum, et sic bulliunt.   (*267*)

4. ALITER OFELLAE: recte friguntur ut paene assae reddantur. liquaminis summi[1] cyathum, aquae cyathum, aceti cyathum, olei cyathum. simul mixtis et immissis in patellam fictilem, frigis et inferes.   (*268*)

5. ALITER OFELLAS: in sartagine abundanti oenogaro. piper asparges et inferes.   (*269*)

6. ALITER OFELLAS: ofellae prius sale et cumino ⟨aspersae⟩[2] infusae in aquam recte friguntur.   (*270*)

V. ASSATURAE

1. ASSATURAM SIMPLICEM: assam a furno salis plurimo conspersam cum melle inferes.[3]   (*271*)

2. ALITER ASSATURAS: petroselini scripulos VI, asareos scripulos VI, zingiberis scripulos VI, lauri bacas V, condimenti ⟨satis⟩, laseris radicis scripulos VI, origani scripulos VI, cyperis

---

[1] *summi* codd., rest. Br.
[2] add. Br.
[3] *simplicem* transferred from after *furno* to after *assaturam* by Br.

that they do not get burned. Pound pepper, lovage, cyperus, cumin, blend with *liquamen* and *passum*. With this sauce put the meat pieces in a saucepan. When they are cooked take them out, dry them, and serve without sauce, sprinkled with pepper. Should the pieces of meat be fat take the skin off when preparing them. You can make this kind of *ofellae* also with belly of pork.

3. MEAT PIECES IN THE MANNER OF WILD BOAR. Marinade in oil and *liquamen*, and add spices when they are cooked. And when they are on the fire add the sauce ⟨described below⟩ and boil again. ⟨The sauce:⟩ Ground pepper, spices, honey, *liquamen*; add cornflour when it boils. You can also boil them in plain water without oil and *liquamen*, and sprinkle with pepper when cooked. Then add the above sauce and let come to the boil again.

4. MEAT PIECES, ANOTHER METHOD. Fry them properly so that they become nearly roasted, ⟨take⟩ 1 cyathus each of best *liquamen*, water, vinegar, and oil, mix together, put in an earthenware pan, fry ⟨again⟩, and serve.

5. MEAT PIECES, ANOTHER METHOD. Cook them in a frying-pan with plenty of *oenogarum*. Sprinkle with pepper and serve.

6. MEAT PIECES, ANOTHER METHOD. Soak the meat pieces in water, having sprinkled them before with salt and cumin. Then fry properly.

V. ROASTS

1. MEAT ROASTED plain in the oven, sprinkled with plenty of salt. Serve with honey.[1]

2. SAUCE FOR ROAST MEAT. 6 scruples each of parsley, hazelwort, ginger, 5 laurel berries, sufficient seasoning, 6 scruples each of asafœtida root, origan, and cyperus, a little

[1] This is worth trying with any kind of meat. The honey brings out the flavour.

11—R.C.B.

scripulos VI, costi modice, pyrethri scripulos III, apii seminis scripulos VI, piperis scripulos XII, liquaminis et olei quod sufficit. (*272*)

3. ALITER ASSATURAS: myrtae siccae bacam exenteratam cum cumino, pipere, melle, liquamine, defrito et oleo teres, et fervefactum amulas. carnem elixam sale subassatam perfundis, piper aspargis et inferes. (*273*)

4. ALITER ASSATURAS: piperis scripulos VI, ligustici scripulos VI, petroselini scripulos VI, apii seminis scripulos VI, anethi scripulos VI, laseris radicis scripulos VI, asareos scripulos VI, pyrethri modice, cyperis scripulos VI, carei scripulos VI, cumini scripulos VI, zingiberis scripulos VI, liquaminis heminam, olei acetabulum. (*274*)

5. ASSATURAS IN COLLARI: elixatur et infunditur in fretali piper, condimentum, mel, liquamen, et attorretur in clibano quousque coquatur. elixum vero collare, si voles, sine conditura assas, et siccum calidum perfundis. (*275*)

VI. IN ELIXAM ET COPADIA

1. IUS IN ELIXAM OMNEM: piper, ligusticum, origanum, rutam, silfium, cepam siccam, vinum, caroenum, mel, acetum, olei modicum. persiccatam et sabano expressam elixam perfundis. (*276*)

2. IUS IN ELIXAM: piper, petroselinum, liquamen, acetum, caryotam, cepulam, olei modicum. perfundis calido iure.
(*277*)

3. IUS IN ELIXAM: teres piper, rutam aridam, feniculi semen, cepam, caryotam, liquamen et oleum.

4. IUS CANDIDUM IN ELIXAM: piper, liquamen, vinum, rutam, cepam, nucleos, conditum, modicum de buccellis maceratis unde stringat, oleum. cum coxerit, ius perfundis. (*278*)

5. ALITER IUS CANDIDUM IN ELIXAM: piper, careum, ligusti-

costmary, 3 scruples of pyrethrum, 6 scruples of celery-seed, 12 scruples of pepper, and sufficient *liquamen* and oil.

3. ANOTHER SAUCE FOR ROAST MEAT. Pound seeded dried myrtle-berries, cumin, pepper, honey, *liquamen*, *defrutum*, and oil, bring to the boil, and thicken with cornflour. Boil the meat first, then roast with salt, and pour the sauce over. Sprinkle with pepper and serve.

4. ANOTHER SAUCE FOR ROAST MEAT. 6 scruples each of pepper, lovage, parsley, celery-seed, dill, asafœtida root, hazelwort, a little pyrethrum, 6 scruples each of cyperus, caraway, cumin, ginger, 1 pint *liquamen*, ½ gill of oil.

5. ROAST NECK. Boil the meat and put in a frying-pan pepper, herbs, honey, *liquamen*, and let the meat roast with this in the oven (*clibanus*) until cooked. If you wish you can roast the boiled neck without the sauce and pour the hot sauce over the dry meat.

VI. SAUCES FOR BOILED MEAT AND MEAT SLICES

1. SAUCE FOR EVERY KIND OF BOILED MEAT. Pepper, lovage, origan, rue, asafœtida, dried onion, wine, *caroenum*, honey, vinegar, a little oil. Dry the boiled meat, press in a cloth, and pour the sauce over.

2. SAUCE FOR BOILED MEAT. Pepper, parsley, *liquamen*, vinegar, Jericho date, Welsh onion, a little oil. Heat up, and pour over the meat.

3. SAUCE FOR BOILED MEAT. Pound pepper, dried rue, fennel-seed, onion, Jericho date, *liquamen*, and oil.

4. WHITE SAUCE FOR BOILED MEAT. Pepper, *liquamen*, wine, rue, onion, pine-kernels, spiced wine, a little soaked bread for thickening, oil. When it is cooked pour over the meat.

5. ANOTHER WHITE SAUCE FOR BOILED MEAT. Pepper,

cum, thymum, origanum, cepulam, dactylum, mel, acetum, liquamen, oleum.   (*279*)

6. IN COPADIIS IUS ALBUM: piper, cuminum, ligusticum, rutae semen, Damascena. infundis vinum, oenomeli et aceto temperabis. ⟨agitabis⟩ thymo et origano.   (*280*)

7. ALITER IUS CANDIDUM IN COPADIIS: piper, thymum, cuminum, apii semen, feniculum, mentam, bacam myrtae, uvam passam. mulso temperas. agitabis ramo satureiae.
     (*281*)

8. IUS IN COPADIIS: piper, ligusticum, careum, mentam, nardostachyum, folium, ovi vitellum, mel, mulsam, acetum, liquamen et oleum. agitabis satureia et porro, amulabis.
     (*282*)

9. IUS ALBUM IN COPADIIS: piper, ligusticum, cuminum, apii semen, thymum, nucleos infusos, nuces infusas et purgatas, mel, acetum, liquamen et oleum.   (*283*)

10. IUS IN COPADIIS: piper, apii semen, careum, satureiam, cneci flos, cepulam, amygdala tosta, caryotam, liquamen, oleum, sinapis modicum. defrito coloras.   (*284*)

11. IUS IN COPADIIS: piper, ligusticum, petroselinum, cepulam, amygdala tosta, dactylum, mel, acetum, liquamen, defritum, oleum.   (*285*)

12. IUS IN COPADIIS: ova dura concidis, piper, cuminum, petroselinum, porrum coctum, myrtae bacas, plusculum mel, acetum, liquamen, oleum.   (*286*)

13. ⟨IUS⟩ IN ELIXAM ANETHATUM CRUDUM: piper, anethi semen, mentam siccam, laseris radicem, suffundis acetum, adicies caryotam, mel, liquamen, sinapis modicum, defrito ⟨et⟩ oleo temperabis. et hoc in collari porcino.   (*287*)

14. IUS IN ELIXAM ALLECATUM: piper, ligusticum, careum, apii semen, thymum, cepulam, dactylum, allecem colatum; melle et vino temperas; apium viridem concisum super aspargis, oleum mittis et inferes.   (*288*)

VII. VENTRICULA

1. VENTREM PORCINUM bene exinanies, aceto et sale, postea

caraway, lovage, thyme, origan, Welsh onion, date, honey, *liquamen*, oil.

6. WHITE SAUCE FOR MEAT SLICES. Pepper, cumin, lovage, rue-seed, damsons. Pour on wine, and blend with *mulsum* and vinegar. ⟨Stir⟩ with thyme and origan.

7. WHITE SAUCE FOR MEAT-SLICES, ANOTHER METHOD. Pepper, thyme, cumin, celery-seed, fennel, mint, myrtle-berry, raisins. Blend with *mulsum*. Stir with a sprig of savory.

8. SAUCE FOR MEAT SLICES. Pepper, lovage, caraway, mint, spikenard, bay-leaf, egg-yolk, honey, honey-water, vinegar, *liquamen*, and oil. Stir with savory and leek. Thicken with cornflour.

9. WHITE SAUCE FOR MEAT SLICES. Pepper, lovage, cumin, celery-seed, thyme, soaked pine-kernels, cleaned soaked nuts, honey, vinegar, *liquamen*, and oil.

10. SAUCE FOR MEAT SLICES. Pepper, celery-seed, caraway, savory, safflower, Welsh onion, toasted almonds, Jericho dates, *liquamen*, oil, a little mustard. Colour with *defrutum*.

11. SAUCE FOR MEAT SLICES. Pepper, lovage, parsley, Welsh onion, toasted almonds, dates, honey, vinegar, *liquamen*, *defrutum*, and oil.

12. SAUCE FOR MEAT SLICES. Chop hard-boiled eggs and add pepper, cumin, parsley, boiled leek, myrtle-berries, a fair amount of honey, vinegar, *liquamen*, and oil.

13. COLD DILL SAUCE FOR BOILED MEAT. Pepper, dill-seed, dried mint, asafœtida root; pour on vinegar, add Jericho date, honey, a little mustard; blend with *defrutum* and oil. This sauce can also be served with neck of pork.

14. ALLEC SAUCE FOR BOILED MEAT. Pepper, lovage, caraway, celery-seed, thyme, Welsh onion, date, strained *allec*; blend with honey and wine. Sprinkle with fresh chopped celery, add oil, and serve.

VII. PIG'S STOMACH

1. WELL EMPTY A PIG'S STOMACH, clean it out with vinegar and

aqua lavas, et sic hac impensa imples: pulpam porcinam tunsam tritam, ita ut enervata commisceas cerebella tria et ova cruda, cui nucleos infundis et piper integrum mittis et hoc iure temperas. teres piper, ligusticum, silfium, anesum, zingiber, rutae modicum, liquamen optimum et olei modicum. reples aqualiculum sic ut laxamentum habeat, ne dissiliat in coctura. surclas ambas[1] et in ollam bullientem summittis. levas et pungis acu, ne crepet. cum ad dimidias coctus fuerit, levas et ad fumum suspendis ut coloretur. et denuo eum perelixabis, ut coqui possit, deinde liquamine, mero, oleo modico ⟨temperabis⟩, et cultello aperies et cum liquamine et ligustico apponis.   (*290*)

2. VENTREM UT TOSTUM FACIAS, in cantabro involve, postea in muriam mittis et sic coque.   (*291*)

VIII. LUMBI ET RENES

LUMBULI ASSI ITA FIUNT: aperiuntur in duas partes ita ut expansi sint, et aspergitur eis piper tritum, nuclei et coriandrum concisum, minutatim factum et semen feniculi tritum. deinde lumbuli recluduntur [assi] et consuuntur et involvuntur omento et sic praedurantur in oleo et liquamine, inde assantur in clibano vel craticula.   (*292*)

IX. PERNA

1. PERNAM, ubi eam cum Caricis plurimis elixaveris et tribus lauri foliis, detracta cute tessellatim incides et melle complebis.

---

[1] *ambas* codd., rest. by Br. (*scil.*, *partes*).

salt, and then wash with water and stuff it with the following
mixture: Minced and pounded pork into which you mix three
brains skinned and freed of stringy matter, raw eggs, pine-
kernels and peppercorns, and blend with the following sauce:
pound pepper, lovage, asafœtida, aniseed, ginger, a little rue,
best *liquamen*, and a little oil. Fill the stomach, leaving some
space so that it does not burst while cooking. Bind both ends
together, and plunge it into a cauldron of boiling water. Lift
out and prick with a needle, taking care that it does not burst.
When it is half cooked take out and hang up to smoke so that
it colours. Then boil again thoroughly until done, adding
finally *liquamen*, wine, and a little oil. Open with a knife, and
serve with *liquamen* and lovage.

2. To MAKE ROAST STOMACH, roll in bran, soak in brine, and
then cook.

VIII. KIDNEYS

GRILLED OR ROASTED KIDNEYS.[1] Cut them open, stretch
them, and stuff them with ground pepper, pine-kernels and
very finely chopped coriander, also ground fennel-seed. Then
close the kidneys, sew together, wrap in sausage-skin and brown
in oil and *liquamen*; afterwards roast in the oven (*clibanus*) or
grill.

IX. HAM

1. BOIL THE HAM[2] with plenty of dried figs and three bay-
leaves. Remove the skin and make criss-cross incisions, which
you fill with honey. Next make a paste of flour and oil and

---

[1] We assume with Guégan that by "lumbi (lumbuli) et renes" the
kidneys with the surrounding fat are meant.

[2] This recipe can also be used with gammon. Quantities: for a
three-pound piece of ham or gammon about ½ lb. figs. For paste:
1 lb. of flour and enough oil to produce a manageable pastry which
could be rolled out a little. Make a coat of pastry about ½ in. thick.
Baking-time: well over an hour in medium oven (pre-heated); boiling
gammon with figs is an excellent idea; even without the subsequent
baking, the flavour is delicious.

deinde farinam oleo subactam contexes et ei corium reddis.   et,
cum farina cocta fuerit, eximas furno et ut est inferes.   (*293*)

2. PERNAE COCTURAM: ex aqua cum Caricis cocta simpliciter,
ut solet, inlata cum buccellis, caroeno vel condito.   melius, si
cum musteis.   (*294*)

X. PETASONEM EX MUSTEIS

PETASONEM elixas cum bilibri hordei et Caricis XXV.   cum
elixatus fuerit, decarnas et arvillam illius candenti vatillo uris
et melle contingis.   quod melius, missum in furnum, melle
oblinas.[1]   cum coloraverit, mittis in caccabum passum, piper,
fasciculum rutae, merum, temperas.   cum fuerit temperatum,
dimidium in petasonem perfundis[2] et alia parte piperati buccellas musteorum fractas[3] perfundis.   cum sorbuerint, quod
mustei recusaverint, petasoni refundis.   (*295*)

XI

LARIDI COCTURA: Tectum aqua cum multo anetho coques,
oleum modicum destillabis et modicum salis.   (*296*)

XII. IECINORA SIVE PULMONES

1. IECINERA HAEDINA VEL AGNINA SIC COQUES: aquam mulsam
facies, et ova ⟨et⟩ partem lactis admisces eis ut incisa iecinera
sorbeant.   coques ex oenogaro, pipere asperso, et inferes.

(*297*)

[1] *obligas* codd., corr. by Br.
[2] *perfundis* codd., rest. by Br.
[3] *fractas* codd., rest. by Br.

cover the ham with this. When the paste is baked take out of
the oven and serve as it is.

2. BOILED HAM. Boiled simply in water with dried figs, as
usual, it is served with biscuits,[1] *caroenum*, or spiced wine, or—
better—with sweet-wine cakes.[2]

X. SHOULDER OF PORK (CURED LIKE HAM) WITH SWEET-WINE CAKES

BOIL THE SHOULDER OF PORK with 2 lb. of barley and 25 dried
figs. When it is done remove the meat from the bone, and
brown its fat on a glowing hot brazier and sprinkle with honey,
or—better—put it in the oven and rub in honey. When it is
browned put in a saucepan *passum*, pepper, a sprig of rue, and
wine. Mix. When the pepper-sauce is mixed, pour half of it
on the shoulder of pork, and the other half over pieces of sweet-
wine cake.[3] When these are saturated pour the rest of the
liquid over the meat.

XI

BOILED LARD. Boil covered in water with plenty of dill, add
a little oil and a little salt.

XII. LIVER AND LIGHTS

1. KID'S OR LAMB'S LIVER. Make honey-water and mix
into it eggs and some milk, and make incisions in the liver and
let it absorb the liquid. Then cook it in *oenogarum*, sprinkle
with pepper, and serve.

---

[1] Or rolls?   [2] See note to the following recipe.
[3] A recipe for these cakes is given by Cato (*De Agricultura*, 121):
"Sweet-wine cakes are made as follows: Moisten 1 peck of wheat
flour with must. Add aniseed, cumin, 2 lb. of fat, 1 lb. of cheese,
and some grated bark of a laurel twig; shape and place each cake on a
bay-leaf; then bake." The quantities for 1 lb. flour work out at
2 oz. fat and 1 oz. cheese.

2. ALITER [IECINERA] IN PULMONIBUS: ex lacte lavas pulmones et colas quod capere possunt, et confringis ova duo cruda, salis grana pauca, mellis ligulam, et simul commisces et imples pulmones. elixas et concidis. teres piper, suffundis liquamen, passum, merum. pulmones confringis et hoc oenogaro perfundis. (298)

XIII. DULCIA DOMESTICA ET MELCAE

1. DULCIA DOMESTICA: palmulas vel dactylos excepto semine, nuce vel nucleis vel pipere trito infercies. sale foris contingis, frigis in melle cocto, et inferes. (300)

2. ALITER DULCIA: musteos Afros optimos rades et in lacte infundis. cum biberint, in furnum mittis, ne arescant, modice. eximes eos calidos, melle perfundis, compungis ut bibant. piper aspergis et inferes. (301)

3. ALITER DULCIA: siligineos rasos frangis, et buccellas maiores facies. in lacte infundis, frigis ex [in] oleo, mel superfundis et inferes. (302)

4. ⟨ALITER⟩ DULCIA: piperato mittis mel, merum, passum, rutam. eo mittis nucleos, nuces, alicam elixatam. concisas nuces Abellanas tostas adicies, et inferes. (303)

5. ALITER DULCIA: piper, nucleos, mel, rutam et passum teres, cum lacte et tracta coques. coagulum coque cum modicis ovis. perfusum melle, aspersum ⟨pipere⟩ inferes. (304)

6. ALITER DULCIA: accipies similam, coques [et] in aqua calida, ita ut durissimam pultem facias, deinde in patellam expandis. cum refrixerit, concidis quasi ⟨ad⟩ dulcia et frigis in oleo optimo. levas, perfundis mel, piper aspergis et inferes. melius feceris, si lac pro aqua miseris. (305)

7. TYROPATINAM: accipies lac, quod adversus patinam

2. LIGHTS. Wash the lights in milk, and let them absorb as much as they can. Then break two raw eggs, add a few grains of salt, a spoonful of honey, work this into a smooth mixture, and stuff the lights with it. Boil in water and chop up. Pound pepper, moisten with *liquamen*, *passum*, and wine. Mince the lights, and pour this *oenogarum* over.

XIII. HOME-MADE SWEETS AND MELCAE

1. HOME-MADE SWEET. Stone dates, and stuff with nuts, pine-kernels, or ground pepper. Roll in salt, fry in cooked honey, and serve.

2. ANOTHER SWEET. Remove the crust from best African sweet-wine cakes[1] and steep them in milk. When they are saturated put them in the oven—not for too long, so that they do not dry up. Take them out hot, pour honey over, prick them to let them absorb the honey. Sprinkle with pepper, and serve.

3. ANOTHER SWEET. Remove the crust from wheaten loaf, break up into largish morsels. Steep in milk, fry in oil, pour honey over, and serve.

4. ANOTHER SWEET. To a pepper mash add honey, wine, *passum*, rue; further pine-kernels, nuts, boiled spelt-grits. Add chopped toasted filbert nuts, and serve.

5. ANOTHER SWEET. Pound pepper, pine-kernels, honey, rue, and *passum*; cook in milk and pastry. Thicken with a few eggs. Pour honey over, sprinkle with pepper, and serve.

6. ANOTHER SWEET. Take best wheat flour and cook it in hot water so that it forms a very hard paste, then spread it on a plate. When cold cut it up for sweets, and fry in best oil. Lift out, pour honey over, sprinkle with pepper, and serve.

7. MILK AND EGG SWEET.[2] Take milk, measure it against the

[1] See note to VII, x.
[2] The title *tyropatina* means 'a dish with cheese'; but the result is a very good custard.

aestimabis, temperabis lac cum melle quasi ad lactantia, ova quinque ad sextarium mittis, si ad heminam, ova tria. in lacte dissolvis ita ut unum corpus facias, in Cumana colas et igni lento coques. cum duxerit ad se, piper aspargis et inferes.

(306)

8. Ova spongia ex lacte: ova quattuor, lactis heminam, olei unciam in se dissolvis, ita ut unum corpus facias. in patellam subtilem adicies olei modicum, facies ut bulliat, et adicies impensam quam parasti. una parte cum fuerit coctum, in disco vertes, melle perfundis, piper aspargis et inferes.

(307)

9. Melcas cum[1] pipere et liquamine, vel sale, oleo et coriandro.   (<i>308</i>)

XIV. Bulbos

1. Bulbos oleo, liquamine, aceto inferes, modico cumino asperso.

2. Aliter: bulbos tundes atque ex aqua coques, deinde oleo frigis. ius sic facies: thymum, puleium, piper, origanum, mel, acetum modice et, si placet, et modice liquamen. piper aspargis et inferes.   (<i>309</i>)

3. Aliter: bulbos elixas in pultarium pressos, mittis thymum, origanum, mel, acetum, defritum, caryotam, liquamen et oleum modice. piper aspargis et inferes. [Varro: "si quid de bulbis, dixi: 'in aqua, qui Veneris ostium quaerunt,' deinde ut legitimis nuptiis in cena ponuntur, sed et cum nucleis pineis aut cum erucae suco et pipere"].   (<i>310</i>) (<i>311</i>)

---

[1] *mel castum* codd., corr. by Br.

pan, mix the milk with honey as if for milk-food, add 5 eggs
to a pint or 3 eggs to ½ pint. Work the eggs with the milk into
a smooth mixture. Strain into an earthenware pot and cook
over a slow fire. When it is set sprinkle with pepper, and
serve.

8. EGG SPONGE WITH MILK. Mix together 4 eggs, ½ pint of
milk, 1 oz. oil. Pour a little oil into a thin frying-pan, bring to
sizzling point, and add the prepared mixture. When it is
cooked on one side turn out on to a round dish, pour honey
over, sprinkle with pepper, and serve.

9. MELCAE.[1] Serve with pepper and *liquamen* or with salt,
oil, and coriander.

XIV. BULBS

1. BULBS.[2] Serve with oil, *liquamen*, vinegar, sprinkled
with a little cumin.

2. ANOTHER METHOD. Pound the bulbs and boil in water,
then fry in oil. Make the following dressing: thyme, pennyroyal, pepper, origan, honey, a little vinegar, and if you wish
a little *liquamen*. Sprinkle with pepper and serve.

3. ANOTHER METHOD. Boil the bulbs and strain them into a
deep saucepan; add thyme, origan, honey, vinegar, *defrutum*,
Jericho date, *liquamen*, and a little oil. Sprinkle with pepper
and serve.

GLOSS. Varro: "Asked about bulbs, I answered: ⟨they can

---

[1] A recipe for *melcae* by Paxamos, in the *Geoponica* (18, 21): "The
so-called *melca* will be ready to hand and better if you pour sharp
vinegar into new earthenware vessels and put them on the hot embers
or over a slow fire—*i.e.*, on glowing charcoal. When the vinegar
begins to bubble take it away from the heat so that it cannot boil over
and pour milk into the vessels and put them in a store-cupboard or
another cupboard or anywhere where they remain undisturbed.
And on the following day you will have melcae that are much nicer
than those prepared with much art."

[2] See note to IV, v, 1.

4. ALITER.   BULBOS FRICTOS: oenogaro inferes.   *(312)*

XV. FUNGI FARNEI VEL BOLETI

1. FUNGI FARNEI: elixi, calidi, exsiccati in garo piperato[1]
accipiuntur, ita ut piper cum liquamine teras.[2]   *(313)*

2. IN FUNGIS FARNEIS: piper, caroenum, acetum et oleum.
          (314)

3. ALITER FUNGI FARNEI: elixi ex sale, oleo, mero, coriandro
conciso inferuntur.   *(315)*

4. BOLETOS FUNGOS: caroenum, fasciculum coriandri viridis.
ubi ferbuerint, exempto fasciculo inferes.   *(316)*

5. BOLETOS ALITER: calyculos eorum liquamine vel sale
aspersos inferunt.   *(317)*

6. BOLETOS ALITER: thyrsos eorum concisos in patellam
novam perfundis, addito pipere, ligustico, modico melle.
liquamine temperabis. oleum modice.   *(318)*

XVI. TUBERA

1. TUBERA radis, elixas, sale aspergis, et surculo infiges.
subassas, et mittes in caccabum oleum, liquamen, caroenum,
vinum, piper et mel. cum ferbuerit, amulo obligas. tubera
exornas et inferes.   *(319)*

2. ALITER TUBERA: elixas et, asperso sale, in surculis adfigis
et subassas. et mittes in caccabum liquamen, oleum viride,
caroenum, vinum modice et piper confractum et mellis modicum, et ferveat. cum ferbuerit, amulo obligas, et tubera com-
punges, ut combibant illud. exornas. cum bene sorbuerint,
inferes. si volueris, eadem tubera omento porcino involves et
assabis et sic inferes.   *(320)*

---

[1] *in garo piper* codd., corr, by Br.   [2] *ita . . . teras*: gloss?

be eaten boiled⟩ in water for those who seek the door of love, or, as they are served with a legitimate wedding meal, but also with pine-kernels or flavoured with rocket and pepper."

4. FRIED BULBS. Serve with *oenogarum*.

XV. TREE FUNGI AND MUSHROOMS

1. TREE FUNGI. They are served boiled, hot, drained dry, with peppered *garum* [*i.e.*, pounded pepper with *liquamen*].

2. DRESSING FOR TREE FUNGI. Pepper, *caroenum*, vinegar, and oil.

3. TREE FUNGI, ANOTHER METHOD. Boiled in water, served with salt, oil, wine, chopped coriander.

4. MUSHROOMS. ⟨Cook in⟩ *caroenum* with a bouquet of fresh coriander. When they have cooked remove the bouquet and serve.

5. MUSHROOMS, ANOTHER METHOD. Serve the stalks with *liquamen* or sprinkled with salt.

6. MUSHROOMS, ANOTHER METHOD. Chop the stalks, place in a new shallow pan, having added pepper, lovage, a little honey. Blend with *liquamen*, add a little oil ⟨and let cook⟩.

XVI. TRUFFLES

1. SCRAPE THE TRUFFLES, boil, sprinkle with salt, and put them on skewers. Grill lightly, then put in a saucepan oil, *liquamen*, *caroenum*, wine, pepper, and honey. When this boils thicken with cornflour, undo the truffles, and serve ⟨with this sauce⟩.

2. TRUFFLES, ANOTHER METHOD. Boil, put on skewers, and grill lightly. Then put in a saucepan *liquamen*, virgin oil, *caroenum*, a little wine and ground pepper, and a little honey. Bring to the boil. When it boils thicken with cornflour. Prick the truffles so that they may absorb this liquid. Undo. When they are saturated serve. If you wish you can wrap these truffles in sausage-skin and grill and serve thus.

3. ALITER ⟨IN⟩ TUBERA OENOGARUM[1]: piper, ligusticum, coriandrum, rutam, liquamen, mel, vinum, oleum modice. calefacies.   (*321*)

4. ALITER TUBERA: piper, mentam, rutam, mel, oleum, vinum modicum.   calefacies et inferes.   (*322*)

5. ALITER TUBERA: elixa cum porro, deinde sale, pipere, coriandro conciso, mero, oleo modico inferes.   (*323*)

6. ALITER TUBERA: piper, cuminum, silfi, mentam, apium, rutam, mel, acetum vel vinum, salem vel liquamen et oleum modice.   (*324*)

XVII. IN COLOCASIO

IN COLOCASIO: piper, cuminum, rutam, mel, liquamen, olei modicum.   cum ferbuerit, amulo obligas.   (*325*)

XVIII. COCLEAS

1. COCLEAS LACTE PASTAS: accipies cocleas, spongizabis, membranam tolles, ut possint prodire.   adicies in vas lac et salem uno die, ceteris diebus [in] lac per se, et omni hora mundabis stercus.   cum pastae fuerint, ut non possint se retrahere, ex oleo friges.   mittes oenogarum.   similiter et † pulpas[2] pasci possunt.   (*326*)

---

[1] ⟨*in*⟩ add. Br., who also took *oenogarum* to be part of the heading—both with analogy to I, xvii, 1, which is the same recipe.

[2] *pulpa* Teubner ed., *pulte* Humelberg; could it be *sapa*? Cp. Pliny, *Nat. Hist.*, IX, 56, 82 (174).

3. OENOGARUM FOR TRUFFLES.[1] Pepper, lovage, coriander, rue, *liquamen*, honey, wine, a little oil. Heat up.

4. ANOTHER DRESSING FOR TRUFFLES. Pepper, mint, rue, honey, oil, a little wine. Heat up and serve.

5. TRUFFLES, ANOTHER METHOD. Boil with leek. Then serve with salt, pepper, chopped coriander, wine, and a little oil.

6. ANOTHER DRESSING FOR TRUFFLES. Pepper, cumin, asafœtida, mint, celery, rue, honey, vinegar or wine, salt or *liquamen*, and a little oil.

XVII. SAUCE FOR TARO[2]

Pepper, cumin, rue, honey, *liquamen*, a little oil. When it boils thicken with cornflour.

XVIII. SNAILS

1. SNAILS FED ON MILK. Take the snails, clean with a sponge, remove the membrane so that they may come out ⟨of their shells⟩. Put in a vessel ⟨with the snails⟩ milk and salt for one day, for the following days add only milk, and clean away the excrements every hour. When the snails are fattened to the point that they cannot get back into their shells fry them in oil. Serve with *oenogarum*. In a similar way they can be fed on meat.[3]

---

[1] This recipe occurs again as I, xvii, 1. The compiler probably took it from here and placed it under the general rules about such sauces, without removing it from its original place.

[2] *Colocasia antiquorum* Schott, an aroid plant, with a tuberous root, the Egyptian taro or culcas. The variety *C. esculenta*, taro (also called Tanyah tuber, dasheen, or Chinese potato), grows in the Pacific islands and is also cultivated in the southern parts of the United States. The taros in this recipe were probably boiled.

[3] The text is apparently corrupt; according to Pliny, *Nat. Hist.*, IX, 56, 82 (174), *sapa* can be used to fatten snails.

12—R.C.B.

2. COCLEAS: sale puro et oleo assabis cocleas: lasere, liquamine, pipere, oleo suffundis.   (*327*)

3. COCLEAS ASSAS: liquamine, pipere, cumino, suffundis assidue.

4. ALITER COCLEAS: viventes in lac siligineum infundes: ubi pastae fuerint, coques.   (*328*)

XIX. OVA

1. OVA FRIXA: oenogarata.

2. OVA ELIXA: liquamine, oleo, mero vel ex liquamine, pipere, lasere.

3. IN OVIS HAPALIS: piper, ligusticum, nucleos infusos. suffundes mel, acetum: liquamine temperabis.   (*329*)

2. SNAILS. Fry them in pure salt and oil, baste with asafœtida, *liquamen*, pepper, and oil.

3. ROAST SNAILS. Baste diligently with *liquamen*, pepper,
cumin.

4. SNAILS, ANOTHER METHOD. Soak alive in milk mixed
with wheat flour; when they are fattened, cook.

XIX. EGGS

1. FRIED EGGS. Serve with *oenogarum*.

2. BOILED EGGS. Serve with *liquamen*, oil, and wine, or
with *liquamen*, pepper, and asafœtida.

3. ⟨SAUCE⟩ FOR SOFT-BOILED EGGS. ⟨Pound⟩ pepper, lovage,
soaked pine-kernels. Add honey and vinegar, blend with
liquamen.[1]

[1] This is a very commendable recipe. Take enough pine-kernels
to give the sauce the consistency of salad-cream. They should be
soaked in water over-night.

LIBER VIII

TETRAPUS

I. in apro. II. in cervo. III. in caprea. IV. in ovifero. V. bubula sive vitulina. VI. in haedo et agno.
VII. in porcello. VIII. leporem. IX. glires.

I. In apro

1. Aper ita conditur: Spongiatur, et sic aspergitur ei sal et
cuminum frictum, et sic manet. alia die mittitur in furnum.
cum coctus fuerit, perfunditur piper tritum, condimentum
aprunum,[1] mel, liquamen, caroenum et passum.   (330)

2. Aliter in apro: aqua marina cum ramulis lauri aprum
elixas quousque madescat. corium ei tolles. cum sale,
sinapi, aceto inferes.   (331)

3. Aliter in apro: teres piper, ligusticum, origanum, bacas
myrtae exenteratas, coriandrum, cepas, suffundes mel, vinum,
liquamen, oleum modice, calefacies, amulo obligas. aprum in
furno coctum perfundes. hoc et in omne genus carnis ferinae
facies.   (332)

---

[1] *condimentum aprunum* bracketed as gloss by earlier editors, rest
as part of the text by Br.

180

BOOK VIII

THE QUADRUPED

I. Boar. II. Venison. III. Wild goat. IV. Wild sheep. V. Beef and veal. VI. Kid or lamb. VII. Sucking-pig. VIII. Hare. IX. Dormice.

I. BOAR

1. BOAR is prepared in the following manner: Sponge it and sprinkle with salt and grilled cumin, and leave it like that. The next day put it in the oven. When it is cooked pour over ⟨a sauce made of⟩ ground pepper, the juice from the boar, honey, *liquamen, caroenum,* and *passum.*

2. BOAR, ANOTHER METHOD. Boil the boar in sea-water[1] with sprigs of laurel until it is tender. Take off the skin. Serve with salt, mustard, and vinegar.

3. BOAR, ANOTHER METHOD. ⟨Take⟩ ground pepper, lovage, origan, seeded myrtle-berries, coriander, onions; moisten with honey, wine, *liquamen,* a little oil; heat, thicken with cornflour. Pour over the boar, which has been cooked in the oven. In this way you can prepare every kind of game.

4. HOT SAUCE FOR ROAST BOAR. Pepper, grilled cumin, celery-seed, mint, thyme, savory, safflower, toasted pine-kernels or toasted almonds, honey, wine, *liquamen,* vinegar, and a little oil.

[1] Cato (*De Agricultura,* 106) gives directions for the treatment of sea-water: "Take 6 gallons of sea-water from the deep sea, where no fresh water comes in. Pound 1½ lb. of salt, put it in, and stir with a stick until a boiled hen's egg will float on it, then stop mixing. Add 12 pints old wine, either from Aminoea or mixed white wine, mix well. Then pour it into a vessel treated with pitch, and seal. If you wish to prepare more sea-water make it according to the proportions given above."

4. In aprum assum iura ferventia facies sic: piper, cuminum frictum, apii semen, mentam, thymum, satureiam, cneci
flos, nucleos tostos vel amygdala tosta, mel, vinum, liquamen,
acetum, oleum modice.   (*333*)

5. Aliter in aprum assum iura ferventia: piper, ligusticum,
apii semen, mentam, thymum, nucleos tostos, vinum, acetum,
liquamen et oleum modice.   cum ius simplex bullierit, tunc
triturae globum mittes et agitas cepae et rutae fasciculo.   si
volueris pinguius facere, obligas ius albo ovorum liquido, moves
paulatim, aspergis piper tritum et inferes.   (*334*)

6. Ius in aprum elixum: piper, ligusticum, cuminum, silfi,
origanum, nucleos, caryotam, mel, sinape, acetum, liquamen et
oleum.   (*335*)

7. Ius frigidum in aprum elixum: piper, careum, ligusticum, coriandri semen frictum, anethi semen, apii semen,
thymum, origanum, cepulam, mel, acetum, sinape, liquamen,
oleum.   (*336*)

8. Aliter ius frigidum in aprum elixum: piper, ligusticum,
cuminum, anethi semen et thymum, origanum, silfi modicum,
erucae semen plusculum, suffundes merum, condimenta viridia
modica, cepam, Ponticas vel amygdala fricta, dactylum, mel,
acetum, merum modicum, coloras defrito, liquamen, oleum.
                                                        (*337*)

9. Aliter ⟨ius⟩ in apro: teres piper, ligusticum, origanum,
apii semen, laseris radicem, cuminum, feniculi semen, rutam,
liquamen, vinum, passum.   facies ut ferveat.   cum ferbuerit,
amulo obligas.   aprum intro foras ⟨tanges⟩ et inferes.   (*338*)

10. Perna apruna ita impletur Terentina: per articulum,
pernae palum mittes ita ut cutem a carne separes, ut possit
condimentum accipere per cornulum et universa impleatur.
teres piper, bacam lauri, rutam: si volueris, laser adicies, liquamen optimum, caroenum et olei viridis guttas.   cum impleta
fuerit, constringitur illa pars, qua impleta est, ex lino et mittitur
in zemam.   elixatur in aqua marina cum lauri turionibus et
anetho.   (*340*)

5. ANOTHER HOT SAUCE FOR ROAST BOAR. Pepper, lovage, celery-seed, mint, thyme, toasted pine-kernels, wine, vinegar, *liquamen*, and a little oil. When the liquid in which the boar is roasting has boiled put the pounded mixture in and stir with a bunch of onions and rue. If you wish to make it thicker bind the juice with white of eggs, stir slowly, sprinkle with ground pepper, and serve.

6. SAUCE FOR BOILED BOAR. Pepper, lovage, cumin, asafœtida, origan, pine-kernels, Jericho date, honey, mustard, vinegar, *liquamen*, and oil.

7. COLD SAUCE FOR BOILED BOAR. Pepper, caraway, lovage, grilled coriander-seed, dill-seed, celery-seed, thyme, origan, Welsh onion, honey, vinegar, mustard, *liquamen*, oil.

8. ANOTHER COLD SAUCE FOR BOILED BOAR. Pepper, lovage, cumin, dill-seed, thyme, origan, a little asafœtida, a good measure of rocket seed; add wine, a few green herbs, onion, hazel-nuts or toasted almonds, dates, honey, vinegar, a little ⟨more⟩ wine; colour with *defrutum*, and add *liquamen* and oil.

9. ANOTHER SAUCE FOR BOAR. Pound pepper, lovage, origan, celery-seed, asafœtida root, cumin, fennel-seed, rue, *liquamen*, wine, *passum*. Bring to the boil. When it boils thicken with cornflour. Moisten the boar ⟨with this sauce⟩ inside and outside and serve.

10. LEG OF BOAR. A leg of boar is stuffed with Terentian stuffing in the following way: Drive a stick through the knuckle of the leg ⟨*i.e.*, at the small end of the leg⟩, to separate the skin from the flesh, so that it can receive the spices through a little funnel and can be filled entirely. Pound pepper, laurel berry, rue; if you wish add asafœtida; moisten with best *liquamen* and a few drops of best oil. ⟨Stuff the leg with this mixture in the manner indicated above.⟩ When it is stuffed sew the opening through which you have stuffed it with flax, and put it in a cauldron. Boil in sea-water with laurel shoots and dill.

II. IN CERVO

1. IUS IN CERVUM: teres piper, ligusticum, careum, origanum, apii semen, laseris radicem, feniculi semen, fricabis, suffundes liquamen, vinum, passum, oleum modice. cum ferbuerit, amulo obligas. cervum coctum intro foras tanges et inferes.

(*341*)

2. IN PLATONEM similiter et in omne genus venationis eadem conditura uteris.   (*342*)

3. ALITER: cervum elixabis et subassabis. teres piper, ligusticum, careum, apii semen, suffundes mel, acetum, liquamen, oleum.   calefactum amulo obligas et carnem perfundes.

(*343*)

4. IUS IN CERVO: piper, ligusticum, cepulam, origanum, nucleos, caryotas, mel, liquamen, sinape, acetum, oleum. (*344*)

5. CERVINAE CONDITURA: piper, cuminum, condimentum, petroselinum, cepam, rutam, mel, liquamen, mentam, passum, caroenum et oleum modice.   amulo obligas, cum iam bulliit.

(*345*)

6. IURA FERVENTIA IN CERVO: piper, ligusticum, petroselinum, cuminum, nucleos tostos aut amygdala. suffundes mel, acetum, vinum, oleum modice, liquamen, et agitabis.   (*346*)

7. EMBAMMA IN CERVINAM ASSAM: piper, nardostachyum, folium, apii semen, cepam aridam, rutam viridem, mel, acetum, liquamen, adicies caryotam,[1] uvam passam et oleum.   (*347*)

8. ALITER IN CERVUM ASSUM IURA FERVENTIA: piper, ligusticum, petroselinum, Damascena macerata, vinum, mel, acetum, liquamen, oleum modice. agitabis porro et satureia.   (*348*)

---

[1] *adiectam (-um) caretam* codd., corr. by R.

II. VENISON

1. SAUCE FOR VENISON. Crush pepper, lovage, caraway, origan, celery-seed, asafœtida root, fennel-seed; pound well, pour on *liquamen*, wine, *passum*, a little oil. When it comes to the boil thicken with cornflour. Moisten the cooked stag inside and out, and serve.

2. FOR FALLOW DEER and for every kind of venison you can use the same sauce.

3. VENISON, ANOTHER METHOD. Boil the stag, and roast lightly. Pound pepper, lovage, caraway, celery-seed; add honey, vinegar, *liquamen*, and oil. When hot thicken with cornflour and pour over the meat.

4. SAUCE FOR VENISON. Pepper, lovage, Welsh onion, origan, pine-kernels, Jericho dates, honey, *liquamen*, mustard, vinegar, oil.

5. SAUCE FOR VENISON. Pepper, cumin, herbs, parsley, onion, rue, honey, *liquamen*, mint, *passum*, *caroenum*, and a little oil. Thicken with cornflour when boiling.

6. HOT SAUCE FOR VENISON. Pepper, lovage, parsley, cumin, toasted pine-kernels or almonds. Add honey, vinegar, wine, a little oil, *liquamen*, and stir.

7. SAUCE FOR ROAST VENISON. Pepper, spikenard, bay-leaf, celery-seed, dried onion, fresh rue, honey, vinegar, *liquamen*; add Jericho dates, raisins, and oil.

8. HOT SAUCE FOR ROAST VENISON, ANOTHER METHOD. Pepper, lovage, parsley, soaked ⟨dried⟩ damsons, wine, honey, vinegar, *liquamen*, a little oil. Stir with a bunch of leek and savory.[1]

---

[1] Quantities for five people: ¼ lb. of damsons (or prunes), 1½ tumblers of red wine, about a dessert-spoon of honey, half a small glass of vinegar (or more when prunes are used), half a small glass of *liquamen*, a little oil. The result is a thickish sauce which is very good. One could probably make it more liquid according to taste by adding more wine. Cooking-time about 1 hour over a low fire.

III. In caprea

1. Ius in caprea: piper, ligusticum, careum, cuminum, petroselinum, rutae semen, mel, sinape, acetum, liquamen et oleum.   (349)

2. Ius in caprea assa: piper, condimentum, rutam, cepam, mel, liquamen, passum, oleum modice. amulum, ⟨cum⟩ iam bulliit.   (350⟩

3. Aliter ius in caprea: piper, condimentum, petroselinum, origanum modicum, rutam, liquamen, mel, passum et olei modicum. amulo obligabis.   (351)

IV. In ovifero [hoc est ovis silvatica]

1. Ius in ovifero fervens: piper, ligusticum, cuminum, mentam siccam, thymum, silfi, suffundes vinum, adicies Damascena macerata, mel, vinum, liquamen, acetum, passum ad colorem, oleum. agitabis fasciculo origani et mentae siccae.
(352)

2. Ius in venationibus omnibus elixis et assis: piperis scripulos VIII, rutam, ligusticum, apii semen, iuniperum, thymum, mentam aridam scripulos senos, pulei scripulos III. haec omnia ad levissimum pulverem rediges et in uno commisces et teres.   adicies in vasculum mel quod satis erit, et his uteris cum oxygaro.   (353)

3. Ius frigidum in ovifero: piper, ligusticum, thymum, cuminum frictum, nucleos tostos, mel, acetum, liquamen et oleum. piper asperges.   (354)

V. Bubula sive vitellina

1. Vitellina fricta: piper, ligusticum, apii semen, cumi-

III. WILD GOAT

1. SAUCE FOR WILD GOAT. Pepper, lovage, caraway, cumin, parsley, rue-seed, honey, mustard, vinegar, *liquamen*, and oil.

2. ANOTHER SAUCE FOR ROAST WILD GOAT. Pepper, herbs, rue, onion, honey, *liquamen*, *passum*, a little oil. Thicken with cornflour when boiling.

3. ANOTHER SAUCE FOR WILD GOAT. Pepper, herbs, parsley, a little origan, rue, *liquamen*, honey, *passum*, and a little oil. Thicken with cornflour.

IV. WILD SHEEP

1. HOT SAUCE FOR WILD SHEEP. Pepper, lovage, cumin, dried mint, thyme, asafœtida; add wine, soaked ⟨dried⟩ damsons, honey, wine, *liquamen*, vinegar, *passum* to colour, and oil. Stir with a bunch of origan and dried mint.

2. SAUCE FOR ALL KINDS OF VENISON, BOILED AND ROAST. 8 scruples of pepper, 6 scruples each of rue, lovage, celery-seed, juniper, thyme, dried mint, 3 scruples of pennyroyal. Reduce all this to a very fine powder, and mix together and pound. Put in the vessel sufficient honey, and use this mixture with *oxygarum*.

3. COLD SAUCE FOR WILD SHEEP. Pepper, lovage, thyme, grilled cumin, toasted pine-kernels, honey, vinegar, *liquamen*, and oil. Sprinkle with pepper.

V. BEEF AND VEAL

(The following recipes are meant for joints or slices of veal or beef, and do not refer to the whole animal.)

1. FRIED VEAL. Pepper, lovage, celery-seed, cumin, origan,

num, origanum, cepam siccam, uvam passam, mel, acetum, vinum, liquamen, oleum, defritum.   (*355*)

2. VITULINAM SIVE BUBULAM CUM PORRIS ⟨VEL⟩ CYDONEIS VEL CEPIS VEL COLOCASIIS: liquamen, piper, laser et olei modicum.   (*356*)

3. IN VITULINAM ELIXAM: teres piper, ligusticum, careum, apii semen, suffundes mel, acetum, liquamen, oleum. calefacies, amulo obligas et carnem perfundes.   (*357*)

4. ALITER IN VITULINA ELIXA: piper, ligusticum, feniculi semen, origanum, nucleos, caryotam, mel, acetum, liquamen, sinapi et oleum.   (*358*)

VI. IN HAEDO VEL AGNO

1. COPADIA HAEDINA SIVE AGNINA pipere, liquamine coques. cum faseolis faratariis, liquamine, pipere, lasere. cum inbracto, buccellas panis et oleo modico.[1]   (*359*)

2–3. ALITER HAEDINAM SIVE AGNINAMEX CALDATAM: mittes in caccabum copadia. cepam, coriandrum minutatim succides, teres piper, ligusticum, cuminum, liquamen, oleum, vinum. coques, exinanies in patina, amulo obligas. [Aliter haedinam sive agninam excaldatam] ⟨agnina⟩ a crudo trituram mortario accipere debet, caprina autem cum coquitur accipit trituram.   (*360*) (*361*)

4. HAEDUM SIVE AGNUM ASSUM: [haedi cocturam].[2] ubi eum ex liquamine et oleo coxeris, incisum infundes in pipere, lasere, liquamine, oleo modice, et in craticula assabis. eodem iure continges. piper asparges et inferes.   (*362*)

5. ALITER HAEDUM SIVE AGNUM ASSUM: piperis semunciam, asareos scripulos VI, zingiberis modicum, petroselini scripulos VI, laseris modice, liquaminis optimi heminam, olei acetabulum.   (*363*)

---

[1] Text of codd. rest. and punctuation changed by Br. (p. 67 with note 99).

[2] *haedi cocturam* considered a gloss by Br. (p. 86).

dried onion, raisins, honey, vinegar, wine, *liquamen*, oil, *defru-tum*.[1]

2. VEAL OR BEEF WITH LEEKS OR QUINCES OR ONIONS OR TAROS.[2] ⟨Serve with⟩ *liquamen*, pepper, asafœtida, and a little oil.

3. SAUCE FOR BOILED VEAL. Pound pepper, lovage, caraway, celery-seed; add honey, vinegar, *liquamen*, and oil. Heat, thicken with cornflour, and pour over the meat.

4. ANOTHER SAUCE FOR BOILED VEAL. Pepper, lovage, fennel-seed, origan, pine-kernels, Jericho dates, honey, vinegar, *liquamen*, mustard, and oil.

VI. KID OR LAMB

1. PIECES OF KID OR LAMB. Cook with pepper and *liquamen*. Serve accompanied by chopped fresh beans with *liquamen*, pepper, and asafœtida, or with a sauce of bread pieces and a little oil.

2—3. HOT KID OR LAMB STEW. Put the pieces of meat into a pan. Finely chop an onion and coriander, pound pepper, lovage, cumin, *liquamen*, oil, and wine. Cook, turn out into a shallow pan, thicken with cornflour. If you take lamb you should add the contents of the mortar while the meat is still raw, if kid, add it while it is cooking.

4. ROAST KID OR LAMB. When you have cooked it in *liquamen* and oil make incisions in the skin and pour over a mixture of pepper, asafœtida, *liquamen*, and a little oil, and grill. Moisten with the same juice, sprinkle with pepper, and serve.

5. ROAST KID OR LAMB, ANOTHER METHOD. ½ oz. pepper, 6 scruples of hazelwort, a little ginger, 6 scruples of parsley, a little asafœtida, ½ pint of best *liquamen*, ½ gill of oil.

---

[1] The meat is probably meant to be fried separately and to have the sauce poured over it afterwards, but it is also very good braised in the sauce.   [2] See note to VII, xvii.

6. Haedus sive agnus syringiatus id est † mammotestus:
exossatur diligenter a gula, sic ut uter fiat, et intestina eius
integra exinaniuntur, ita ut in caput intestina sufflentur, et per
novissimam partem stercus exinanibitur. aqua lavantur diligenter et sic implentur admixto liquamine, et ab umeris consuitur et mittitur in clibanum. cum coctus fuerit, perfunditur
ius bulliens: lac, piper tritum, liquamen, caroenum, defritum
modice, sic et oleum, et iam bullienti mittis amulum. vel
certe mittitur in reticulo vel in sportella et diligenter constringitur et bullienti zemae cum modico salis summittitur. cum bene
illic tres undas bullierit, levatur, et denuo bullit cum umore
supra scripto. bulliente conditura perfunditur.   (*364*)

7. Aliter haedus sive agnus syringiatus: lactis sextarium
unum, mellis unc. IV, piperis unc. I, salis modicum, laseris
modicum. ius in † ipsius: olei acetabulum, liquaminis acetabulum, mellis acetabulum, dactylos tritos octo, vini boni
heminam, amulum modice.   (*365*)
8. Haedus sive agnus crudus: oleo, pipere fricabis et
asparges foris salem purum multo cum coriandri semine. in
furnum mittis, assatum inferes.   (*366*)
9. Haedum sive agnum Tarpeianum: antequam coquatur,
ornatus consuitur. piper, rutam, satureiam, cepam, thymum
modicum. et liquamine collues haedum, macerabis in furno[1]
in patella, quae oleum habeat. cum percoxerit, perfundes in
patella impensam, teres satureiam, cepam, rutam, dactylos,
liquamen, vinum, caroenum, oleum. cum bene duxerit
impensam, in disco pones, piper asperges et inferes.   (*367*)

10. Haedum sive agnum Parthicum: mittes in furnum.
teres piper, rutam, cepam, satureiam, Damascena enucleata,
laseris modicum, vinum, liquamen, et oleum [vinum]. fervens
colluitur in disco, ex aceto sumitur.   (*368*)

[1] *in furno in patella* codd., rest. by F. R.

6. BONED SUCKING KID OR LAMB. Bone carefully from the gullet, so that it becomes like a sack, and empty the intestines completely by blowing into them from the head, so that the excrement will be emptied through the back passage. Wash carefully and fill with water, and an admixture of *liquamen*. Sew up the animal at the shoulders, and put it in the oven. When it is cooked pour on the following hot sauce: Milk, ground pepper, *liquamen*, *caroenum*, a little *defrutum*, and also a little oil; when this comes to the boil add cornflour to thicken.

Or you can put the animal in a net or basket, bind together carefully, and put it in a boiling cauldron with a little salt. When it has well boiled up three times lift it out and boil again in the above sauce. It is served with the boiling sauce poured over.

7. ANOTHER METHOD FOR KID OR LAMB, BONED. Cook in 1 pint of milk, 4 oz. honey, 1 oz. pepper, a little salt, a little asafœtida. Sauce: ½ gill of *liquamen*, ½ gill of honey, 8 pounded dates, ½ pint of good wine, a little cornflour to thicken.

8. KID OR LAMB ⟨SPICED⟩ RAW. Rub with oil and pepper, sprinkle outside generously with pure salt mixed with coriander-seed. Put in the oven, roast, and serve.

9. KID OR LAMB À LA TARPEIUS.[1] Before cooking truss and sew up. ⟨Pound⟩ pepper, rue, savory, onion, a little thyme, add *liquamen*, and moisten the animal with this. Cook until tender in the oven in a shallow pan which contains oil. When it is done pour over ⟨in the pan⟩ the following mixture: pounded savory, onion, rue, dates, *liquamen*, wine, *caroenum*, and oil. When this mixture has well thickened turn into a round dish, sprinkle with pepper, and serve.

10. KID OR LAMB, PARTHIAN MANNER. Put in the oven. Pound pepper, rue, onion, savory, stoned damsons, a little asafœtida, wine, *liquamen*, and oil. Place the animal on a round dish. Pour sauce over while hot, and serve with vinegar.

[1] The identity of this Tarpeius has not been established.

11. Haedum laureatum ex lacte: haedum curas, exossas, interanea eius cum coagulo tolles, lavas. adicies in mortarium piper, ligusticum, laseris radicem, bacas lauri duas, pyrethri modicum, cerebella duo vel tria. haec omnia teres, suffundes liquamen, temperabis ex sale. super trituram colas lactis sextarios duos, mellis ligulas duas. hac impensa intestina reples et super haedum componis in gyro, et omento ⟨vel⟩ charta cooperis, surclas. in caccabum vel patellam compones haedum, adicies liquamen, oleum, vinum. cum ad mediam cocturam venerit, teres ⟨piper⟩, ligusticum, et ius de suo sibi suffundes.   mittes defriti modicum, teres, reexinanies in caccabum. cum percoctus fuerit, exornas, amulo obligas et inferes.   (369)

VII. In porcello

1. Porcellum farsilem duobus generibus: curas, a gutture exenteras, a cervice ornas. antequam praedures, subaperies auriculam sub cutem, mittes impensam Terentinam in vesicam bubulam et fistulam aviarii rostro vesicae alligabis, per quam exprimes in aurem quantum ceperit. post a charta praecludes et infiblabis et praeparabis aliam impensam. sic facies: teres piper, ligusticum, origanum, laseris radicem modicum, suffundes liquamen, adicies cerebella cocta, ova cruda, alicam coctam, ius de suo sibi, ⟨si⟩ fuerint, aucellas, nucleos, piper integrum; liquamine temperas. imples porcellum, charta obduras et fiblas. mittes in furnum. cum coctus fuerit, exornas, perunges et inferes.   (372)

2. Aliter porcellum: Salem, cuminum, laser.

3. Porcellum liquaminatum: de porcello eicis utriculum, ita ut aliquae pulpae in eo remaneant. teres piper, ligusticum, origanum, suffundes liquamen, adicies unum cerebellum, ova

11. KID WITH BAY AND MILK. Prepare the kid, bone, remove the entrails, including the stomach, wash. Put in a mortar pepper, lovage, asafœtida root, two bay-berries, a little pyrethrum, two or three brains; pound all this, add *liquamen*, season with salt. Strain 2 pints of milk and 2 tablespoonfuls of honey over the contents of the mortar. Stuff the guts with this mixture, and arrange them on the head of the kid in a circle. Cover with sausage-skin or paper, bind together, and place the kid in a saucepan or a shallow pan, adding *liquamen*, oil, and wine. Half-way through the cooking pound pepper, lovage, and pour on some of the cooking-liquor. Add a little *defrutum*; mix well. Empty into the saucepan. When it is done remove paper and binding material, thicken the sauce with cornflour, and serve.

VII. SUCKING-PIG

1. SUCKING-PIG STUFFED IN TWO WAYS. · Clean, gut from the gullet, and truss from the neck. Before you brown it open the ear a little under the skin, put Terentian stuffing in an ox-bladder, and bind to the opening of the bladder a bird-keeper's reed pipe. Through this press into the ear as much ⟨of the stuffing⟩ as it will hold. Then close with paper and fasten, and prepare another stuffing in the following manner. Pound pepper, lovage, origan, a little asafœtida root, moisten with *liquamen*, add cooked brains, raw eggs, cooked spelt-grits, stock, small birds if you have them, also pine-kernels, whole peppercorns; blend with *liquamen*. Stuff the piglet, wrap tightly in paper, and fasten. Put in the oven. When it is cooked remove paper and fastenings, pour a little oil on, and serve.

2. SUCKING-PIG, ANOTHER METHOD. ⟨Cook seasoned with⟩ salt, cumin, asafœtida.

3. SUCKING-PIG IN LIQUAMEN. Remove the entrails of the piglet, but so that some of the offal is left in. Pound pepper, lovage, origan, moisten with *liquamen*, add 1 brain, 2 eggs, mix

13—R.C.B.

duo, misces in se. porcellum praeduratum imples, fiblabis, in sportella ferventi ollae summittis. cocto fiblas tolles, ut ius ex ipso manare[1] possit. pipere aspersum inferes. (373)

4. PORCELLUM ELIXUM FARSILEM: de porcello utriculum eicies, praeduras. teres piper, ligusticum, origanum, suffundes liquamen, cerebella cocta quod satis sit, similiter ova dissolves, liquamine temperabis, farcimina cocta integra praecides. sed ante porcellum praeduratum liquamine delavas, deinde imples, infiblas, in sportella ferventi ollae summittes. coctum spongizas, sine pipere inferes. (374)

5. PORCELLUM ASSUM TRACTOMELINUM: porcellum curatum a gutture exenteras, siccas. teres piperis unciam, mel, vinum, impones ut ferveat, tractam siccatam confringes et partibus caccabo permisces. agitabis surculo lauri viridis, tam diu coques, donec levis fiat et impinguet. hac impensa porcellum imples, surculas, obduras charta, in furnum mittes, exornas et inferes. (375)

6. PORCELLUM LACTE PASTUM ELIXUM CALIDUM IURE FRIGIDO CRUDO APICIANO: adicies in mortarium piper, ligusticum, coriandri semen, mentam, rutam, fricabis, suffundes liquamen, adicies mel, vinum, et liquamine ⟨temperabis⟩. porcellum elixum ferventem sabano mundo siccatum perfundes et inferes. (376)

7. PORCELLUM VITELLIANUM: porcellum ornas quasi aprum, sale asperges, in furno assas. adicies in mortarium piper, ligusticum, suffundes liquamen, vino et passo temperabis. in caccabo cum olei pusillo ferveat. et porcellum assum iure asperges, ita ut sub cute ius recipiat. (377)

8. PORCELLUM FLACCIANUM: porcellum ornas in modum apri, sale asperges et in furnum mittes. dum coquitur, adicies in mortarium piper, ligusticum, careum, apii semen, laseris

---

[1] *manere* codd., corr. by Humelberg.

well. Brown the piglet, then stuff, fasten with skewers, and
hang in a basket in a boiling cauldron. When cooked remove
the skewers so that the juice can run out. Sprinkle with
pepper and serve.

4. SUCKING-PIG BOILED AND STUFFED. Disembowel the pig;
brown. Pound pepper, lovage, origan, moisten with *liquamen*,
add sufficient cooked brains, also break eggs, blend with *liquamen*, add cut-up sausages that have been cooked whole. First
wash the browned pig with *liquamen*, then stuff, skewer, and
hang it in a basket in a boiling cauldron. When it is cooked
sponge and serve without pepper.

5. ROAST SUCKING-PIG WITH A PASTRY AND HONEY STUFFING.
Disembowel the cleaned pig from the gullet, and dry. Pound
1 oz. pepper, honey, wine, bring to the boil, crumble dried
pastry, and mix it with the ingredients in the pan. Stir with
a sprig of fresh laurel, then cook until it thickens and becomes
smooth. Stuff the pig with this mixture, skewer, wrap
tightly in paper, put in the oven. ⟨When cooked⟩ remove the
skewers and paper and serve.

6. SUCKING-PIG FED ON MILK, BOILED AND HOT, WITH COLD,
UNCOOKED DRESSING À LA APICIUS. Put in the mortar pepper,
lovage, coriander-seed, mint, rue, pound, moisten with *liquamen*, add honey, wine and blend with *liquamen*. Dry the
hot boiled pig with a clean cloth, pour the dressing over, and
serve.

7. SUCKING-PIG À LA VITELLIUS. Prepare the piglet like a
boar, sprinkle with salt, roast in the oven. Put in the mortar
pepper, lovage, moisten with *liquamen*, blend with wine and
passum. Bring to the boil in the saucepan with a little oil.
Pour this sauce over the roast piglet, allowing the sauce to
penetrate under the crackling.

8. SUCKING-PIG À LA FLACCUS.[1] Prepare the piglet like a
boar, sprinkle with salt, and put in the oven. While it is
cooking put in the mortar pepper, lovage, caraway, celery-seed,

[1] The identity of Flaccus has not been established.

radicem, rutam viridem, fricabis, suffundes liquamen, vino et
passo temperabis. In caccabo cum olei modico ferveat.
amulo obligas. porcellum cocto ab ossibus tanges,[1] apii semen
teres ita ut fiat pulvis, asperges et inferes.   (*378*)

9. Porcellum laureatum: porcellum exossas, quasi oeno-
garatum ornas, praeduras. laurum viridem in medio franges
satis, in furno assas, et mittes in mortarium piper, ligusticum,
careum, apii semen, laseris radicem, bacas lauri. fricabis, suffundes liquamen, et vino et passo temperabis. adicies in
caccabo cum olei modico, ut ferveat. obligas. porcellum
lauro eximes et iure ab ossibus tanges et inferes.   (*379*)

10. Porcellum Frontinianum: exossas, praeduras, ornas.
adicies in caccabum liquamen, vinum, obligas fasciculum porri,
anethi, media coctura mittes defritum. coctum lavas et siccum
mittes. piper asperges et inferes.   (*380*)

11. Porcellum aenococtum: porcellum praeduras, ornas;
adicies in caccabum oleum, liquamen, vinum, aquam, obligas
fasciculum porri, coriandri, media coctura colorabis defrito.
adicies in mortarium piper, ligusticum, careum, origanum, apii
semen, laseris radicem, fricabis, suffundes liquamen, ius de suo
sibi; vino et passo temperabis; exinanies in caccabum, facies ut
ferveat. cum ferbuerit, amulo obligas. porcellum composi-
tum in patina perfundes, piper asperges et inferes.   (*381*)

12. Porcellum Celsinianum: ornas, infundes pipere, ruta,

---

[1] *porcellum cocto ab ossibus tanges,* and in the following recipe, *iure
ab ossibus tanges*: the precise meaning of these expressions is not clear
to me. If no other sauce were given in these recipes one might in-
terpret 'pour stock from bones over the piglet.' But since no other
direction for the sauces is given, *coctum* and *ius* must refer to the
sauces described in the recipes. Could it be that *ab ossibus tangere*
is a term comparable to *leporem a dorso tangis* in VIII, viii, 7 ?

asafœtida root, fresh rue; pound, moisten with *liquamen*, blend with wine and *passum*. Bring to the boil in a saucepan with a little oil. Thicken with cornflour. When the sauce is cooked pour over the pig, pound celery-seed to powder, sprinkle over, and serve.

9. SUCKING-PIG WITH BAY. Bone the pig and prepare as for sucking-pig in *oenogarum*. Brown. ⟨Garnish with⟩ sufficient fresh bay-leaves broken in half, roast in the oven. Put in the mortar pepper, lovage, caraway, celery-seed, asafœtida root, bay-berries; pound, moisten with *liquamen*, blend with wine and *passum*. Put in a saucepan with a little oil and bring to the boil. Thicken with cornflour. Take the piglet out of the bay-leaves, pour the sauce over, and serve.

10. SUCKING-PIG À LA FRONTO.[1] Bone, brown, truss. Put in a saucepan *liquamen*, wine, and a bouquet of leeks and dill. ⟨Cook the sucking-pig in this.⟩ Half-way through the cooking add *defrutum*. When cooked, wash and dry. Sprinkle with pepper and serve.

11. SUCKING-PIG COOKED IN A METAL CASSEROLE. Brown the pig and truss. Put in the pan ⟨in which you cook the pig⟩ oil, *liquamen*, wine, water, and a bouquet of leeks and coriander. Half-way through the cooking add *defrutum* to colour. Put in the mortar pepper, lovage, caraway, origan, celery-seed, asafœtida root; pound, moisten with *liquamen* and some of the cooking-liquor. Blend with wine and *passum*. Empty this into the pan, bring to the boil, and when it boils thicken with cornflour. Dress the pig on a shallow dish and pour the sauce over. Sprinkle with pepper and serve.

12. SUCKING-PIG À LA CELSINUS.[2] Truss and stuff with

---

[1] See note to VI, ix, 12.

[2] Celsinus is the signatory of the *Testamentum Porcelli* in Jerome, *c. Rufinum*, 1, 17, p. 473.

cepa, satureia, sicuto † suo, et ova infundes per auriculam, et
ex pipere, liquamine, vino modico in acetabulum temperas, et
sumes.   *(382)*

13. PORCELLUM ASSUM: teres piper, rutam, satureiam, cepam,
ovorum coctorum media, liquamen, vinum, oleum, conditum.
bulliat.   conditura porcellum in boletari perfundes et inferes.
(383)

14. PORCELLUM HORTOLANUM[1]: porcellus hortolanus exossatur per gulam in modum utris.   mittitur in eo pullus isiciatus
particulatim concisus, turdi, ficedulae, isicia de pulpa sua,
Lucanicae, dactyli exossati, fabriles bulbi, cocleae exemptae,
malvae, betae, porri, apium, cauliculi elixi, coriandrum, piper
integrum, nuclei, ova XV superinfunduntur, liquamen piperatum. [ova mittuntur tria][2] et consuitur et praeduratur.   in
furno assatur.   deinde a dorso scinditur, et iure hoc perfunditur.   piper teritur, ruta, liquamen, passum, mel, oleum modicum.   cum bullierit, amulum mittitur.   *(384)*

15. IUS FRIGIDUM IN PORCELLUM ELIXUM ITA FACIES: teres
piper, careum, anethum, origanum modice, nucleos pineos,
suffundes acetum, liquamen, caryotam, mel, sinape factum,
superstillabis oleum, piper asperges et inferes.   *(385)*

16. PORCELLUM TRAIANUM SIC FACIES: exossas porcellum et
aptabis sicuti aenococtum et ad fumum suspendes, et adpendeas, et quantum adpendeas, tantum salis in ollam mittes.
et elixas ut coquatur, et siccum in lance inferes ⟨pro⟩ salso
recente.   *(386)*

___

[1] *sic* codd.; perhaps *Hortalanum?*   Cp. Br., p. 93, note 139.
[2] *ova mittuntur tria* codd., *trita* Giarratano in Teubner ed.; Br.
(p. 86) suggested treating it as gloss.

pepper, rue, onion, savory and . . . ,[1] and stuff the head pouring eggs through the ear, and mix in a cup pepper, *liquamen*, and a little wine, ⟨cook⟩ and serve.

13. ROAST SUCKING-PIG. Pound pepper, rue, savory, onion, yolks of boiled eggs, *liquamen*, wine, oil, spiced wine. Bring to the boil. Pour this sauce over the pig arranged on the serving-dish, and serve.

14. SUCKING-PIG FED ON VEGETABLES (? *or* À LA HORTALUS[2]). Bone the pig from the gullet so as to make a sack. Stuff it with meat from a chicken cut up in pieces, thrushes, fig-peckers, forcemeat made of the pig's entrails, Lucanian sausages, stoned dates, dried bulbs, snails taken out of their shells, mallows, beets, leeks, celery, boiled cabbage, coriander, peppercorns, pine-kernels, finally put in 15 eggs and *liquamen* mixed with ground pepper. Sew it up and brown. Then roast in the oven. When done cut it open at the back and pour over the following sauce: pounded pepper, rue, *liquamen*, *passum*, honey, a little oil. When boiling thicken with cornflour.

15. COLD SAUCE FOR BOILED SUCKING-PIG prepare in the following way. Pound pepper, caraway, dill, a little origan, pine-kernels. Moisten with vinegar and *liquamen*, add Jericho dates, honey, prepared mustard, drip oil over it, sprinkle with pepper, and serve.

16. SUCKING-PIG À LA TRAJAN. Make thus: Bone the pig and prepare as for pig cooked in a metal casserole,[3] and hang up to smoke. Weigh it, and put its weight in salt into the cauldron. And boil until done, then dry and dish up in the serving-dish instead of fresh salt fish.

[1] The text is corrupt, and the recipe seems to be shortened; *infundere*, to 'pour in,' is really the word for 'soaking,' so that it could mean the pig is steeped in the herbs and some liquid; but it seems here to refer to the eggs which must be introduced through the ear. The sense of the last phrase is quite obscure to me.

[2] If the text is to be emended to *Hortalanum* the recipe would be one invented by M. Hortensius Hortalus, mentioned by Tacitus (*Annales*, 2, 37) and Suetonius (*Tiberius*, 47).

[3] No. 11 above.

17. In porcello lactante: piperis unc. I, vini heminam, olei optimi acetabulum maius, liquaminis acetabulum, aceti acetabulum minus.   *(387)*

VIII. Leporem

1. Leporem madidum: in aqua praecoquitur modice, deinde componitur in patina, [ac] coquendus ⟨ex⟩ oleo in furno, et cum prope sit coctus ex alio oleo. pertangito de conditura infra scripta: teres piper, ⟨ligusticum⟩, satureiam, cepam, rutam, apii semen, liquamen, laser, vinum et modice olei. aliquotiens versatur, in ipsa percoquitur conditura.   *(395)*

2. Item aliam ad eum impensam: cum prope tolli debeat, teres piper, dactylum, laser, uvam passam, caroenum, liquamen, oleum. suffundes, et, cum bullierit, piper asperges et inferes. *(396)*

3. Leporem farsum: nucleos integros, amygdala, nuces sive glandes concisas, piperis grana solida, pulpam de ipso lepore, et ovis fractis obligatur, de ⟨inde tegitur⟩ omento porcino, in furno ⟨assatur⟩. sic iterum impensam facies: rutam, piper satis, cepam, satureiam, dactylos, liquamen, caroenum vel conditum. diu combulliat donec spisset, et sic perfunditur. sed lepus in piperato liquamine maneat.[1]   *(397)*

4. Ius album in assum leporem: piper, ligusticum, cuminum, apii semen, ovi duri medium. trituram colligis et facies globum ex ea. in caccabulo coques liquamen, vinum, oleum, acetum modice, cepulam concisam, postea globulum condimentorum mittes et agitabis origano vel satureia. si opus fuerit, amulas.   *(398)*

5. Aliter in leporem: ex sanguine et iecinere et pulmonibus leporinis minutal: adicies in caccabum liquamen et oleum ⟨et⟩ cocturam, porrum et coriandrum minutatim concides, iecinera et pulmones in caccabum mittes. cum cocta fuerint, teres piper, cuminum, coriandrum, laseris radicem,

---

[1] *liquamine maneat* E, *liquamine et lasere maneat* V.

17. Sauce for very young sucking-pig. 1 oz. pepper, ½ pint of wine, a little over ½ gill of best oil, ½ gill of *liquamen*, just under ½ gill of vinegar.

VIII. Hare

1. Hare in sauce. Scald the hare in water, then place in a shallow pan, roast in the oven in oil. When it is nearly done add some more oil, and pour over the following sauce: Pound pepper, lovage, savory, onion, rue, celery-seed, *liquamen*, asafœtida, wine, and a little oil. Turn several times, and finish cooking in this sauce.

2. The same in another sauce. When the hare is nearly ready to be taken out pour on ⟨the following sauce⟩: Pounded pepper, dates, asafœtida, raisins, *caroenum*, *liquamen*, oil. When it has come to the boil sprinkle with pepper and serve.

3. Stuffed hare. ⟨The stuffing⟩: Whole pine-kernels, almonds, chopped nuts or beech-nuts, whole peppercorns, the chopped giblets of the hare, bind with eggs. Then wrap the hare in pig's omentum and roast in the oven. Make the following sauce: Rue, sufficient pepper, onion, savory, dates, *liquamen*, *caroenum* or spiced wine; let this boil together long enough for it to thicken, and pour over the hare, which is served in this *liquamen*-pepper sauce.

4. White sauce for roast hare. Pepper, lovage, cumin, celery-seed, yolk of 1 hard-boiled egg. Pound this and work into a ball. Cook in a small saucepan *liquamen*, wine, oil, and a little vinegar, a chopped Welsh onion, then add the ball of spices and stir with origan or savory. If necessary thicken with cornflour.

5. Hare, another method: Minced liver and lights of the hare with its blood. Put in a saucepan *liquamen* and oil and stock, finely chop leek and coriander and add liver and lights. When this is done pound pepper, cumin, coriander, and asafœtida root, mint, rue, pennyroyal, moisten with

mentam, rutam, puleium, suffundes acetum, adicies iecinera leporum et sanguinem, teres. ⟨adicies⟩ mel et ⟨ius⟩ de suo sibi, aceto temperabis, exinanies in caccabum, pulmones leporum minutatim concisos in eundem caccabum mittes, facies ut ferveat. cum ferbuerit, amulo obligas, piper asperges et inferes.   (*399*)

6. ALITER LEPOREM EX SUO IURE: leporem curas, exossas, ornas, mittes in caccabo, adicies oleum, liquamen, cocturam, fasciculum porri, coriandrum, anethum. dum coquitur, adicies in mortarium piper, ligusticum, cuminum, coriandri semen, laseris radicem, cepam aridam, mentam, rutam, apii semen, fricabis, suffundes liquamen, adicies mel, ius de suo sibi, defrito, aceto temperabis. facies ut ferveat. cum ferbuerit, amulo obligabis. exornas, ius perfundes, ⟨piper⟩ asperges et inferes.   (*400*)

7. LEPOREM PASSENIANUM: leporem curas, exossas, extensum ornas; suspendes ad fumum. cum coloraverit, facies ut dimidia coctura coquatur. levas, asperges salem, assas,[1] oenogaro tanges, adicies in mortarium piper, ligusticum, fricabis, suffundes liquamen, vino et liquamine temperabis. in caccabum. adicies oleum modicum, facies ut ferveat. cum ferbuerit, amulo obligas. leporem assum a dorso tangis, piper asperges et inferes.   (*401*)

8. LEPOREM ISICIATUM: eadem conditura condies pulpam, nucleos infusos admisces, omento teges vel charta, colliges lacinias et surcula.   (*402*)

9. LEPOREM FARSILEM: leporem curas, ornas, quadratum imponis. adicies in mortarium piper, ligusticum, origanum, suffundes liquamen, adicies iecinera gallinarum cocta, cerebella cocta, pulpam concisam, ova cruda tria, liquamine temperabis. omento teges et charta et surclas. lento igni subassas. adicies in mortarium piper, ligusticum, fricabis, suffundes liquamen, vino et liquamine temperabis, facies ut ferveat. cum ferbuerit,

---

[1] *massam* codd.; corr. by Br.

vinegar, add the hare's liver and blood, pound together. Add
honey and some of the cooking-liquor, stir in vinegar, empty
into a saucepan, put the finely chopped hare's lights into the
same pan, and bring to the boil. When it boils thicken with
cornflour. Sprinkle with pepper and serve.

6. HARE IN ITS OWN JUICE. Clean the hare, bone, truss,
put in the pan. Add oil, *liquamen*, stock, a bunch of leeks,
coriander, dill. While it is cooking put in the mortar pepper,
lovage, cumin, coriander-seed, asafœtida root, dried onion,
mint, rue, celery-seed; pound. Moisten with *liquamen*, add
honey, some of the cooking-liquor, blend with *defrutum* and
vinegar, bring to the boil. When boiling thicken with cornflour. Undo the hare, pour the sauce over, sprinkle with
pepper, and serve.

7. HARE À LA PASSIENUS.[1] Clean the hare, bone, truss it with
its legs stretched, hang up to smoke. When it has got colour
let it cook until half done. Take out, sprinkle with salt, roast,
and pour over ⟨the following⟩ *oenogarum*: Put in the mortar
pepper and lovage; pound; moisten with *liquamen*, blend with
wine and *liquamen*, put in the saucepan, adding oil. Bring to
the boil. When boiling thicken with cornflour. Pour over
the back of the roast hare. Sprinkle with pepper and serve.

8. MINCED HARE. Spice the ⟨minced⟩ meat of the hare
with the same sauce, add soaked pine-kernels, wrap in sausage-
casing or paper, fasten the edges, and bind together. ⟨Roast.⟩

9. STUFFED HARE. Clean the hare and truss. Place on a
square board. Put in the mortar pepper, lovage, origan,
moisten with *liquamen*, put in cooked chicken-liver, cooked
brains, the chopped liver and lights of the hare, three raw eggs,
blend with *liquamen*. ⟨Stuff the hare with this mixture.⟩
Wrap it in sausage-skin and paper, bind together, and roast
over a slow fire. Put in the mortar pepper, lovage; pound,
moisten with *liquamen*, blend with wine and *liquamen*, bring

[1] The identity of Passienus has not been established.

amulo obligas, et leporem subassatum perfundes. piper asperges et inferes. (*403*)

10. ALITER LEPOREM ELIXUM: ornas, adicies in lance oleum, liquamen, acetum, passum, cepam concides et rutam viridem, thymum subcultratum, et sic adpones. (*404*)

11. LEPORIS CONDITURA: teritur piper, ruta, cepula, [et] iecur leporis, liquamen, caroenum, passum, olei modicum. amulum, cum bullit. (*405*)

12. LEPOREM ⟨PIPERE⟩ SICCO SPARSUM: et hunc praecondies sicut haedum Tarpeianum. antequam coquatur, ornatus suitur. piper, rutam, satureiam, cepam, thymum modicum, liquamine collues, postea in furnum ⟨mittes⟩, coques et impensa tali circumsparges: piperis semunciam, rutam, cepam, satureiam, dactylos IV, uvam passam ustam coloratam[1] super vatillum, vinum, oleum, liquamen, caroenum. frequenter tangitur ut condituram suam omnem tollat, postea ex pipere sicco in disco sumitur. (*406*)

13. ALITER LEPOREM CONDITUM: coques ex vino, liquamine, aqua, sinapi modico, anetho, porro cum capillo suo. cum ⟨in⟩ se coxerit, condies: piper, satureiam, cepae rotundum, dactylos, Damascena duo, vinum, liquamen, caroenum, olei modice. stringatur amulo, modicum bulliat. conditura lepus in patina perfunditur. (*407*)

IX. GLIRES

GLIRES: isicio porcino, item pulpis ex omni membro glirium, trito cum pipere, nucleis, lasere, liquamine farcies glires, et sutos in tegula positos mittes in furnum aut farsos in clibano coques.[2] (*408*)

---

[1] *iustam coloratum* codd.; corr. by Br.
[2] Punctuation changed by Br.

to the boil. When boiling thicken with cornflour and pour over the roast hare. Sprinkle with pepper and serve.[1]

10. BOILED HARE. Truss ⟨and boil⟩. Put in the serving-dish oil, *liquamen*, vinegar, *passum*, chopped onion and fresh rue, chopped thyme, and so serve.

11. SAUCE FOR HARE. Pound pepper, rue, Welsh onion, the liver of the hare, add *liquamen*, *caroenum*, *passum*, and a little oil. Thicken with cornflour when boiling.

12. HARE SPRINKLED WITH DRY PEPPER. Prepare the hare as for kid *à la* Tarpeius.[2] Before cooking it truss and sew up. Moisten it with a mixture of pepper, rue, savory, onion, a little thyme and *liquamen*, then put it in the oven, cook, and pour all over the following mixture: ½ oz. pepper, rue, onion, savory, 4 dates, raisins browned over a brazier, wine, oil, *liquamen*, and *caroenum*. Baste the hare with this mixture frequently, so that it absorbs the entire liquid. Then lift out and serve on a round dish with dry pepper.

13. HARE IN SAUCE, ANOTHER METHOD. Cook the hare in wine, *liquamen*, water, with a little mustard ⟨seed⟩, dill, and whole leek. While it is cooking prepare the following sauce: Pepper, savory, round onion, dates, two damsons, wine, *liquamen*, *caroenum*, and a little oil. Thicken with cornflour, allow to boil slightly. Pour the sauce over the hare in the serving-dish.

IX. DORMICE

Stuff the dormice with minced pork, the minced meat of whole dormice, pounded with pepper, pine-kernels, asafœtida, and *liquamen*. Sew up, place on a tile, put in the oven, or cook, stuffed, in a small oven (*clibanus*).

---

[1] Quantities for the sauce: 1½ tumblers of red wine, a cocktail-glass of *liquamen*, pepper and lovage to taste. May be thickened to a jelly-like consistency. For the stuffing about ¾ lb. of chicken liver. Roasting-time for the hare: 2½–3 hours.

[2] VIII, vi, 9.

THALASSA

I. in lucusta. II. in torpedine. III. in lolligine. IV. in sepiis. V. in polypo. VI. in ostreis. VII. omne genus conchyliorum. VIII. in echino. IX. in mitulis. X. in sarda cordula. XI. embractum Baianum.

I. [Ius] in lucusta

1. Ius in lucusta et cammaris[1]: indura cepam pallachanam concisam. † eius[2] piper, ligusticum, careum, cuminum, caryotam, mel, acetum, vinum, liquamen, oleum, defritum. hoc ius adicito sinapi in elixuris. (*409*)

2. Lucustas assas sic facies: aperiuntur lucustae, ut adsolet, cum testa sua et infunditur eis piperatum, coriandratum, et sic in craticula assantur. cum siccaverint, adicies ius in craticula quotiens siccaverint quousque assantur bene, ⟨et⟩ inferes.

(*410*)

3. Lucustam elixam cum cuminato: piper, ligusticum,

---

[1] *cappari* codd., corr. by Br.
[2] *eius* codd., *adicies* suggested by R.

BOOK IX

THE SEA

I. Sea-crayfish. II. Electric ray. III. Squid. IV.
Cuttlefish. V. Octopus. VI. Oysters. VII. For all
kinds of shell-fish. VIII. Sea-urchin. IX. Mussels.
X. Bonito, young tunny-fish. XI. *Embractum Baianum.*

I. Sea-crayfish

1. Sauce for sea-crayfish and large prawns.[1] Brown a
chopped spring-onion. Add pepper, lovage, caraway, cumin,
Jericho date, honey, vinegar, wine, *liquamen*, oil, *defrutum*.
Serve this sauce, with mustard added, with boiled ⟨sea-crayfish
or prawns⟩.

2. Grilled sea-crayfish are prepared as follows. The
sea-crayfish are opened as usual and left in their shells, and
moistened with a pepper and coriander sauce[2] and thus grilled.
Whenever they get dry pour some more sauce over until they
are well done, then serve.

3. Boiled sea-crayfish with cumin sauce. Pepper, lovage,
parsley, dried mint, plenty of cumin, honey, vinegar, *liquamen*.
If you wish add a bay-leaf and malabathrum.

4. Minced sea-crayfish-tail balls. Remove first the
harmful scrotum,[3] then boil the flesh, chop, and form balls with
liquamen, pepper, and eggs.

5. Dressing for boiled sea-crayfish. Pepper, cumin, rue,
honey, vinegar, *liquamen*, and oil.

---

[1] See notes to II, i, 1.

[2] The pepper and coriander sauce to be made on the principle of
the cumin sauce of the following recipe, taking plenty of coriander
and pepper instead of cumin.   [3] (?) text corrupt.

petroselinum, mentam siccam, cuminum plusculum. mel,
acetum, liquamen. si voles, folium et malabathrum addes.
                                                    (411)
    4. ALITER LUCUSTAM: ISICIA DE CAUDA EIUS SIC FACIES: folium
noci † uvam[1] prius demes et elixas deinde pulpam, concides,
cum liquamine, pipere et ovis isicia formabis.   *(412)*
    5. IN LUCUSTA ELIXA: piper, cuminum, rutam, mel, acetum,
liquamen et oleum.   *(413)*
    6. ALITER IN LUCUSTA: piper, ligusticum, cuminum, mentam,
rutam, nucleos, mel, acetum, liquamen et vinum.   *(414)*

II. IN TORPEDINE

    1. IN TORPEDINE: teritur piper, ruta, cepula arida. ⟨addes⟩
mel, liquamen, passum, vinum modice, olei boni guttas. cum
bullire coeperit, amulo obligas.   *(415)*
    2. IN TORPEDINE ELIXA: piper, ligusticum, petroselinum,
mentam, origanum, ovi medium, mel, liquamen, passum,
vinum, oleum. si voles, addes sinape, acetum. si calidum
volueris, uvam passam addes.   *(416)*

III. IN LOLLIGINE

    1. IN LOLLIGINE IN PATINA: teres piper, rutam, mel modicum,
liquamen, caroenum, olei guttas.
    2. IN LOLLIGINE FARSILI: piper, ligusticum, coriandrum, apii
semen, ovi vitellum, mel, acetum, liquamen, vinum et oleum.
obligabis.   *(417)*

IV. IN SEPIIS

    1. IN SEPIA FARSILI: piper, ligusticum, apii semen, careum,
mel, liquamen, vinum, condimenta coctiva. calefacies, et sic
aperies sepiam et perfundes.   *(418)*
    2. SIC FARCIES EAM SEPIAM COCTAM: cerebella elixa enervata

---

[1] *folliclum* [*nocivam uvam*] Schuch; *follem nocivum?* Teubner ed.
in the app. crit.

6. ANOTHER DRESSING FOR SEA-CRAYFISH. Pepper, lovage, cumin, mint, rue, pine-kernels, honey, vinegar, *liquamen*, and wine.

II. ELECTRIC RAY

1. SAUCE WITH ELECTRIC RAY. Pound pepper, rue, dried Welsh onion, add honey, *liquamen*, *passum*, a little wine, a few drops of good oil. When it begins to bubble thicken with cornflour.

2. DRESSING ⟨COLD OR HOT⟩ WITH BOILED ELECTRIC RAY. Pepper, lovage, parsley, mint, origan, yolk of egg, honey, *liquamen*, *passum*, wine, and oil. If you wish add mustard and vinegar. If you want it hot add raisins.

III. SQUID

1. SQUID IN THE PAN. Pound pepper, rue, a little honey, *liquamen*, and *caroenum*, add a few drops of oil, ⟨and cook the squid in this in a shallow pan in which you also serve it⟩.[1]

2. STUFFED SQUID SAUCE.[2] Pepper, lovage, coriander, celery-seed, yolk of egg, honey, vinegar, *liquamen*, wine, and oil. Thicken.

IV. CUTTLEFISH

1. SAUCE WITH STUFFED CUTTLEFISH. Pepper, lovage, celery-seed, caraway, honey, *liquamen*, kitchen herbs. Heat up, open the cuttlefish, and pour over.

2. STUFFING FOR COOKED CUTTLEFISH. Pound boiled brains —having first skinned them—with pepper, to which you add enough raw eggs, peppercorns, and tiny rissoles. ⟨Stuff the

---

[1] Cooking-time about 1 hour.

[2] The stuffing is not given, but may presumably be similar to that of the stuffed cuttlefish, iv, 2.

14—R.C.B.

teres cum pipere, cui commisces ova cruda quod satis erit, piper
integrum, isicia minuta, et sic consues et in bullientem ollam
mittes ita ut coire impensa possit.   (*419*)

3. SEPIAS ELIXAS AB AHENO: in frigidam missas cum pipere,
lasere, liquamine, nucleis.   ova ⟨addes⟩, et condies ut voles.
    (*420*)

4. ALITER SEPIAS: piper, ligusticum, cuminum, coriandrum
viride, mentam aridam, ovi vitellum, mel, liquamen, vinum,
acetum et oleum modicum.   et, ubi bullierit, amulo obligas.
    (*421*)

V. IN POLYPO

IN POLYPO: pipere, liquamine, lasere.   inferes.   (*422*)

VI. IN OSTREIS

IN OSTREIS: piper, ligusticum, ovi vitellum, acetum, liquamen, oleum et vinum.   si volueris, et mel addes.   (*423*)

VII. IN OMNE GENUS CONCHYLIORUM

IN OMNE GENUS CONCHYLIORUM: piper, ligusticum, petroselinum, mentam siccam, cuminum plusculum, mel, ⟨acetum⟩,[1]
liquamen.   si voles, folium et malabathrum addes.   (*424*)

VIII. IN ECHINO

1. IN ECHINO: accipies pultarium novum, oleum modicum,
liquamen, vinum dulce, piper minutum.   facies ut ferveat.
cum ferbuerit, in singulos echinos mittes, agitabis, ter bulliat.
cum coxeris, piper asperges et inferes.   (*425*)

2. ALITER ⟨IN⟩ ECHINO: piper, costum modice, mentam
siccam, mulsum, liquamen, spicam Indicam et folium. (*426*)

3. ALITER ⟨IN⟩ ECHINO: lotum mittes in aqua calida, coques,

[1] *acetum* add. Br. from IX, 1, 3.

cuttlefish⟩, sew up, and plunge in a deep saucepan of boiling water, so that the stuffing can solidify.

3. CUTTLEFISH BOILED IN THE CASSEROLE. Put to cool ⟨and serve⟩ with ⟨a dressing of⟩ pepper, asafœtida, *liquamen*, and pine-kernels. Add eggs and seasoning to taste.

4. ANOTHER SAUCE FOR CUTTLEFISH. Pepper, lovage, cumin, fresh coriander, dried mint, yolk of egg, honey, *liquamen*, wine, vinegar, and a little oil. When it boils thicken with cornflour.

V. OCTOPUS

SERVE OCTOPUS with pepper, *liquamen*, and asafœtida.

VI. OYSTERS

DRESSING FOR OYSTERS. Pepper, lovage, yolk of egg, vinegar, *liquamen*, oil, and wine; if you wish add also honey.

VII. FOR ALL KINDS OF SHELL-FISH

DRESSING FOR ALL KINDS OF SHELL-FISH. Pepper, lovage, parsley, dried mint, plenty of cumin, honey, vinegar, *liquamen*. If you wish add also a bay-leaf and malabathrum.

VIII. SEA-URCHIN

1. SEA-URCHIN. Take a new deep saucepan, put in a little oil, *liquamen*, sweet wine, and ground pepper. Bring to the boil. When it boils pour ⟨some of this⟩ into each sea-urchin, stir, let come up three times. When they are done sprinkle with pepper and serve.

2. ANOTHER SAUCE FOR SEA-URCHIN. Pepper, a little cost-mary, dried mint, *mulsum*, *liquamen*, spikenard, and bay-leaf.

3. SEA-URCHIN, ANOTHER METHOD. Wash and plunge in hot

levas, in patella compones, addes folium, piper, mel, liquamen, olei modice, ova, et sic obligas. in thermospodio coques, piper asperges et inferes.   (*427*)

4. IN ECHINO SALSO: echinum salsum cum liquamine optimo, caroeno, pipere temperabis et adpones.   (*428*)

5. ALITER: echinis salsis liquamen optimum admisces, et quasi recentes apparebunt, ita ut a balneo sumi possint. (*429*)

IX. IN MITULIS

IN MITULIS: liquamen, porrum concisum, cuminum, passum, satureiam, vinum. mixtum facies aquatius et ibi mitulos coques.   (*430*)

X. IN SARDA CORDULA MUGILE

1. IN SARDIS: SARDAM FARSILEM SIC FACERE OPORTET: sarda exossatur, et teritur puleium, cuminum, piperis grana, menta, nuces, mel. impletur et consuitur. involvitur in charta et sic supra vaporem ignis in operculo componitur. conditur ex oleo, caroeno, allece.   (*431*)

2. SARDA ITA FIT: coquitur sarda et exossatur. teritur piper ⟨cum⟩ ligustico, thymo, origano, ruta, caryota, melle, et in vasculo ovis concisis ornatur impensa: vinum modice, acetum, defritum et oleum viride.   (*432*)

3. IUS IN SARDA: piper, origanum, mentam, cepam, aceti modicum et oleum.   (*433*)

4. IUS IN SARDA: piper, ligusticum, mentam aridam, cepam coctam, mel, acetum, oleum. perfundes, asperges ovis duris concisis.   (*434*)

5. IUS IN CORDULA ASSA: piper, ligusticum, apii semen, mentam, rutam, caryotam, mel, acetum, vinum et oleum. convenit et in Sarda.   (*435*)

6. IUS IN MUGILE SALSO: piper, ligusticum, cuminum, cepam,

water, let cook, take out and place in a shallow pan, add bay-leaf, pepper, honey, *liquamen*, a little oil, add eggs to bind. Cook in the hot ashes. Sprinkle with pepper and serve.

4. DRESSING FOR SALTED SEA-URCHINS. Serve salted sea-urchins with a dressing of best *liquamen*, *caroenum*, and pepper.

5. ANOTHER METHOD. To salted sea-urchins add best *liquamen*, and they will look like fresh ones, so that they can be eaten after the bath.

IX. MUSSELS

Mix *liquamen*, chopped leek, cumin, *passum*, savory, and wine, dilute the mixture with water, and cook the mussels in it.

X. BONITO, YOUNG TUNNY-FISH, GREY MULLET

1. STUFFED BONITO. Bone the fish. Pound pennyroyal, add cumin, peppercorns, mint, nuts, honey. Stuff the fish with this mixture and sew up. Wrap in paper and cook in the steam[1] in a covered pan. Season with oil, *caroenum*, and *allec*.

2. BONITO. Prepare thus: Cook the fish and bone it. Pound pepper with lovage, thyme, origan, rue, Jericho date, honey, put it into a small vessel and add chopped hard-boiled eggs, a little wine, vinegar, *defrutum*, and best oil.

3. DRESSING FOR BONITO. Pepper, origan, mint, onion, a little vinegar, and oil.

4. DRESSING FOR BONITO. Pepper, lovage, dried mint, cooked onion, honey, vinegar, oil. Pour over the fish and garnish with chopped hard-boiled eggs.

5. DRESSING FOR YOUNG GRILLED TUNNY-FISH. Pepper, lovage, celery-seed, mint, rue, Jericho date, honey, vinegar, wine, and oil. This goes also with bonito.

6. DRESSING FOR SALT GREY MULLET. Pepper, lovage,

[1] See note to II, ii, 2.

mentam, rutam, calvam, caryotam, mel, acetum, sinape et oleum.   *(437)*

7. ALITER IUS IN MUGILE SALSO: piper, origanum, erucam, mentam, rutam, calvam, caryotam, mel, oleum, acetum et sinape.   *(438)*

XI. IUS IN SILURO, IN PELAMYDE ET IN THYNNO SALSIS

piper, ligusticum, cuminum, cepam, mentam, rutam, calvam, caryotam, mel, acetum, sinape, oleum.   *(439)*

XII. IUS IN MULLO TARICHO

piper, rutam, cepam, dactylum, sinapi, trito commisces echino ⟨et⟩ oleo.   et sic perfundes piscem frictum vel assatum.   *(440)*

XIII. SALSUM SINE SALSO

1. iecur coques, teres, et mittes piper et[1] liquamen aut salem. addes oleum.   iecur leporis aut haedi aut agni aut pulli; et, si volueris, in formella piscem formabis.   oleum viride supra adicies.   *(441)*

2. ALITER VICE SALSI: cuminum, piper, liquamen teres.   et passum modice vel caroenum et nuces tritas plurimas misces et simul conteres et salsari defundes.   oleum modice superstillabis et inferes.   *(442)*

3. ALITER SALSUM SINE SALSO: cumini tantum quantum quinque digitis tollis, piperis ad dimidium eius et unam spicam alei purgatam teres.   liquamen superfundes, oleum modice superstillabis.   hoc aegrum stomachum valde reficit et digestionem facit.   *(443)*

---

[1] *aut* codd., corr. by Br.

cumin, onion, mint, rue, filbert nut, Jericho date, honey, vinegar, mustard, and oil.

7. ANOTHER DRESSING FOR SALT GREY MULLET. Pepper, origan, rocket, mint, rue, filbert nut, Jericho date, honey, oil, vinegar, and mustard.

XI. SAUCE FOR SALT SHEAT-FISH, YOUNG TUNNY-FISH,[1] TUNNY-FISH

Pepper, lovage, cumin, onion, mint, rue, filbert nut, Jericho date, honey, vinegar, mustard, oil.

XII. DRESSING WITH SALT RED MULLET

Pepper, rue, onion, date, mustard, mix with pounded sea-urchin and oil, and pour this over the fried or grilled fish.

XIII. SALT FISH WITHOUT FISH

1. Cook liver, grind and add pepper and *liquamen* or salt. Add oil. Use hare, kid, lamb, or chicken-liver: and mould into a fish in a small mould if liked. Sprinkle virgin oil over it.

2. ANOTHER SUBSTITUTE FOR SALT FISH. Pound cumin, pepper, and *liquamen*, and mix with it a little *passum* or *caroenum* and plenty of ground walnuts, pound together, pour into brine. Add a few drops of oil and serve.

3. ANOTHER SUBSTITUTE FOR SALT FISH. Pound as much cumin as you can pick up with five fingers, half the quantity of pepper, and one peeled clove of garlic. Pour on *liquamen*, add a few drops of oil. This is excellent for a sick stomach, and facilitates digestion.

---

[1] Young tunny-fish: the *pelamys* is a tunny-fish under a year old but older than the young tunny-fish (*cordula*) of x, 5.

XIV. Embractum Baianum

Embractum Baianum: ostreas minutas, sphondylos, urticas in caccabum mittes, nucleos tostos concisos, rutam, apium, piper, coriandrum, cuminum, passum, liquamen, caryotam, oleum.   (*444*)

XIV. Embractum Baianum

Put in a saucepan minced oysters, mussels, sea-urchins, chopped toasted pine-kernels, rue, celery, pepper, coriander, cumin, *passum*, *liquamen*, Jericho date, oil. ⟨Cook and serve.⟩[1]

[1] This may possibly have been meant to be eaten cold.

HALIEUS

I. in piscibus diversis. II. in murenam. III. in
anguillam.

I. IN PISCIBUS

1. IUS DIABOTANON IN PISCE FRIXO: piscem quemlibet curas,
salsas, friges. teres piper, cuminum, coriandri semen, laseris
radicem, origanum, rutam, fricabis, suffundes acetum, adicies
caryotam, mel, defritum, oleum, liquamen, temperabis,
refundes in caccabum, facies ut ferveat. cum ferbuerit, piscem
frictum perfundes. piper asperges et inferes. (445)

2. IUS IN PISCE ELIXO: piper, ligusticum, cuminum, cepulam,
origanum, nucleos, caryotam, mel, acetum, liquamen, sinapi,
oleum modice. ius calidum si velis, uvam passam. (446)

3. ALITER IN PISCE ELIXO: teres piper, ligusticum, coriandrum
viride, satureiam, cepam, ovorum vitella cocta, passum,
acetum, oleum et liquamen. (447)

4. ⟨ALITER⟩ IUS IN PISCE ELIXO: piscem curabis diligenter,
mittes in mortarium salem, coriandri semen, conteres bene,
volves eum, adicies in patinam, cooperies, gypsabis, coques in

BOOK X

THE FISHERMAN

I. Various fish. II. *Murenae*. III. Eel.

I. FISH

1. SAUCE WITH HERBS FOR FRIED FISH. Take any fish you like, clean, salt, fry. Pound pepper, cumin, coriander-seed, asafœtida root, origan, rue; pound well, moisten with vinegar, add Jericho date, honey, *defrutum*, oil, *liquamen*, mix well, pour into a saucepan, bring to the boil. When it boils pour over the fried fish. Sprinkle with pepper and serve.

2. SAUCE FOR BOILED FISH. Pepper, lovage, cumin, Welsh onion, origan, pine-kernels, Jericho dates, honey, vinegar, *liquamen*, mustard, and a little oil. If you want hot sauce add raisins ⟨and heat through⟩.[1]

3. ANOTHER SAUCE FOR BOILED FISH. Pound pepper, lovage, fresh coriander, savory, onion, yolks of hard-boiled eggs, *passum*, vinegar, oil, and *liquamen*.

4. FISH COOKED IN ITS OWN JUICE.[2] Prepare the fish carefully. Put in a mortar salt and coriander-seed; pound. Roll the fish in this, place it in a pan, cover and seal, and cook in the oven. When it is cooked remove. Sprinkle with very strong vinegar and serve.

5. ANOTHER SAUCE FOR BOILED FISH. Clean the fish, put in a

---

[1] Quantities for 5 people: 4–5 large dates, 2–3 sprigs of lovage, 2 oz. pine-kernels, 1 spring onion—instead of Welsh onion—a pinch of cumin, mustard and vinegar to taste.

[2] The Latin title of this recipe reads 'another sauce for boiled fish'; but as there is no sauce, nor is the fish boiled, this title cannot be correct. This recipe is excellent with haddock or hake; cooking-time about 30 minutes.

furno. cum coctus fuerit, tolles, aceto acerrimo asperges et inferes.   *(448)*

5. ALITER IUS IN PISCE ELIXO: cum curaveris piscem, adicies in sartaginem ⟨coriandri⟩ semen, aquam, anethum viride et ipsum piscem. cum coctus fuerit, asperges aceto et inferes.   *(449)*

6. IUS ALEXANDRINUM IN PISCE ASSO: piper, cepam siccam, ligusticum, cuminum, origanum, apii semen, pruna Damascena enucleata, mulsum, acetum, liquamen, defritum, oleum, et coques.   *(450)*

7. ALITER IUS ALEXANDRINUM IN PISCE ASSO: piper, ligusticum, coriandrum viride, uvam passam enucleatam, vinum, passum, liquamen, oleum, et coques.   *(451)*

8. ALITER IUS ALEXANDRINUM IN PISCE ASSO: piper, ligusticum, coriandrum viride, cepam, Damascena enucleata, passum, liquamen, acetum, oleum, et coques.   *(452)*

9. IUS IN GONGRO ASSO: piper, ligusticum, cuminum frictum, origanum, cepam siccam, ovorum vitella cocta, vinum, mulsum, acetum, liquamen, defritum, et coques.   *(453)*

10. IUS IN CORNUTAM: piper, ligusticum, origanum, cepam, uvam passam enucleatam, vinum, mel, acetum, liquamen, oleum, et coques.   *(454)*

11. IUS IN MULLOS ASSOS: piper, ligusticum, rutam, mel, nucleos, acetum, vinum, liquamen, oleum modice. calefacies et perfundes.   *(455)*

12. ALITER IUS IN MULLOS ASSOS: rutam, mentam, coriandrum, feniculum, omnia viridia, piper, ligusticum, mel, liquamen et oleum modice.   *(456)*

13. IUS IN PELAMYDE ASSA: piper, ligusticum, origanum, coriandrum viride, cepam, uvam passam enucleatam, passum, acetum, liquamen, defritum, oleum, et coques. hoc ius convenit et in elixa. si vis, et mel addes.   *(457)*

frying-pan coriander-seed, water, fresh dill, and the fish.
When it is cooked sprinkle with vinegar and serve.

6. ALEXANDRIAN SAUCE FOR GRILLED FISH. Pepper, dried
onion, lovage, cumin, origan, celery-seed, stoned damson,
mulsum, vinegar, *liquamen*, *defrutum*, oil. ⟨Pound, mix,⟩ and
cook.

7. ANOTHER ALEXANDRIAN SAUCE FOR GRILLED FISH. Pepper,
lovage, fresh coriander, stoned raisins, wine, *passum*, *liquamen*,
oil. ⟨Pound, mix, and⟩ cook.

8. ANOTHER ALEXANDRIAN SAUCE FOR GRILLED FISH. Pepper,
lovage, fresh coriander, onion, stoned damsons, *passum*, *liquamen*, vinegar, oil. ⟨Pound, mix, and⟩ cook.[1]

9. SAUCE WITH GRILLED CONGER EEL. Pepper, lovage,
grilled cumin, origan, dried onion, yolks of boiled eggs, wine,
mulsum, vinegar, *liquamen*, *defrutum*. ⟨Pound, mix, and⟩
cook.

10. SAUCE WITH CORNUTA.[2] Pepper, lovage, origan, onion,
stoned raisin, wine, honey, vinegar, *liquamen*, oil. ⟨Pound,
mix, and⟩ cook.

11. SAUCE FOR GRILLED RED MULLET. Pepper, lovage, rue,
honey, pine-kernels, vinegar, wine, *liquamen*, a little oil.
Heat through and pour over the fish.

12. ANOTHER SAUCE FOR GRILLED RED MULLET. Rue, mint,
coriander, fennel, all fresh, pepper, lovage, honey, *liquamen*,
and a little oil.

13. SAUCE FOR GRILLED YOUNG TUNNY-FISH.[3] Pepper,
lovage, origan, fresh coriander, onion, stoned raisin, *passum*,
vinegar, *liquamen*, *defrutum*, oil. ⟨Pound, mix, and⟩ cook.
This sauce can also be served with boiled fish. Add honey,
if liked.

[1] About ¾ lb. of damsons is sufficient a basis for the sauce for
about 4 people; be careful not to use too much vinegar, as damsons
are rather acid. If prunes are used instead of damsons a little more
vinegar is required.

[2] This fish—although mentioned by Pliny—cannot be identified
with certainty.

[3] Cp. note to IX, xi.

14. Ius in percam: piper, ligusticum, cuminum frictum, cepam, pruna Damascena enucleata, vinum, mulsum, acetum, oleum, defritum, et coques.   *(458)*

15. Ius in pisce rubellione: piper, ligusticum, careum, serpyllum, apii semen, cepam siccam, vinum, passum, acetum, liquamen, oleum. amulo obligas.   *(459)*

II. ⟨In murenam⟩

1. Ius in murena assa: piper, ligusticum, satureiam, crocomagma, cepam, pruna Damascena enucleata, vinum, mulsum, acetum, liquamen, defritum, oleum, et coques.   *(460)*

2. Aliter ius in murena assa: piper, ligusticum, pruna Damascena, vinum, mulsum, acetum, liquamen, defritum, oleum, et coques.   *(461)*

3. Aliter ius in murena assa: piper, ligusticum, nepetam montanam, coriandri semen, cepam, nucleos pineos, mel, acetum, liquamen, oleum, et coques.   *(462)*

4. Aliter ius in murena elixa: piper, ligusticum, anethum, apii semen, rhus Syriacum, caryotam, mel, acetum, liquamen, oleum, sinape, defritum.   *(463)*

5. Aliter ius in murena elixa: piper, ligusticum, careum, apii semen, coriandrum, mentam aridam, nucleos pineos, rutam, mel, acetum, vinum, liquamen, oleum modice. calefacies et amulo obligas.   *(464)*

6. ⟨Aliter⟩ ius in murena elixa: piper, ligusticum, careum, cuminum, nucleos, caryotam, sinape, mel, acetum, liquamen et oleum et defritum.   *(465)*

III

1. Ius in lacertos elixos: piper, ligusticum, cuminum, rutam viridem, cepam, mel, acetum, liquamen, oleum modice. cum bullierit, amulo obligas.   *(467)*

14. SAUCE FOR PERCH. Pepper, lovage, grilled cumin, onion, stoned damsons, wine, *mulsum*, vinegar, oil, *defrutum*. ⟨Pound, mix, and⟩ cook.

15. SAUCE FOR SEA-BREAM. Pepper, lovage, caraway, serpyllum, celery-seed, dried onion, wine, *passum*, vinegar, *liquamen*, oil. Thicken with cornflour.

II. MURENAE

1. SAUCE FOR GRILLED MURENA. Pepper, lovage, savory, dried saffron,[1] onion, stoned damsons, wine, *mulsum*, vinegar, *liquamen*, *defrutum*, oil. ⟨Pound, mix,⟩ and cook.

2. ANOTHER SAUCE FOR GRILLED MURENA. Pepper, lovage, damson, wine, *mulsum*, vinegar, *liquamen*, *defrutum*, oil. ⟨Pound, mix,⟩ and cook.

3. ANOTHER SAUCE FOR GRILLED MURENA. Pepper, lovage, mountain catmint, coriander-seed, onion, pine-kernels, honey, vinegar, *liquamen*, oil. ⟨Pound, mix,⟩ and cook.

4. SAUCE FOR BOILED MURENA. Pepper, lovage, dill, celery-seed, Syrian sumach, Jericho date, honey, vinegar, *liquamen*, oil, mustard, *defrutum*.

5. ANOTHER SAUCE FOR BOILED MURENA. Pepper, lovage, caraway, celery-seed, coriander, dried mint, pine-kernels, rue, honey, vinegar, wine, *liquamen*, a little oil. Heat through and thicken with cornflour.

6. ANOTHER SAUCE FOR BOILED MURENA. Pepper, lovage, caraway, cumin, pine-kernels, Jericho date, mustard, honey, vinegar, *liquamen*, oil, and *defrutum*.

III

1. SAUCE FOR BOILED HORSE-MACKEREL. Pepper, lovage, cumin, fresh rue, onion, honey, vinegar, *liquamen*, a little oil. When boiling thicken with cornflour.

[1] Saffron = crocomagma—*i.e.*, saffron after extraction of oil.

2. Ius in pisce elixo: piper, ligusticum, petroselinum, origanum, cepam aridam, mel, acetum, liquamen, vinum, oleum modice. cum bullierit, amulo obligas. et in lance inferes.   (*466*)

3. Ius in pisce asso: piper, ligusticum, thymum, coriandrum viride, mel, acetum, liquamen, vinum, oleum, defritum. calefacies et agitabis rutae surculo et obligabis amulo.   (*468*)

4. Ius in thynno: piper, cuminum, thymum, coriandrum, cepam, uvam passam,[1] acetum, mel, vinum, liquamen, oleum. calefacies; amulo obligabis.   (*469*)

5. Ius in thynno elixo: piper, ligusticum, thymum, condimenta moretaria, cepam, caryotam, mel, acetum, liquamen et oleum et sinape.   (*470*)

6. Ius in dentice asso: piper, ligusticum, coriandrum, mentam, rutam aridam, malum Cydonium coctum, mel, vinum, liquamen, oleum. calefacies, amulo obligabis.   (*471*)

7. In dentice elixo: piper, anethum, cuminum, thymum, mentam, rutam viridem, mel, acetum, liquamen, vinum, oleum modice. calefacies et amulo obligabis.   (*472*)

8. Ius in pisce aurata: piper, ligusticum, careum, origanum, rutae bacam, mentam, myrtae bacam, ovi vitellum, mel, acetum, oleum, vinum, liquamen. calefacies et sic uteris.   (*473*)

9. Ius in pisce aurata assa: piper, coriandrum, mentam aridam, apii semen, cepam, uvam passam, mel, acetum, vinum, liquamen et oleum.   (*474*)

10. Ius in scorpione elixo: piper, careum, petroselinum, caryotam, mel, acetum, liquamen, sinape, oleum, defritum.
      (*475*)

11. In pisce oenogarum: teres piper, rutam, mel commisces, passum, liquamen, caroenum, et igni mollissimo calefacies.
      (*476*)

12. ⟨Aliter⟩ in pisce oenogarum: ut supra facies. cum bullierit, amulo obligabis.

---

[1] *passum* in Teubner edition is probably a misprint.

2. SAUCE FOR BOILED FISH. Pepper, lovage, parsley, origan, dried onion, honey, vinegar, *liquamen*, wine, a little oil. When boiling, thicken with cornflour. Pour over the fish in the serving-dish and serve.

3. SAUCE FOR GRILLED FISH. Pepper, lovage, thyme, fresh coriander, honey, vinegar, *liquamen*, wine, oil, *defrutum*. Heat and stir with a sprig of rue and thicken with corn-flour.

4. SAUCE FOR TUNNY-FISH. Pepper, cumin, thyme, corian-der, onion, raisin, vinegar, honey, wine, *liquamen*, oil. Heat through and thicken with cornflour.

5. SAUCE FOR BOILED TUNNY-FISH. Pepper, lovage, thyme, spices used for *moretarium*,[1] onion, Jericho date, honey, vinegar, *liquamen*, oil, and mustard.

6. SAUCE FOR GRILLED DENTEX. Pepper, lovage, coriander, mint, dried rue, cooked quince, honey, wine, *liquamen*, oil. Heat through, thicken with cornflour.

7. SAUCE FOR BOILED DENTEX. Pepper, dill, cumin, thyme, mint, fresh rue, honey, vinegar, *liquamen*, wine, a little oil. Heat and thicken with cornflour.

8. SAUCE FOR GOLD-BREAM. Pepper, lovage, caraway, origan, rue-berry, mint, myrtle-berry, yolk of egg, honey, vinegar, oil, wine, *liquamen*. Heat through, and so serve.

9. SAUCE FOR GRILLED GOLD-BREAM. Pepper, coriander, dried mint, celery-seed, onion, raisin, honey, vinegar, wine, *liquamen*, and oil.

10. SAUCE FOR BOILED SCORPION FISH. Pepper, caraway, parsley, Jericho date, honey, vinegar, *liquamen*, mustard, oil, *defrutum*.

11. OENOGARUM FOR FISH. Pound pepper, rue, mix with honey, *passum, liquamen, caroenum*, and heat over a very low fire.

12. ANOTHER OENOGARUM FOR FISH. Prepare as above. When it boils thicken with cornflour.

---

[1] See I, xxi.

15—R.C.B.

IV. ⟨IN ANGUILLAM⟩

1. IUS IN ANGUILLAM: piper, ligusticum, apii semen, anethum, rhus Syriacum, caryotam, mel, acetum, liquamen, sinape et defritum.   (477)

2. ⟨ALITER⟩ IUS IN ANGUILLAM: piper, ligusticum, rhus Syriacum, mentam siccam, rutae bacas, ovorum vitella cocta, mulsum, acetum, liquamen, oleum. coques.   (478)

IV. Eel

1. SAUCE FOR EEL.   Pepper, lovage, celery-seed, dill, Syrian sumach, Jericho date, honey, vinegar, *liquamen*, oil, mustard, and *defrutum*.

2. ANOTHER SAUCE FOR EEL.   Pepper, lovage, Syrian sumach, dried mint, rue-berries, yolks of boiled eggs, *mulsum*, vinegar, *liquamen*, oil. ⟨Pound, mix, and⟩ cook.

INDEX

NOTE

The numbers refer to pages; '*n.*' following a page reference indicates a footnote. The principal items are arranged in groups under headings: **Fish, Fruit and Nuts, Game, Herbs and Spices, Kitchen Utensils and Tableware, Latin and Greek Authors, Latin Culinary Terms, Meat, Poultry and Game-birds, Pulse, Sauces, Sea-food, Sweets and Cakes, Vegetables, Wine and Wine Preparations.**

ALEXANDRIA, bread from, 95; marrows, in fashion of, 77; sauces for grilled fish, in fashion of, 221

alica—see Spelt(-grits)

amulum (=starch, translated 'corn-flour'), manufacture of, 27

BARLEY, with boiled shoulder of pork (*petaso*), 169; soup, 117, 137

bread, Alexandrian, 95; Picentine, 93

CELSINUS, sucking-pig à la, 197, 199

cereal-dishes: *apothermum*, 67. *See also* Barley, Spelt(-grits)

cheese, 26 f., 169 *n.* 2; *patella* with, 103; in *patina* with milk, 101; in *sala cattabia*, 93–95; sweet, 59; Vestine, 26, 95; *tyropatina*, 171 *n.*

Commodus, *conchicla* à la, 135

Cyrenaica, silphium from, 28, 57, 157

EGG-DISHES: boiled, 179; egg sponge with milk, 173; fried, 179; milk and egg sweet, 171; sauce for soft-boiled, 179

Fish (general), cooked in its own juice, 219; fricassee of, 111; grilled, with horse-parsley, 83; *patinae* of, 105 ff.; preservation of, 51; sauces for, 219 ff.

Fish (various kinds):

anchovy (*apua*), 99, 105

aurata—see Gold-bream

bonito, 213

bream, gold—*see* Gold bream

bream, sea-—*see* Sea-bream

conger eels, sauce with grilled, 221

cornuta, sauce with, 221

dentex (a Mediterranean fish of the genus *acanthopteryges*, still popular in Mediterranean countries), *patina* of, 109; sauces for, 225

eel, sauces for, 227. *See also* Conger eels

electric ray, sauce with, 209; dressing with boiled, 209

gold bream (*aurata=chrysophrys aurata*, a kind of sea-bream, native to the Mediterranean), *patina* of, 109; sauces for, 225

hake (*piscis asellus*), fillets of, in *patina* with milk, 101

horse-mackerel, sauce for, 223

lagita, patinae of, 105, 107

mullet, grey, *patina* of, 109; salt, dressing for, 213 ff.

mullet, red, sauces for grilled, 221; *patina* of, 105; salt, dressing for, 215

murenae (lampreys? They were among the most popular fish with the Romans. Wealthy people kept them in ponds and

juniper (*iuniperus*), 187
laser, laserpitium—see Asafœtida;
  Silphium
laurel (fresh), 195
laurel-berry, 69, 159, 161, 183,
  193, 197
laurel shoots, 183
laurel, sprigs of, 181
lauri baca—see Laurel-berry
lauri folium, laurus viridis—see
  Bay-leaf
leaf, aromatic (*folium*), 45, 55, 57,
  59, 147. *See also* Bay-leaf
lentiscus, bacae lentisci—see Mastic-
  berries
ligusticum—see Lovage
lovage (*Ligusticum levisticum*
  Linn.), *passim*
malabathrum, 57, 207, 211
mallow, flowers of (*flores malvarum*), 133. *See also under*
  Vegetables
mastic (*mastix*), 45
mastic berries (*bacae lentisci*), 85
mint (*menta*), *passim*
mustard (*sinapi*), 55, 69, 83, 139,
  141, 143, 145, 151, 153, 159,
  165, 181, 183, 185, 187, 189,
  199, 205, 207, 209, 215, 219,
  223, 225, 227; preparation of,
  49
myrtle-berries (*bacae myrtae*), 55,
  65, 145, 147 n., 163, 165, 181,
  225
nard, Indian (*spica Indica*), 147.
  See also Spikenard
nardostachyum—see Spikenard
nepeta—see Catmint
nepeta montana—see Catmint,
  mountain
ocimum—see Basil
onion (*cepa*), 77, 81, 85, 87, 97,
  103, 105, 107, 109, 117, 131,
  135, 143, 145, 147, 149, 155,
  163, 181, 183, 185, 187, 189,
  191, 199, 201, 203, 205, 213,
  215, 221, 223, 225. *See also
  under* Vegetables

onion, spring (*cepa pallachana*),
  107, 207
onion, Welsh (*cepula*), 163, 165,
  183, 185, 201, 205, 209, 219
origan (*origanum*), *passim*
parsley (*petroselinum*), *passim*
pennyroyal (*puleium*), 77, 79, 117,
  125, 127, 173, 187, 201, 213
pepper (*piper*), *passim*
petroselinum—see Parsley
puleium—see Pennyroyal
pyrethrum (*Anacyclus pyrethrum*
  DC), 65, 119, 163, 193
rhus Syriacum—see Sumach,
  Syrian
rocket (*eruca*), 55, 145, 175, 183,
  215
rue (*ruta*) (stalks and leaves of),
  passim
rue-berry (*baca rutae*), 103, 225,
  227
rue-seed (*semen rutae*), 145, 165,
  187
safflower (*cneci flos, cnecon*), 51,
  147, 165, 181
saffron (*crocus*), 45, 55
saffron, dried (*crocomagma*), 223
savory (*satureia*)—*passim*
Serpyllum (*Thymus serpyllum*),
  223
sesame (*sesamum*), 149
seseli (*seseli, sil montanum, siler,*
  the name of several umbelliferous plants—*e.g.,* *Laserpitium
  siler* Linn., and *Tordylium
  officinale* Linn.), 59, 117; (*sil
  montanum*), 77
shallot (*cepa Ascalonia*), 105, 115
sil, sil montanum—see Seseli
silphium, Cyrenaican, 28 f., 57,
  157; Persian (=asafœtida), 28,
  57, 157; how to make one
  ounce last, 51. *See also* Asafœtida
sinapi—see Mustard
sinapi viride—see Mustard plant
  under Vegetables

the first Apicius passage, p. 66, it can only mean 'to boil'; Schuch altered the text in this case and transformed the chicken bones into date-stones, which would easily go bad and acquire a bad smell. In the second passage, p. 142, the meaning is not so clear; with turnips, 'losing their bad smell' might mean 'losing their pungency.' But is it possible that the passage should be interpreted 'boil the turnips so that they can be peeled'? The passage in the excerpts of Vinidarius reads : '*ofellas assas exbromabis diligenter et in sartagine mittes*'; could '*exbromare*' here mean 'to skin'?

exornare, this verb is used in the Cookery Book in a way not illustrated in the *Thesaurus Linguae Latinae*; it is used in connexion with sucking-pig and hare which had been wrapped in paper, skewered, or trussed, and with skewered truffles, to indicate that the wrappings and skewers are to be removed before serving, 174, 192, 194, 202. In two cases the verb is clearly used as an opposite to 'ornare.' Only once is it used in the more usual sense, p. 70, where it means 'arrange.'

ornare, this means in Apicius usually 'to prepare for cooking,' especially 'to truss (bird, hare, etc.),' 140, 142, 148, 150, 152, 190, 192, 194, 196, 202, 204; only once the verb means 'to garnish,' 212—in this latter sense cf. '*adornare*,' used once in p. 102.

steam, to cook over the (*ad, supra,*

vaporem ignis pones), 64, 212; (*impones ad vaporem*), 98

thermospodium—see Ashes, hot

Lepcis Magna, *liquamen* manufactured at, 21

Lucretius, *patella à la*, 107

Meat, general: boiled, sauces for, 163 ff.; fillets, 157; fricassees, 111 ff.; pieces (*ofellae*), 159 ff.; preservation of, 49; ragout in the manner of Ostia, 159; rissoles, various, 63 ff.; roasts, 161 ff.; salt, how to make sweet, 51; slices, sauces for, 165

Meat, various kinds:

beef, 187, 189

brains, in *conchicla*, 135, 137; in cream of horse-parsley, 95; in kid with bay and milk, 193; in *patinae*, 95, 99, 103, 105, 109; in pease mould, 127, 131; rissoles of, 63; sausages of, 69; in soups, 123, 125; stewed with cucumbers, 77; in stuffings, (for chicken), 155, (for cuttle-fish), 209, (for hare), 203, (for marrows), 121, (for pig's stomach), 167, (for sucking-pig), 193, 195

coloefium (leg of pork or top part of pig's trotters (?)), 116

dormice, stuffed, 32, 205

ham (*perna*), boiled and baked, 167 f.

ham (*petaso*), boiled, with sweet-wine cakes, 169

kid, various recipes for, 189 ff.

kidneys, grilled or roasted, 167

lamb in thick soup with pastry and milk, 123; various recipes for, 189 ff.

lard, boiled, 169

lights, 171; of hare, 201, 203

liver, of chicken, in *patinae*, 101, 103; in sauce for roast crane or duck, 145; in stuffing for hare, 203; of hare, 201, 203,

for sucking-pig, 199; cabbage-leaves, leeks rolled in, 81; *patina* of, 97; various kinds of, 79 *n*. 2; as vegetable and salad, 79 ff.

carduus—*see* Artichoke

caroetae—*see* Carrots

carrots (*caroetae*), 91

cauliculi—*see* Cabbage

celery, green: with beans from Baiae, 139; as laxative, 75; purée, 85; in stuffing for sucking-pig, 199; in vegetable stew, 119

chicory—*see* Endive

citrium—*see* Pumpkin—*see also* Citron, *under* Fruits and Nuts

colocasia, colocasium (It has also been suggested that the name denotes Egyptian lotus, *nelumbium speciosum* Willd.)—*see* Taro

cucumbers (*cucumeres*), cooked, 77; *patina* of, 97; as salad, 77 ff.; in sauce for roast crane or duck, 143

cucumeres—*see* Cucumbers

cucurbitae—*see* Marrows

cymae—*see* Cabbage

endive (chicory, *intubum*), dressed as salad; 87

fabaciae virides—*see* Beans, green

faenum graecum—*see* Fenugreek

faseoli—*see* Beans, French

fenugreek, 139

fungi farnei (according to Pliny, both edible and poisonous fungi were sometimes named after the trees on or near which they grew; *farnus* has been identified either as an ash-tree or a kind of oak)—*see* Fungi, tree

fungi, tree (*fungi farnei*), boiled, 175; dressing for, 175

green, to make bright green, 73; how to preserve, 53

herbs, wild (*rusticae*), *patina* of, 97; raw with dressing, or cooked, 85

holisatrum, holiserae, holus atrum—*see* Horse-parsley

horse-parsley, cream of, 95; *patina* with, 103; purée, 85; raw with a dressing, 83

intubum (It is either *Cichorium intybus* Linn., chicory, or *Cichorium endivia* Linn., endive.)—*see* Endive

lactuca—*see* Lettuce

leek, in barley soup, 117; with beans, 139; with beets, 83; boiled, in sauce for meat slices, 165; in *bouquet garni* or chopped as seasoning, 67, 69, 143, 149, 151, 153, 155, 185, 197, 201, 205; in broth, 73, 75; in *conchicla* of peas, 135; in fricassees, 111, 113, 115; with lentils, 127; with peas (dried), 127, 129, 131, 133; in sauce, 213; stewed with quinces, 111; in stuffing for sucking-pig, 199; truffles boiled with, 177; veal or beef with, 189; as vegetable, 81; in vegetable stew, 117

lettuce (*lactuca*), *patina*, 95; purée, with onions, 85; as salad, 87

mallow, in barley soup, 117; hearts of, in *patina* with milk, 99; leaves to line a pan, 119; in stuffing for sucking-pig, 199; as vegetable, 79

malva—*see* Mallow

marrows (*cucurbitae*), with boiled chicken, 153; *patina* of, 99; stuffed, 121; various recipes, 75 ff.

melo (denotes probably a small, round melon, also called *melopepo*)—*see* Melons

melons (*pepones, melones*), dressed as salad, 79

mushrooms (*boleti*), various recipes for, 175

mustard plant (green), *patina* of, 97

napus (either = *rapa*; or *Brassica napus*, var. *esculenta*, swede; we

Made in the USA
Middletown, DE
14 April 2019